STUDIES IN PUBLIC ADMINISTRATION
Volume VI

*

EDITORIAL COMMITTEE

Leonard D. White   Marshall E. Dimock

Floyd W. Reeves

GOVERNMENT CORPORATIONS
AND FEDERAL FUNDS

THE UNIVERSITY OF CHICAGO PRESS
CHICAGO, ILLINOIS

✶

THE BAKER & TAYLOR COMPANY
NEW YORK

THE CAMBRIDGE UNIVERSITY PRESS
LONDON

THE MARUZEN-KABUSHIKI-KAISHA
TOKYO, OSAKA, KYOTO, FUKUOKA, SENDAI

THE COMMERCIAL PRESS, LIMITED
SHANGHAI

GOVERNMENT CORPORATIONS AND FEDERAL FUNDS

*

By JOHN McDIARMID

Department of Politics
Princeton University

THE UNIVERSITY OF CHICAGO PRESS
CHICAGO · ILLINOIS

To A. M. M. *and* E. W. M.

INTRODUCTION

WHENEVER government undertakes an activity which is financially profitable there is always some interest, or group of interests, which may be expected to raise the voice of protest. It is usually a different matter when the undertaking has ceased to be a money-making one; "principle" loses its potency. So long as profit is to be made, however, you will hear the familiar battle cry, "The government is competing unfairly with its citizens; get the government out of business." This was heard when, about the middle of the last century, the state began to take over toll roads and water-supply systems. The same objection was voiced when privately run schools began to feel the competition of free public education. Today public opinion accepts these services, and a few others like the post office, as being essentially public. Gradually, almost imperceptibly, they have gravitated from the private into the public category. Moreover, citizens expect them to be efficiently and satisfactorily run. And, generally speaking, they are. The explanation is close at hand: when a public service is recognized as "legitimate," and when the demand for good service is strong, then government shows that it can be as efficient as any other group of persons, whether they be labeled "private" or otherwise.

In the United States and Great Britain, "municipal socialism," that is, the operation of local utilities, has been largely a development of the last sixty or seventy years, while the trend toward "state socialism," in actual practice, is of even more recent origin, most of it having occurred since the turn of the century. Rapid impetus to the movement has set in only since the World War and is found primarily in the fields of banking and credit, communication, transportation, and power. In Great Britain, for example, conservatives and socialists alike have conspired to bring electricity, broadcasting, London transport, and the coal industry within the "public" fold. Few observers expect the process to stop there.

With pronounced trends toward state trading, the intensity of complaints against government competition has grown apace, particularly in the United States. And much of the attack has been of the old variety, emotional and unspecific. Verbal symbols designed to secure an antagonistic response toward government activity still constitute the chief weapons of the opposition. Government is inefficient in its very nature; bureaucracy is the ruination of government; money spent on public services means so much less toward business prosperity. These are some of the more familiar refrains, and the objective of energetic public relations experts is to repeat them so frequently that they will be accepted as axiomatic.

But the old refrains have lost some of their appeal. Citizens see model schools, modern hydroelectric generating stations, efficient port facilities, all owned and operated by public authorities, and their skepticism grows. If this can be done in some cases, why not in others?

Before going much further toward state trading, it is important that we secure the right answer. It is not a simple one, of this I feel certain. Both the capitalists and the socialists, so called, have been guilty of oversimplification. What we need is a general theory of enterprises, cutting across the fields tagged "public" and "private." Such a theory would show that success or efficiency—which governments are supposed to be unable to achieve—is actually composed of and dependent upon a number of elements. This is not the place to attempt such an intricate analysis.

There is, however, one common condition which both private and public enterprises should assiduously seek if they are to be really efficient, namely, a sufficient degree of freedom with which to undertake experiments, adjust to changing circumstances, and make the best use of the undertaking's personnel and management assets. The market is traditionally, necessarily, uncertain. Those who ply their wares therein must expect changes of style, disasters of nature, unforeseen misfortunes, failures of trust, defects of organization, unfair methods of competition, and new discoveries. Successful exploitation of an opportunity often depends upon the availability of cash reserves or the instant securing of credits. The dealer in the market soon learns that he who fails to snatch a profitable opening loses it to others who are stronger or more alert.

Financial freedom is at the center of every other freedom. If you lack liberty to spend your capital or income within relatively broad limits, in all probability you will not be able to purchase the brains with which to secure success. If you must purchase what someone else thinks you should, just because it sells at the lowest price, you will not invariably secure what you can sell enthusiastically or use with confidence. If you do not have reserves or credit with which to expand, you are not likely to be on a sharp lookout for profitable opportunities. If you are not free to hire whom you will, you may suffer from lack of loyalty and teamwork.

Nothing encourages men like responsibility. Nothing inspires men more than free opportunity. Few things are more chilling to initiative than limitations imposed from the outside, regulations which lack discrimination and flexibility. It is a well-known trait of human nature that capacity rebels against outside control. These considerations apply with as much force to government as they do to industry.

Inflexibility is the curse of bureaucracy. Bureaucracy is inherent in bigness, but some of its objectionable consequences can be eliminated by adequate contriving. The deadening factors are outside control, hard and fast regulations, lack of that flexibility which accompanies freedom. Unless rigidity is constantly fought and means are found to insure flexibility, business enterprises become as bureaucratic as the worst of governments.

The trading enterprises of public authorities can be given a sufficient degree of freedom, thus assuring all the flexibilities we have championed, if only the desire is there to accord it. Even government trading departments, integrated as they are with the rest of the administrative machinery, can be accorded more latitude than the ordinary political departments. The administrative and financial experience of the British post office since the reforms of 1932 is one of the most recent and striking cases in point.

The dangers of bureaucracy and inflexibility are not nearly so great in the case of smaller undertakings, such as those of municipalities. The problem becomes most difficult, however, when trading services are planted within the garden of a huge bureaucracy like that of the federal government at Washington.

In any large enterprise, whether business or governmental, there is an ever present danger of giving the central financial agency too much power, too much authority over operations. Rigidity at the center results in paralysis at the extremities, at the very point at which the service is rendered and flexibility needs to be greatest. The rigidity of central financial control operates with especial objectionableness upon public trading enterprises; for reasons already discussed, they need greater freedom and flexibility than the others. There is a growing recognition of this need for special treatment. Mr. McDiarmid shows clearly how Congress has tried to relax the central financial control and also guarantee the fiscal autonomy of government corporations engaged in financial and business activities. But, as his study so strikingly shows, the problem is a complex one, and there is more than one side to the issue. The reader may well be grateful to him for not leaving the matter up in the air. With logical clearness and admirable objectivity he analyzes the several alternatives and indicates the one which to him seems preferable.

The feature of the corporation which is most renowned is that of limited liability. This has been a distinct advantage in private industry, where it has stimulated entry into new fields, for it has provided entrepreneurs and investors with an opportunity to reap the benefits of risk-taking and rapid exploitation with only a proportional, usually only infinitesimal, possibility of being held personally and financially accountable. Statesmen now pondering public policy are wondering, quite naturally, whether diminution of risk has not been carried too far and whether corporate freedom in many cases does not amount to license.

Another outstanding characteristic of the corporation is its legal, financial, and administrative autonomy. A corporation is a separate, distinct, integrated entity. Being separate and self-contained, it naturally possesses the potentialities of freedom and enterprise which we have been praising. In the long run, this autonomy of corporations is likely to prove of greater social significance and value than the privilege of limited liability. My own belief is that in the coming years society will have to invent more socially desirable methods of defining the permissible area of corporate enterprise and of increasing the trusteeship accountability of managers and owners. On the other hand, there is a good deal of evidence to show that restrictions on operating and financial autonomy are fraught with the gravest of social dangers.

It is a tribute to the potential business efficiency inherent in the corporate device that government reliance upon the public corporation has tended to increase with the extension of state trading. Statesmen have realized that bureaucratic influences inhering in a system of central control and integrated administration are difficult to reform. Progress is slow unless there is an effective demand for more and better public services. Either because they feel pessimistic about the possibilities of reform or because the urgency of taking over a trading service does not permit of delay, national legislators have more and more turned to the autonomous device, the public corporation. They have said, in effect, "Let us use the same kind of legal entity, freedom of management, and independence of finance which contribute to the success of the best-managed private enterprises." It is an argument that is hard to answer. Small wonder, then, that defenders of the *status quo* often become more alarmed about government's use of efficient methods than about the doctrinaire writings of revolutionists!

The use of the public corporation is a development of almost world-wide proportions. In some cases, notably in the United States, the government owns all the shares of stock and is solely responsible for management. This type is referred to as the government-owned corporation, or simply "government corporation" (the latter usage being preferred by Mr. McDiarmid). In other cases, both government and a private company or individuals contribute to the investment and share in the management; this form of public corporation goes under the name of "mixed enterprise." It is the outstanding public utility development in post-war Europe and is found prominently in a dozen countries on the Continent. The United States has an experiment resembling it in the Boston Elevated Railway, but this particular enterprise also has resemblances to the third variety of public corporation I shall mention, namely, the public utility trust or public board. The public utility trust, variously denominated "public board," "public concern," and "public corporation," is found outstandingly in Great Britain, where it is exemplified by such socialized services as the Port of London Authority, the Central Electricity Board, the British Broadcasting Corporation, and the London Passenger Transport Board. All these are not identical in their form of ownership and method of constituting the directing board, but in a general way it may be said that the public utility trust is a public board or corporation in which the shares of stock are owned by private investors, without voting rights, and the enterprise is managed by a policy board appointed by the government and, sometimes, with the collaboration of interests designated by it. The principal exception to this definition is the British Broadcasting Corporation, which has no privately subscribed stock. However, it, like the other public corporations, is free from "treasury control" and possesses managerial autonomy.

There is no reason for using the corporate device unless a

high degree of autonomy and flexibility is required for the function under consideration. This is another way of saying that the public corporation should be confined to trading activities and that it should not be employed indiscriminately, needlessly. This sound rule of social policy has been violated in some cases within recent years, and a repetition of such mistakes is to be avoided. An old, established rule of statecraft is that *ad hoc* agencies should be kept at a minimum. Every agency that wants to be free from the integrated structure of the government and the control of central staff agencies must be able to make out a case for itself, showing that the advantages considerably outweigh the disadvantages. At the present stage of development in American public administration, and confronted as we are with the need of important economic changes, there is a convincing case, I think, for the continued independence of the more important and permanent public corporations. But, in general, administrative integration and party responsibility are so important that the establishment of separate governmental units should be discouraged.

We should not only guard ourselves against a too frequent and promiscuous use of the corporate device but we should insist that corporations adhere to type or else be converted into ordinary departmental setups. There is no use maintaining the appearance of a corporation, unless the enterprise retains the corporation's virtues of autonomy and flexibility. Stripped of these, the so-called corporation will have lost its social justification.

It is to be expected that public corporations now in existence will fluctuate between increased autonomy and bureaucratic control. This is only inevitable, I suppose, in countries where one party and then another comes into power. Those business and political factions which consider their interests adversely affected by a given public commercial undertaking will quite likely attempt to weaken the corporate character of the venture. Next to putting it out of business altogether, this is an effective method of attack. It is useless to think that our standards of political morality are high enough to prevent this kind of sabotage from being attempted.

Our citizens and our lawmakers, our administrators and our judges, all need to be educated in the essentials of the public corporation, its characteristic virtues and advantages. It is a separate, distinct entity, free to operate efficiently and flexibly. It is guided by a "little legislature," a board of directors or trustees, which formulates its basic policies in accordance with the charter and the intentions of the legislature, and which acts as the controlling agency in protecting the public interest. This goes a long way toward compensating for the lack of central integration and control. It is free to issue certificates of indebtedness, retain its net profits, make contracts, purchase without restriction, enjoy all the financial rights of a private corporation. It is free to pay good salaries, recruit the best people it can get, hire and fire to its advantage. Finally, since it is a legal person, its life is perpetual, it does not depend upon annual appropriations, and it can be sued for its violations of the law.

These are advantages of prime social significance. So important are they that they outweigh many an objection which may be brought. If we are going to employ the public corporation in pursuance of public policy, let us try to be authentic. Mr. McDiarmid's study shows clearly what the essentials are, so far as financial management is concerned.

MARSHALL E. DIMOCK

PREFACE

THIS study was begun when I was a graduate student in public administration at the University of Chicago. As temporary research assistant to the National Resources Board my interest in government corporations had been heightened by three months spent in Knoxville studying the Tennessee Valley Authority. Particularly, the controversy between that corporation and the Comptroller-General had directed my attention to the problem of financial powers with which this monograph is primarily concerned.

In planning the study, in defining its scope, and indeed in every phase of the research and composition, I have had the invaluable guidance of my teacher and friend, Marshall E. Dimock, to whom I am greatly indebted. Most of my information has been obtained from official publications and through innumerable interviews with public officials. I am grateful to many of the latter for their sufferance of my questions and for liberal contribution of their own views and experiences. In several instances I was given access to unpublished material which proved to be of great value.

Without implicating many friends in the profession who have made helpful suggestions, I desire nevertheless to express my appreciation of their interest and encouragement. My sister, Florence Gooch, generously contributed her efficient assistance in the preparation of the manuscript, while Dorothy McDiarmid has helped in far too many ways to enumerate. My wife has graciously undertaken the uninspiring task of proofreading, to which she unfortunately fell heir.

My thanks are due the editor of the *American Political Science Review* for permission to use sections of the study which have appeared in that journal, and also to the Brookings Institution, Harper and Brothers, Alfred A. Knopf, and the

Macmillan Company for allowing me to quote from several of their published works. Finally, I am grateful to the directors of the Public Administration Fund of the University of Chicago for making publication possible.

JOHN McDIARMID

PRINCETON
July 8, 1938

TABLE OF CONTENTS

CHAPTER I

INTRODUCTION TO THE PROBLEM
OF FINANCIAL FREEDOM

A STRIKING feature of the expansion of governmental services in recent years has been the increasing use of the government corporation as an administrative agency. Particularly has the corporate device been utilized in the public operation of economic enterprises, and in most respects the organization, management, and control of such undertakings are more nearly comparable with those of a private business than with the departmental form of governmental administration.

This development has not been confined to any one nation but may be seen in various European countries and the commonwealths of the British Empire, as well as in the United States. To be sure, forms of ownership and control differ markedly. Thus, a characteristic type in Great Britain is the public utility trust, with its nonvoting privately owned securities, and its government-appointed directors, or "trustees."[1] A second variation, found principally in Germany and France, is the mixed undertaking, which is characterized by joint private and public ownership, and over which control, though likewise shared, rests ultimately with the government. Finally, the purest type is the corporation completely owned and controlled by the government, and in the utilization of this instrument the United States has been among the leaders.

The importance of the government corporation as a federal agency has been little recognized, in spite of the fact that a large number have been created to administer a variety of func-

[1] Examples are the Central Electricity Board, the London Passenger Transport Board, and the British Broadcasting Corporation (see Marshall E. Dimock, *British Public Utilities and National Development* [London: Allen & Unwin, Ltd., 1933]).

tions including the operation of rail and water carriers, ship-building and maintenance, provision of housing facilities, distribution of electrical power, relief activities, banking and credit operations in the fields of industry, agriculture, and home-financing, and a host of others far too numerous to mention. The 1936 report of the Secretary of the Treasury reveals that the proprietary interest of the United States in corporations and credit agencies either completely or for the most part government-owned amounts to $4,223,000,000. At the same time, the total assets of these agencies are over $11,791,000,-000.[2] These are staggering sums even in this era of high finance and huge governmental expenditures.

Of the great corporations, the majority have been created since the inauguration of President Roosevelt in 1933. The most notable exception, namely, the Reconstruction Finance Corporation, was organized in 1932, but has been continued and so greatly expanded that it has become virtually a part of the New Deal mechanism. This utilization of the corporate device in the government's attack on the economic crisis is very similar to the earlier experience of World War days. At that time, such corporations as the War Finance Corporation, the United States Housing Corporation, the Emergency Fleet Corporation, the United States Grain Corporation, and the Sugar Equalization Board were created as temporary agencies for carrying on vital activities with a maximum of speed and accomplishment. The success of these early corporations in cutting through red tape and vigorously pursuing their objectives has undoubtedly been a major factor in the recent expansion of the corporate device to meet another emergency—this time economic rather than military.

In any event, the study of the administrative aspects of the government corporation is now one of current rather than of purely historical interest. This device, so frequently used, has been all too little understood. The problem achieves even

---

[2] Figures as of June 30, 1936 (*Annual Report of the Secretary of the Treasury, 1936*, p. 454).

greater significance in the light of the increasing number of proposals that additional corporations be created. Thus, bills introduced into the Seventy-fourth and Seventy-fifth congresses have provided for a Federal Unemployment Insurance Corporation, a Farmers' and Consumers' Financing Corporation, a Farmers' Security Corporation, a Farm Tenant Home Purchase Corporation, a Surplus Reserve Loan Corporation, a Fishery Credit Corporation, and a Federal Housing Development Corporation. Numerous bills have been introduced proposing valley authorities similar to the Tennessee Valley Authority for practically every major river system in the United States, while others would authorize United States purchase of the stock of the federal reserve banks. It has been suggested that the Panama Canal be incorporated.[3] Finally, the much-discussed railroad question has occasionally prompted the proposal of a national railroad corporation as the best solution. Thus, Mr. Celler introduced into the Seventy-third Congress a bill to establish a "Federal Railroad Corporation," and Senator Wheeler's bill in the Seventy-fourth Congress would have created a corporation to be known as "United States Railways."

GOVERNMENT ECONOMIC ENTERPRISES

As we have indicated, the government corporation has been primarily employed in the administration of economic enterprises which are commonly thought of as outside the range of regular "governmental" activities. The inevitable result has been that these corporations have been thrown into the arena wherein are fought the most bitterly contested battles with business interests and the disciples of laissez faire. The corporate device as such becomes lost in impassioned discussions of "government encroachment in the field of private enterprise," or "government competition with private business." Opponents of government operation in general are wont to

[3] Dimock, *Government-operated Enterprises in the Panama Canal Zone* (Chicago: University of Chicago Press, 1934).

voice their opposition to the government corporation because it has become to them the concrete symbol of that operation.[4]

The extent to which those governmental services which compete with private businesses should be expanded (or contracted) is of the greatest importance in our present-day society.[5] While discussion of this problem goes on apace, however, the fact remains that the United States Government is actually carrying on a tremendous number and variety of business and commercial activities. The trend seems to be almost inexorably in the direction of increasing such activities but whether this continues to be true or not, and even if a certain amount of curtailment should set in, there will remain more than enough business activities to warrant a thorough consideration of the administrative desirability of the corporate device.

CONSTITUTIONAL AND LEGAL QUESTIONS

In addition to problems of social and political philosophy, the government corporation raises important constitutional and legal questions. The contention has indeed been made that "there is no place in our constitutional government for the performance of governmental functions by means of corpora-

[4] This may be illustrated by a resolution of the Philadelphia Board of Trade, which reads in part as follows:

"Whereas we are opposed to the use by the Federal Government of corporations, incorporated under the laws of the several states, to carry out Federal purposes in competition with private enterprise: Therefore be it

Resolved, That such corporations as were organized since March 4, 1933, by officials or agencies of the United States for its use shall be liquidated within 90 days and that henceforth, except by express authorization of Congress, no other or like corporation shall be organized for any purpose by or on behalf of the United States (quoted in Congressional Record, LXXIX, 4048).

[5] The exploration of the opposing views on this question, with their attendant economic and emotional implications, would be a fascinating project, but it is not that to which we have addressed ourselves in this study. Interested readers should examine the report of the Shannon Committee, appointed in 1932 to investigate "government competition with private enterprise" (House Report 1985 [72d Cong. 2d sess.]).

tions."[6] Such a conclusion seems far fetched in view of the actual use which has been made of the corporate device. Certainly there has been considerable discussion as to the constitutionality of many governmental activities in which a corporation is employed. Justification has been sought under various constitutional powers—national defense, commerce power, fiscal powers, and the general welfare clause.[7] Here again, however, the moot question has been that of the power of the government to engage in a particular activity, not the constitutionality of the corporate device itself. Rather has the latter never been seriously questioned, where no doubt existed as to the right of the government to perform the functions involved.[8]

Legal questions raised by the government corporation are numerous, and many remain unsolved. The combination of private and public features, liability to suit, property matters, employee relationships, and taxation questions are among the most important aspects from which litigation has resulted.[9] The Fleet Corporation has been the trial horse in many instances, and a study of the cases in which that agency has been concerned would in itself be a sizeable project. With regard to the more recent corporations, novel corporate structures and widely varying functions undoubtedly foreshadow the raising of complicated problems for judicial settlement.[10]

[6] O. R. McGuire, "Government by Corporations," *Virginia Law Review*, XIV (1928), 186. See also the late Senator Schall's bitter attack on "these corporations that are going to make our United States of America a United States of Russia" (*Congressional Record*, LXXIX, 4051).

[7] See M. S. Culp, "Creation of Government Corporations by the National Government," *Michigan Law Review*, XXXIII (1935), 473.

[8] Cf. *McCulloch* v. *Maryland*, 4 Wheaton 316; *Smith* v. *Kansas City Title Trust Co.*, 225 U.S. 180; *Luxton* v. *N. River Bridge Co.*, 153 U.S. 525; see also the many cases involving the Feet Corporation.

[9] These questions have been discussed by John Thurston, "Government Proprietary Corporations," *Virginia Law Review*, XXI (1935), 351, 465; see also "The Corporation as a Federal Administrative Device," *University of Pennsylvania Law Review*, LXXXIII (1935), 346 ff.; "Government Corporations in Business," *Columbia Law Review*, XXXII (1932), 881.

[10] "The Corporation as a Federal Administrative Device," *op. cit.*, p. 357.

While it would seem that some legal questions must inevitably arise if the corporate device is to be utilized by the federal government, nevertheless much additional confusion has been caused by the failure of Congress to supply what Mr. O. P. Field has called "a proper statutory foundation."[11] Laws relating to existing corporations present a veritable maze of provisions, differing in fundamentals as well as in details.[12]

ADMINISTRATIVE CHARACTERISTICS OF THE GOVERNMENT CORPORATION

Aside from questions of social policy, aside from constitutional and legal matters, there remains the significant question of the relative merits and demerits of the government corporation from the point of view of administration. This device has been used in the past; it is found in many varieties today; its further use is indicated for the future. What are its advantages and disadvantages as compared to older forms of governmental organization?

On the one hand, it has been declared that the government corporation is simply a shield for extravagant and irresponsible administration, as well as for corruption.[13] As opposed to this view, other students have been impressed with the greater aggressiveness and efficiency made possible by the use of the

[11] "Government Corporations: A Proposal," *Harvard Law Review*, XLVIII (1935), 775.

[12] It is interesting to note Mr. Field's suggestion that "Congress should enact a carefully drawn statute under which all corporations federally owned and operated should be incorporated." There is room for grave doubt as to whether a general statute with all the provisions recommended by Mr. Field could be drawn without imposing upon the corporations a rigidity and arbitrary uniformity which would prove harmful. However, the searching study by a congressional committee which Mr. Field proposes would at least pave the way to the formation by Congress of valuable guiding principles.

[13] See the late James M. Beck's appraisal (*Our Wonderland of Bureaucracy* [New York: Macmillan Co. 1932], p. 128). The late Senator Schall made several vigorous attacks upon government corporations from the floor of the Senate, but it is difficult to extricate his charges of waste and administrative inefficiency from the larger questions involving his bitter opposition to the policies of the Roosevelt administration (see *Congressional Record*, LXXIX, 1546 ff., 3973 ff., 4048 ff.).

corporate device. With a form of organization similar to that of a private company, a governmental enterprise may be conducted along business lines with great dispatch and vigor. Congressional interference in the details of administration is made more difficult, and the way is paved for the removal of the undertaking from political considerations. Flexibility and speed of action are made possible through managerial discretion and the absence of regular governmental procedures and red tape. The right to sue and be sued in the corporate name is enjoyed. Inefficient details of the civil service requirements need not be followed. Finally, the government corporation enjoys a large measure of financial freedom, with many potentially salutary effects.

For these reasons, it has appeared to many that a considerable number of the trading and quasi-commercial activities of government could best be administered through the corporate device. A clear statement of this view has been made by Professor Marshall E. Dimock,[14] but it is rather widely held and not surprisingly characterizes the ideas of most of the higher officials among the various corporate agencies. The point which is extremely significant for our study is the importance placed upon freedom in financial matters. Thus Professor Dimock has stated that "the principal advantages of a government-owned corporation over an ordinary government department are to be found in the ease and independence with which the undertaking's financial affairs and purchasing operations can be conducted." When it is recalled that adverse critics likewise place greatest emphasis upon financial freedom—this time in terms of deprecation—the importance of the problem as to what financial powers government corporations should enjoy may readily be seen.

Specifically, the financial features frequently found in the government corporation which are of particular interest from the standpoint of administrative freedom are: initial capitali-

---

[14] *Government-operated Enterprises in the Panama Canal Zone*, chap. ix: "Principles Underlying Government-owned Corporations."

zation and consequent removal from the necessity of annual
appropriations; power to borrow money; ability to retain earnings as working capital or for reserves; freedom, in the matter
of expenditures, from general governmental regulations and
restrictions; and freedom, in accounting and auditing matters,
from the control of regular governmental accounting officials.
Among the many corporations, there is far from uniformity
in these matters, as the ensuing chapters will reveal, but the
major questions involved are continually reappearing.

THE GENERAL ACCOUNTING OFFICE

While the initial problem is that of the sources of capital for
carrying on the various corporate enterprises,[15] the remaining
questions involving expenditures, receipts or earnings, and accountability resolve largely into the relationship with the General Accounting Office of the United States. To be sure, clear
statutory pronouncements on these matters are controlling,
but in their absence, or in the event of provisions which may be
variously interpreted, the Comptroller-General has entered the
picture, with his legal interpretations and his administrative
rulings. Sometimes, as in the case of the T.V.A., the manner of
expenditures will be the chief point at issue; in other instances,
for example, the case of the Commodity Credit Corporation,
disposition of earnings has been principally in dispute; occasionally, as in the case of the Inland Waterways Corporation,
relations with the Comptroller-General are virtually nonexist-
ent. Questions of accounting and auditing, involving the nature of a governmental as compared to a private audit, are continually in the background, and embrace the other aspects of
the problem.

The powers and the functions of the General Accounting
Office are numerous and varied. While definitive classification
is exceedingly difficult, the following list has been worked out
as covering the duties and activities specified by law:[16]

[15] See below, chap. iii.

[16] D. H. Smith, *The General Accounting Office* (Baltimore: Johns Hopkins
Press, 1927), p. 78.

1. Control of Treasury receipts and issues
2. Settlement and adjustment of claims
3. Audit of receipts
4. Quasi-judicial and legal activities
5. Accounting
6. Investigations and reports
7. Custodial and recording functions

These activities have been described in detail elsewhere, but a few of the more important points for our study should be noted. Section 305 of the Budget and Accounting Act of 1921 provides as follows: "All claims and demands whatever by the Government of the United States or against it, and all accounts whatever in which the Government of the United States is concerned either as debtor or creditor, shall be settled and adjusted in the General Accounting Office." This provision is the basis for much of the Comptroller-General's control over expenditures, since he has the power to disallow disbursements to which he takes exception. Payments may actually have been made, but, when exception is taken by the General Accounting Office, the disbursing officer must either recover the amount or be held personally liable therefor.

In controlling expenditures, the Comptroller-General demands strict compliance with all general statutes and regulations on the subject. An exhaustive enumeration of such acts and rules would include hundreds of statutory provisions and the majority of the rulings which are to be found in sixteen lengthy volumes containing the decisions of the Comptroller-General. A brief and selective examination, however, should be useful in indicating the nature of the restrictions and procedures which surround expenditure of funds by the ordinary departments and bureaus of the federal government.

Among the legislative provisions relating to expenditures are the following. Purchases and contracts for supplies or services must be made after advertising and allowing sufficient time for the submission of bids, unless immediate delivery or performance is required by the public exigency.[17] All contracts made shall be deposited promptly in the General Accounting Office.[18] American materials and manufactured goods must be purchased for public use, unless the head of a department or establishment finds it inconsistent with the public interest, or the cost unreasonable.[19] No advance of public money shall be made in any case whatever.[20] It is obligatory upon governmental departments to purchase articles manufactured by the federal prison industries when they are available, before making similar purchases elsewhere.[21] All printing, except such classes of work as shall be excepted by the Joint Committee on Printing, must be done at the Government Printing Office.[22] Law books, reference books, and periodicals cannot be purchased from generally or specifically appropriated funds unless purchase is expressly authorized by law.[23] Purchase of newspapers and periodicals from contingent funds when such newspapers and periodicals are not "necessary to the business of the office" is limited to $100 annually in the case of department heads and $30 annually in the case of other executive officers.[24] No employee of the Pinkerton Detective Agency, or similar agency, shall be employed in any government service.[25] No appropriated money may be used for compensation of any publicity expert unless specifically appropriated for that purpose,[26] nor shall any appropriated funds be used to compensate or pay the expenses of accountants or other experts in inaugurating new or changing old methods of transacting the business of the United States.[27] The maintenance, repair, or operation of pas-

---

[17] Revised Statutes, sec. 3709 (hereafter referred to as R.S.). Such statutes of general application usually contain a qualifying clause, such as "except as otherwise provided by law." Specific authorization in other acts frequently makes a general statute inapplicable in particular instances. This qualification should be understood as implied throughout the present discussion.

[18] R.S. sec. 3743.

[19] 41 U.S.C.A. sec. 10a.

[20] R.S. sec. 3648.

[21] 43 Stat. 6; 46 Stat. 391.

[22] 40 Stat. 1270.

[23] 31 U.S.C.A. sec. 678.

[24] 5 U.S.C.A. sec. 102.

[25] 5 U.S.C.A. sec. 53.

[26] 5 U.S.C.A. sec. 54.

[27] 5 U.S.C.A. sec. 55.

senger-carrying vehicles is prohibited unless authorized by law.[28]

No land may be purchased by a governmental department or agency unless under a law authorizing such purchase.[29] No site may be purchased for the purpose of erecting a public building until the written opinion of the Attorney-General shall be had in favor of the validity of the title, nor until consent of the state legislature has been given.[30] All legal services connected with the procurement of title to a site for a public building shall be rendered by United States district attorneys.[31] Expenditures on a public building may not be made until plans and estimates have been submitted to the supervisory architect of the Treasury Department and approved by the Secretary of the Treasury.[32] Furniture for all new public buildings must be procured in accordance with plans and specifications approved by the supervisory architect of the Treasury.[33] Dealing with the use of public property, rather than specifically with the expenditure of funds, one statute prohibits the letting of leases for other than cash rentals.[34]

Contracts for repair of public buildings and works must include a stipulation for liquidated damages for delay.[35] Contractors for the construction and repair of public buildings must furnish good and sufficient bond.[36] No contract shall be made for the rent of any building or part of a building in the District of Columbia until an appropriation is made therefor by Congress.[37]

In a more complete enumeration of general statutory regulations regarding expenditures, mention would have to be made, for example, of provisions relating to travel, subsistence, and employee compensation, but the foregoing list should be sufficiently illustrative. Of even greater importance for our pres-

[28] 38 Stat. 508.
[29] 41 U.S.C.A. sec. 14.
[30] 40 U.S.C.A. sec. 255.
[31] 40 U.S.C.A. sec. 256.
[32] 40 U.S.C.A. sec. 267.
[33] 40 U.S.C.A. sec. 283.
[34] 40 U.S.C.A. sec. 303b.
[35] 32 Stat. 326.
[36] 40 U.S.C.A. sec. 270.
[37] 19 Stat. 370.

ent purposes is a consideration of the role of the Comptroller-General in interpreting, enforcing, and supplementing such legislative provisions. The extent of this power, as conceived by the General Accounting Office, is indicated in the following excerpt from a committee hearing:

> *Question:* "As to the expenditure of appropriated money, according to your interpretation of the law, the Comptroller-General's Office, is the court of last resort?"
>
> ASSISTANT COMPTROLLER-GENERAL LURTIN R. GINN: "Absolutely, except you gentlemen up here. . . . ."[38]

In an early ruling, Comptroller-General McCarl held that the decision as to whether expenditures of public funds are authorized by law and are for the objects or purposes for which the appropriations sought to be charged are available, is a matter for determination solely by the Comptroller-General, "and may not be adjudicated by any court."[39] The immensity of this power is readily apparent when it is remembered that all claims must be settled in the General Accounting Office, that accounts of all expenditures are rendered to that office, and that the Comptroller-General may disallow individual expenditures if in his opinion they are made illegally or without authorization. For illustrative purposes, let us consider some of the regulations and decisions of the Comptroller-General and his predecessor, the Comptroller of the Treasury.

If advertisement for purchases omits any factor considered by the Comptroller-General to be an essential competitive factor, none of the bids received can be accepted, and a readvertisement must be made.[40] The desire to match equipment on hand does not warrant purchase without competition.[41] Immediate delivery does not excuse the formal execution of a contract.[42] The lowest responsible bid meeting specifications must be accepted, and, when any other than the lowest bid is

---

[38] *Hearings before House Committee on Expenditures in the Executive Departments, on H.R. 12180* (70th Cong., 1st sess., March 28 and 31, 1928).

[39] 3 Comptroller General's Decisions 545 (hereafter referred to as C.G.).

[40] 8 C.G. 649.   [41] 3 C.G. 304.   [42] 3 C.G. 314.

accepted, a detailed statement of reasons must be submitted to the General Accounting Office.[43] Contracts deposited in the General Accounting Office should be accompanied by an abstract of all the bids received, or by the bids themselves.[44] Leasing of premises for use of governmental agencies must be after advertising and competition.[45] An act authorizing the purchase of lands (as for reclamation purposes) does not authorize the expense of procuring options for rights of way, water rights, or lands needed.[46] Payment for an option to purchase supplies is also illegal unless specifically authorized.[47] Commercial purchase of brushes is illegal without a showing that the federal penitentiary was unable to furnish such brushes; the law does not contain any provision exempting purchases on account of emergencies.[48] Public funds may not be used to purchase insurance on property.[49]

All claims of common carriers must be transmitted to the General Accounting Office for settlement before payment.[50] Repairs in kind in lieu of cash rentals for private use of public building space are illegal as being repairs for which appropriations have not been made.[51] Treatment of the walls and ceilings of a public building with sound-deadening felt is not an item of repair or preservation but an improvement and is not payable from an appropriation for repairs and preservation of public buildings.[52]

Finally, the General Accounting Office prescribes standard forms for advertising, purchasing, reimbursement, contracts, and accounts, and such forms must be used by the government departments.

The foregoing statutes and regulations, together with innumerable others of a similar nature, constitute the circumscribed bounds within which the various government depart-

---

[43] 4 C.G. 254.   [44] 5 C.G. 566.   [45] 14 C.G. 769.
[46] 9 Comptroller of the Treasury's Decisions 569 (hereafter referred to as C.D.).
[47] 23 C.D. 116.   [48] 14 C.G. 271.
[49] 4 C.G. 690.   [51] 8 C.G. 633, citing R.S., sec. 3733.
[50] Regulation of January 1, 1923.   [52] 2 C.G. 301.

ments expend public funds. Many of them are wholesome and even necessary, but whether wholesome or not, the fact remains that as a unit they comprise the restrictions, procedural details, and consequent delays that have been popularly characterized as "governmental red tape." They lend some support to the charge, frequently made, that government is inefficient and cannot conduct business enterprises with the success characteristic of a well-managed and progressive private company.

Regularized procedures and restrictions are most beneficial or least unsatisfactory when they are applied to activities which are largely of a routine or stable nature. When a government bureau performs the same function with little change from year to year, its necessary expenditures can be accurately estimated, and the manner in which such expenditures are to to be made can be well defined in advance. Many bureaus in the federal government have activities of this relatively static character, and speed and dispatch are comparatively unimportant in the everyday conduct of affairs.

In the realm of private business, however, speed and flexibility are of the essence of success. Customers must be pleased with prompt service; changes in method, products, and services must be made as their desirability becomes apparent; forms must be dispensed with from time to time in order to achieve results; immediate advantage must be taken of favorable markets; extensions and improvements must be made as business warrants; excessive delays, tentative commitments, and complicated procedures result in increased costs and in loss of goodwill and business. In short, a commercial and competitive enterprise requires flexibility and initiative if it is to be successful.

These principles of successful business management cannot be neglected by government when it undertakes enterprises of a commercial nature. The analogy is not perfect, obviously, because of the differing purposes of public and private enterprises, and because of the need for adequate controls to insure responsibility in the use of public funds. Nevertheless, the minutiae of regulations which apply to routine governmental activities cannot be imposed upon governmental business enterprises without damaging results.

In the light of the foregoing observations, the large discretionary power of the Comptroller-General over governmental expenditures becomes extremely significant. For those agencies within his jurisdiction he is the final authority on such questions as the following. Can legal authorization be found for a given expenditure? When is an otherwise proper expenditure, for example, the payment of an appraisal fee, "unreasonably large" and hence illegal? When does the public exigency require emergency purchases without competition? Is a particular low bidder a responsible bidder? Does a particular bid meet specifications? Are particular specifications unjustifiably narrow, thus destroying competition? Do administrative requirements in a particular case justify acceptance of other than the lowest bid?

In addition to control over expenditures, it may be seen that section 305 of the Budget and Accounting Act also gives to the General Accounting Office a certain jurisdiction over receipts from claims owed the government. Thus, the Comptroller-General may object to any compromise of such claims when in his opinion the interests of the government are not adequately protected.

The countersignature of the Comptroller-General is required for requisition of appropriated funds from the Treasury and for warrants covering miscellaneous funds into the Treasury. Power rests with the Comptroller-General to withhold approval of requisitions of appropriated funds, but this is construed as an extraordinary remedy for misuse of previously acquired moneys, and the power is not commonly exercised. Probably the fact that the Secretary of the Treasury may override the Comptroller-General's refusal of requisitions has been of some influence in the matter.[53] As for receipts, the Comptroller-Gen-

[53] The Comptroller-General has been unsuccessful in his attempts to have Congress remove this overriding power of the Secretary of the Treasury (see

eral has been diligent in demanding compliance with sections 3617 and 3618 of the Revised Statutes, which require, with a few exceptions, the covering of funds from "whatever source" into the Treasury as miscellaneous receipts. As we shall see, the applicability of these provisions to the earnings of government corporations has proved to be an important and much-disputed issue.

In the matter of accounting, the Comptroller-General in 1921 inherited the duties previously imposed upon Treasury accounting officials relating to keeping the personal ledger accounts of disbursing and collecting officers and, in addition, was directed to "prescribe the forms, systems, and procedure for administrative appropriation and fund accounting in the several departments and establishments, and for the administrative examination of fiscal officers' accounts and claims against the United States." With the power to require information at any time, the Comptroller-General makes a continuous audit of the financial transactions of the various branches of the government and submits, in addition to his annual report, such special reports as may be required from time to time by Congress, the President, or the Bureau of the Budget.

It is generally recognized that the "auditing" functions exercised by the General Accounting Office are primarily in the nature of a legal examination. A clear statement is to be found in Mr. D. H. Smith's monograph, as follows:

While the detailed accounting procedure of the General Accounting Office follows normal practice in most respects, it differs fundamentally (as with all government accounting) from business or private accounting. Government accounting is essentially legal in its nature. Its guiding principle is legislative authorization as contrasted with business accounting, which operates so largely under lump-sum appropriations entrusted to the discretionary authority of the spending officers. Private accounting is primarily concerned with solvency and profits (thus cost—and

---

Hearings before House Committee on Expenditures in the Executive Departments, on H.R. 12180 [70th Cong., March 28 and 31, 1928]).

expediency), while government accounting is controlled by legality and regularity. Private accounting may, possibly, ignore a rule or regulation if increased profits or decreased costs result. Public accounting, with solvency assured and profits unconsidered, dare not ignore law or regulation, especially since a separate body, Congress, is given power over the purse and jealously guards it.[54]

Thus, the interpretation of appropriation acts of Congress becomes perhaps the most important single function of the Comptroller-General. In the words of Mr. McCarl himself, "The true function of the Comptroller is that of a control officer; that is, to determine the availability of general appropriations to pay claims without further Congressional action. This involves, of course, the consideration of the merits of the claim, but however meritorious a claim, it cannot be allowed by the Comptroller unless there is some appropriation or statutory authority therefor."[55] Because of its importance, the Comptroller's power to interpret appropriation acts has been the subject of much dispute.[56]

It is difficult to reconcile the foregoing considerations with the position taken by Comptroller-General McCarl in 1929 in declaring that "the audit given to expenditures made by governmental departments and establishments does not materially differ from that given and authorized by a private concern, both being similar in their nature and applicable along the same lines."[57] Certainly this view has been vigorously assailed by officials of the various government corporations, who contend that the government audit is fundamentally different from a commercial audit. Whereas a governmental audit is concerned primarily with statutory authorization for a given

[54] *Op. cit.*, p. 111.

[55] Typewritten letter of January 28, 1927, quoted in Smith, *op. cit.*, p. 83.

[56] See Harvey C. Mansfield, "Judicial Review of the Comptroller General," *Cornell Law Quarterly*, XX (1935), 459 ff. For a discussion of the conflict between the accounting officers and the Attorney-General of the United States see A. G. Langeluttig, *The Department of Justice of the United States* (Baltimore: Johns Hopkins Press, 1927), chap. xiii.

[57] *House Document 111* (71st Cong.), p. 48.

expenditure, a private audit is concerned with the honesty and expediency with which corporation funds are expended. Thus, an unusual outlay, made in an emergency and with beneficial results, must be disallowed for lack of authority in a governmental audit, yet a similar expenditure could be recognized as efficient and sanctioned in a commercial audit. Procedures and rules must be followed, in anticipation of a governmental audit, "regardless of efficiency," whereas in a private audit such rigidity is not necessarily imposed. Illustrative of practices disallowable in a governmental audit on purely legal grounds are: leasing of property for other than cash rentals, the compromise of claims, and the alteration of contracts other than "in the interest of the government" (i.e., as interpreted by the accounting officers).

GOVERNMENT CORPORATIONS AND THE GENERAL ACCOUNTING OFFICE

The relationships between the various government corporations and the General Accounting Office will be traced in some detail in the later chapters of this study. Suffice it here to introduce the problem.

While the statutes empowering the Comptroller-General might be interpreted in themselves as extending the jurisdiction of his office to corporations financed with public funds, the Supreme Court in 1927 refused such an interpretation, as affecting the wartime corporations, and explained that, "indeed, an important if not the chief reason for employing these incorporated agencies was to enable them to employ commercial methods and to conduct their operations with a freedom supposed to be inconsistent with accountability to the Treasury under its established procedure of audit and control over the financial transactions of the United States."[58] The Comptroller-General himself has asserted his lack of jurisdiction in some cases, yet in other instances he has maintained that regular governmental statutes are applicable and place the

[58] *Skinner & Eddy Corporation* v. *McCarl*, 275 U.S. 1.

corporations concerned under his supervision. Particularly has the nature of various special audits required by law been the subject of controversy between the General Accounting Office and corporate officials.

In addition to questions of legal interpretation, there has arisen that of the desirability of General Accounting Office control of corporate financial transactions. Comptroller-General McCarl's position has been as follows:

> There are other governmental activities successfully operating under the statutory audit governing appropriated moneys and it is believed that the Government will gain much if the excepted corporations are brought within the general statutes, the effect and principles of which are no more restrictive than the commercial rules, but are capable of enforcement through not otherwise available enforcement agencies.[59]

Consequently, he repeatedly recommended to Congress that all government corporations be placed under his complete control in financial and accounting matters.

On the other hand, corporate officials have felt that such control in the hands of the General Accounting Office would seriously handicap their administrative efficiency and would result in delays and increased overhead and operating expenses.[60] Hence, Congress has been presented with counterarguments whenever the Comptroller's recommendations for increased and more clearly defined control are up for consideration.

The attitude of Congress in this matter is not very clear. The apparent intention of the framers of the various laws creating government corporations has usually been to permit freedom from General Accounting Office control. On the other hand, the nature of special statutory audits has not been unequivocally stated, nor has it been thoroughly understood by

[59] *House Document 111* (71st Cong.), p. 49.

[60] This may be illustrated by the Fleet Corporation's reply to the Comptroller-General's first audit report. Among other things, it was contended that "the Comptroller-General in many instances has assumed authority to question the administrative judgment" of corporation officials (*House Document 695* [71st Cong.], p. 34).

many members of Congress.[61] To be sure, certain congressmen have definitely formulated opinions on the subject, and
many of these will emerge in the chapters which are to follow.
However, the words of the late Representative Buchanan, upon
the occasion of his introducing a provision to prevent the
T.V.A. from utilizing earnings without congressional appropriation, are pertinent: "Mr. Chairman, this is the first of a
series of amendments which I expect to offer, and will continue
to offer, *until we adopt a national policy that will apply to every
corporation organized and conducted by the Government.*"[62]

Among the many disputable issues, one thing stands out as
incontrovertible; every government corporation should be held
adequately responsible and accountable for its trusteeship of
public funds. To this proposition the General Accounting Office, the corporate officials, and all reasonable persons will
agree. The central problem then becomes one of insuring this
accountability while at the same time reducing to a minimum
red tape and interference with administrative flexibility. It will
be the purpose of the following chapters to examine the financial powers which our federal corporations have enjoyed and to
see what lessons may be learned from over thirty years' experience.

[61] In a special report to Congress, Comptroller-General McCarl stated regarding the Fleet Corporation: "It has recently become evident that many members of the Congress have assumed the General Accounting Office was not only
authorized by law to do so, but was requiring observance of regulatory statutes
in connection with the uses of appropriated moneys by the corporation. Such is
not the condition" (*House Document 217* [72d Cong.], pp. 1–3).

[62] *Congressional Record*, LXXIX, 10967. (Italics ours.)

CHAPTER II

HISTORICAL SKETCH OF GOVERNMENT CORPORATIONS[1]

THE PRE-WAR ERA

ALTHOUGH commonly thought of as a recent phenomenon, governmental participation in the corporate field actually began with the first corporation ever created by the United States. Soon after the Bank of North America was authorized by the Continental Congress in 1781, Superintendent of Finance Morris purchased approximately five-eighths of the capital stock in the name of the government. The United States was thus majority owner of the corporation until the objection of other investors forced the withdrawal of public funds in July, 1782.[2]

Two other early banking enterprises provided occasion for investment of federal funds. Government-owned stock of the First and Second Banks of the United States amounted to $2,000,000 and $7,000,000, respectively—20 per cent of the total capital in each case. As in the case of the Bank of North America, no attempt was made to exercise governmental control. Thus, governmental participation in all three of these early banking enterprises was characterized by a simple invest-

[1] The overwhelming majority of corporations owned or controlled by the United States Government are concerned with activities of a business or commercial nature. Included in this number are those of greatest financial importance, those which present the most difficult problems of control and management, and those which are subject to the most public interest and controversy. Consequently, in the analysis which is to follow, we have confined our attention to business or proprietary corporations and have disregarded such charitable and educational corporations as the National Red Cross, the National Academy of Sciences, the Textile Foundation, Inc., Howard University, Columbia Institute for the Deaf, and the Washington National Monument Society.

[2] See L. Lewis, Jr., *A History of the Bank of North America* (Philadelphia: J. B. Lippincott & Co., 1882).

ment in stock and may be distinguished from the later development wherein the business corporation is used as an administrative agency of the government under more or less complete control.

The first instance of complete United States ownership and operation of a business corporation occurred in 1904, at which time the Panama Railroad Company became a government-owned corporation in a manner as simple as it is unique. All stock and property of this existent privately owned and operated company was included in the property and rights in the Canal Zone purchased by the United States for $40,000,000, and the deed was done. Subsequently, the Panama Railroad Company has been operated as a business enterprise under the control of the Secretary of War and a board of directors selected by him.[3] Aside from the railroad line proper, the company owns a steamship line, a baggage transfer service, stables, docks and piers, coal plants, a telephone system and electric clocks, real estate and hotels, a cattle industry and dairy farms, commissaries, and plantations. Since 1904, dividends totaling $12,144,905 have been paid into the United States Treasury,[4] and a careful investigator has been moved to remark that "probably no corporation in American history has had a more colorful financial record than the Panama Railroad Company."[5]

While all the stock of the federal reserve banks is owned by member banks,[6] and thus they cannot be considered as government-owned corporations, several features of the system may

[3] See M. E. Dimock, *Government-operated Enterprises in the Panama Canal Zone* (Chicago, 1934).

[4] *Annual Report, Panama Railroad Company, 1936*, p. 6.

[5] Dimock, *op. cit.*, p. 28.

[6] Although United States ownership of stock was made possible under the original act, such ownership was never consummated in view of the ample supply of private capital. It might be noted, however, that bills have been introduced into the Seventy-fourth and Seventy-fifth congresses proposing that the government take over the outstanding capital stock of all federal reserve banks (see, e.g., H.R. 5010 and H.R. 7627 [75th Cong.]).

be noted briefly in passing. Created in 1913, the federal reserve banks are under the close supervision of the board of governors of the Federal Reserve System, a government agency, by whom three of the nine directors of each bank are appointed. Originally, all the net earnings after payment of 6 per cent cumulative dividends and the building-up of a specified surplus were to accrue to the United States "as a franchise tax," and while an amendment of 1933 provided for the payment of all net earnings into surplus funds,[7] in case of liquidation the surplus of a reserve bank (after payment of all expenses and accrued dividends) reverts to the United States Government. Furthermore, the capital stock, surplus, and income of reserve banks are exempt from federal, state, and local taxation, except taxes upon real estate.

The next step in corporate ownership was taken by the federal government in 1917, at which time the federal land banks were organized by the Federal Farm Loan Board in accordance with statutory provisions.[8] Government ownership of the stock of these banks, as authorized by law, resulted from the hesitancy of private capital, and, of the original capitalization of $9,000,000, $8,892,130 was supplied by the United States Treasury.[9] However, the percentage of government-owned stock was gradually decreased by the double process of redemption and the increase of private capital subscriptions, with the consequence that from 1919 until 1932 the United States was a minority holder. In the latter year an additional subscription of $125,000,000 was made by the government, and, while redemption is again in the process, at the end of 1936 the United States owned 52 per cent of the total stock outstanding. This variability of stock ownership, together with government purchase of land-bank bonds has presented a difficult problem of control, with the result that close supervision and a large

[7] 48 Stat. 164.   [8] See 39 Stat. 362.

[9] *Second Annual Report of F.C.A.*, *1934*, p. 23. For a discussion of the early operation of federal land banks see Harold A. Van Dorn, *Government Owned Corporations* (New York: Alfred A. Knopf, 1926), chap.ii.

measure of control have been maintained by the Federal Farm Loan Board and its successor, the Farm Credit Administration.[10] The federal land banks are permanent institutions designed to provide long-term mortgage credit for agriculture at rates of interest kept as low as possible yet in keeping with the cost of borrowed funds and a margin to cover operating expenses. Some idea of the results may be gathered from figures showing the total number and amount of loans closed from 1917 through 1936—844,839 and $2,965,082,918, respectively. Loans outstanding on December 31, 1936, totaled $2,064,157,-944.[11] It may be noted that joint-stock land banks, also organized in 1917 and now in the process of liquidation, while they are institutions entirely owned by private capital, have been similarly under the close supervision of the Federal Farm Loan Board and the Farm Credit Administration.

Thus we have noted the gradual and sparing use by the federal government of the corporate device prior to the World War. The necessity for vigorous measures during that great international conflict resulted in the creation of several great corporations, completely owned and controlled by the United States, to a brief consideration of which we now turn.

WARTIME CORPORATIONS[12]

The first of the wartime corporations to be created was the United States Shipping Board Emergency Fleet Corporation, organized by the Shipping Board in accordance with statutory authorization and incorporated in the District of Columbia on

[10] Five temporary directors for each bank were originally oppointed by the Federal Farm Loan Board. In 1923 a change resulted in the selection of four directors by the board to represent the public interest and three by the farm loan associations as their representatives. Finally, in 1934 a further change was effected, resulting in the selection of a director-at-large and two district directors by the governor of the F.C.A. to represent the public interest; a fourth by the governor to represent national farm loan associations and borrowers through agencies; one by production credit associations; one by borrowers from regional banks for co-operatives; and the seventh by national farm loan associations and borrowers through agencies (*Second Report of F.C.A., 1934*, pp. 27–28).

[11] *Fourth Annual Report of F.C.A., 1936*, p. 119.

[12] For a detailed discussion of these corporations see Van Dorn, *op. cit.*

April 16, 1917. All of the $50,000,000 of capital stock was sub-
scribed for in behalf of the United States, and exclusive governmental control was maintained through the Shipping Board,
which exercised complete supervision over acts of the corporation. The broad purposes for which both agencies were created
were identical and were outlined in the Shipping Board Act of
1916. Congress had suddenly discovered the paucity of the
United States merchant marine and had been moved to action
through a desire to remedy that situation while promoting at
the same time the development of a strong naval reserve in the
event of war. In the administration of the act, the activities
actually allotted to the corporation were those of construction
and operation of vessels, and with $2,625,451,000 appropriated
by Congress a tremendous construction program was vigorously and rapidly pursued. Shipyards, shipways, and vessels
themselves sprang up almost overnight in a fever of activity of
which it has been said that "history records few undertakings
which rival it in size and none which approach it in speed of
execution."[13] With the end of the war, the primary reason for
construction disappeared, and gradually the main functions of
the corporation became the maintenance and operation of vessels in its possession and attempted sale of those for which no
profitable use could be found. By act of February 11, 1927, the
name of the organization was changed to "United States Shipping Board Merchant Fleet Corporation," and after the aboli-
tion of the Shipping Board in 1933[14] the corporation operated
for a time under the Department of Commerce. Finally, the
Fleet Corporation was dissolved in 1936, and all its functions
were assumed by the newly created United States Maritime
Commission.[15] As an indication of its work, major activities of
the Fleet Corporation during the fiscal year 1934 consisted of
the administration of the marine insurance fund,[16] the opera-

---

[13] *Ibid.*, p. 47.   [14] Executive Order No. 6166, June 10, 1933.

[15] See 49 Stat. 1985 (1936).

[16] This fund, insuring the government's legal or equitable interest in vessel
tonnage, was authorized by act of June 5, 1920 (41 Stat. 988).

tion of government lines and terminals, the custody of the government's laid-up fleet, and the settlement and adjustment of claims of various kinds. In operating five lines with a total of thirty-eight cargo vessels in 1934, the corporation had a total operating loss of approximately $2,200,000 as compared with a loss of about $5,387,000 for the previous year.[17] Evaluations of the Fleet Corporation's achievements vary from those presenting its record as one which lends "considerable encouragement" to the proponents of governmental use of the corporate device[18] to those which, on the other hand, vehemently denounce "this wasteful and bureaucratic activity" with its "stupendous losses."[19]

The second of the great wartime corporations was the Food Administration Grain Corporation, later called the United States Grain Corporation, which was incorporated under the laws of Delaware in accordance with an executive order of President Wilson, August 14, 1917. All the original capital stock of $50,000,000 was subscribed for in the name of the United States, as was the $100,000,000 additional stock authorized by President Wilson on June 21, 1918, and the $350,-000,000 further added upon the formation in 1919 of the United States Grain Corporation with capitalization of $500,000,000. Complete control was insured by presidential appointment or approval of directors. The main purposes of the Grain Corporation were the provision of an adequate supply of cereal foods, in the face of ominous crop shortages, for both the United States and its allies and the carrying-out of the congressional mandates regarding a guaranteed price for wheat in the years of 1918 and 1919. In the thirty-three months of its active existence, a huge organization was built up which handled a total commodity turnover, including the value of both pur-

[17] See *Annual Report of the Secretary of Commerce, 1934*, p. 184.

[18] Van Dorn, *op. cit.*, p. 80.

[19] James M. Beck, *Our Wonderland of Bureaucracy* (New York: Macmillan Co., 1932), pp. 132–34.

chases and sales, of over $7,500,000,000.[20] All buying opera-
tions were ceased on May 31, 1920, and the long process of
liquidation was begun. In contrast to the Fleet Corporation
the operations of the Grain Corporation resulted in a profit, as
evidenced by the return to the United States Treasury of the
original investment of $500,000,000, plus other assets totaling
$57,591,135.48.[21]

On April 5, 1918, Congress again entered the corporate field
by creating the War Finance Corporation, with capital stock of
$500,000,000 entirely subscribed by the United States.[22] Con-
trol was exercised through presidential appointment, with
Senate consent, of four directors who, with the Secretary of the
Treasury as chairman, constituted the board. The War Finance Corporation was designed as a temporary credit agency
for extending financial assistance to "essential industries necessary or contributory to the prosecution of the war," mainly by
making advances, as provided in the organic act, to banks,
bankers, and trust companies which had themselves rendered
such financial assistance. Only in exceptional cases were loans
to be made directly to the industries concerned. After the close
of the war, the corporation was expressly authorized by Congress to make loans in support of the export trade[23] and later
the agricultural and livestock industries.[24] An indication of the
magnitude of the transactions of the War Finance Corporation
may be had from the *Annual Report for 1929*, in which year the
corporation was dissolved and liquidation, begun in January,
1925, turned over to the Secretary of the Treasury. Advances
under the war powers amounted to $306,756,020.76, while total
advances, including in addition those for export, agricultural,
and livestock purposes, represented an outlay of $690,431,-
099.84. Earnings of the corporation to November 30, 1929,
were $64,880,194.61, but this amount does not represent a

[20] F. M. Surface, *The Grain Trade during the World War* (New York:
Macmillan Co., 1928), p. vi.

[21] *Ibid.*, p. 464. Figures as of 1921.

[22] 40 Stat. 506.

[23] 40 Stat. 1313 (1919).

[24] 42 Stat. 181 (1921).

profit to the government, and it is estimated rather that, upon final liquidation, when interest has been considered, the lending operations of the corporation will have been conducted substantially at cost to the government.[25]

A fourth wartime corporation was the United States Housing Corporation, organized and incorporated in the state of New York by the Secretary of Labor, July 8, 1918. Through subscription by the Secretary of Labor for 998 shares of its no-par stock, one share each being subscribed for by the president and the treasurer of the corporation, $100,000,000 appropriated by Congress was placed at the disposal of the corporation. Control was exercised through the selection of directors by the Secretary of Labor. The purpose of the United States Housing Corporation was to remedy distressing and almost prohibitive housing conditions by providing better facilities for industrial workers employed in arsenals, navy yards, and industries "connected with and essential to the national defense," and also for employees of the government residing in the District of Columbia. Construction work was begun immediately, and, although all new projects were ceased in July, 1919, as a result of a congressional mandate to liquidate, provision of houses for approximately six thousand families, or about thirty thousand persons, was accomplished. Of the original investment of $100,000,000, over $73,000,000[26] has been returned to the United States Treasury, the remainder representing a loss by the corporation.[27]

[25] *Annual Report of W.F.C., 1929*, p. 3.

[26] Liquidation is still in process. By June 30, 1934, $73,029,728.28 had been returned (*Annual Report of the Secretary of Labor, 1934*, p. 104).

[27] The president of the corporation has called this "a unique record for what was essentially a war agency" (*Annual Report of the Secretary of Labor, 1925*, p. 44). Other evaluations vary; James M. Beck has said, "Needless to say, the United States has sustained large losses in this paternalistic business adventure" (*op. cit.*, p. 137); Van Dorn, after reviewing the conditions and difficulties under which the corporation labored, concluded that "it is doubtful if any private agency, even given the necessary capital could have done as well" (*op. cit.*, p. 169); Rosner, writing in 1933, stated: "Here is a chapter in our history which the rugged individualist would like us to forget. The story is well worth retelling.

Another corporation established as part of the food control program of the war period was the Sugar Equalization Board, incorporated under the Food Administration in the state of Delaware, on July 31, 1918. All the capital stock of $5,000,000 was subscribed for in the name of the United States by the President, and complete control was exercised through selection of the board of directors and through supervision by the Food Administration. The main purposes of the Sugar Equalization Board were to facilitate distribution and to insure an equal price on sugar from all sources, foreign and domestic—a price such that the consumer would receive the benefit of the lower-cost sugar while the high-cost producer would receive a price which would encourage production. Price stabilization was achieved through outright purchase by the board of the entire Cuban cane-sugar crop of 1918–19 and through licensing of the domestic beet-sugar industry. In its year of major activity, the board purchased a sugar crop valued at approximately $500,000,000, and while preventing an inordinate rise in sugar prices accumulated a surplus of about $40,000,000.[28] In 1926 the capital of $5,000,000, with additional assets amounting to $6,370,621.39, was returned to the United States Treasury.

The two remaining wartime corporations were organized on dates so near the armistice of November 11, 1918, that their active life was exceedingly brief. The United States Spruce Production Corporation was incorporated in the state of Washington on August 20, 1918, with capital stock of $10,000,000 entirely subscribed for by the United States. Its purpose was to make available for the United States and its allies aircraft lumber for war uses, but actual operations had been under way for only eleven days when the signing of the armistice initiated the

----

.... In seven years the New York State Housing Board has provided under its jurisdiction homes for 1900 families, which is less than one-third the number built by the United States Housing Corporation in a year" (*World Tomorrow*, XVI, 445, 446).

[28] Van Dorn, *op. cit.*, p. 197.

liquidating process. Finally, the Russian Bureau, Inc., was organized by the War Trade Board in October, 1918, with capital stock of $5,000,000, again entirely subscribed for by the United States. Its purpose was to stabilize the economic situation in Russia through trade in American exports and Siberian raw materials, but, like the Spruce Production Corporation, it became inactive because of the armistice. In both instances, complete governmental control had been insured through the selection of directors.

An important factor common to all the corporations created during the war was their temporary nature. Organized to facilitate the general mobilization process, these agencies of government have long ceased to exercise their active functions, although, as has been indicated, that termination of activity was not in every case abruptly effected at the end of the war. Thus, their chief interest today is historical, and their importance lies in the valuable lessons that may be learned from the experience of their active existence.

THE POST-WAR PERIOD

In contrast to the temporary wartime corporations are the federal intermediate credit banks, which were created in 1923, designed as a permanent part of the credit structure of the nation.[29] Each of the twelve banks was capitalized at $5,000,000, and the total stock of $60,000,000[30] was subscribed by the Secretary of the Treasury on behalf of the United States. Operating under boards of directors composed of the same individuals who constitute the boards for the federal land banks,[31] the intermediate credit banks have been similarly under the supervision and control of the Federal Farm Loan Board and its successor, the Farm Credit Administration. They were cre-

---

[29] For a detailed discussion see F. Baird and C. L. Benner, *Ten Years of Federal Intermediate Credits* (Washington: Brookings Institution, 1933).

[30] In June and July of 1934, $10,000,000 additional stock was subscribed for by the governor of the F.C.A. in behalf of the United States (see *Second Report of F.C.A.*, pp. 49–50).

[31] See above, p. 24, n. 10.

ated for the purpose of supplying a type of credit falling between long-term loans as advanced by the land banks and the short-term loans of commercial banks—that is, "intermediate credit," defined arbitrarily as loans of from six months to three years' duration.[32] Credit is extended to local financial institutions engaged in making loans to farmers, and direct loans are made to co-operative marketing and purchasing associations. Through 1936, a total of over $3,115,000,000 had been advanced as loans to co-operative associations and loans to and discounts for financing institutions.[33] From dates of organization to 1931, the twelve banks paid into the United States Treasury as franchise taxes $2,496,779 out of earnings, and on June 30, 1937, they had accumulated $9,943,901.18 as earned surpluses, reserves for contingencies, and undivided profits.[34]

The next corporate venture of the federal government in the post-war period occurred in 1924, when the Inland Waterways Corporation was created by Congress. All the capital stock—originally $5,000,000 but subsequently increased to $12,000,-000[35]—is subscribed by the United States, while control and direction of the corporation are vested in the Secretary of War, who may delegate any or all of his functions in that connection to the chairman of the board-president and the board of managers, all of whom he appoints.[36] The Inland Waterways Corporation was created for the purpose of conducting a common-carrier business on the Mississippi River system, partly as a result of the inheritance from war days of a governmental barge

---

[32] 42 Stat. 1456. The lower limit of six months was removed by 46 Stat. 816 (1930).

[33] *Fourth Annual Report of F.C.A., 1936*, p. 11.

[34] *Farm Credit Quarterly, June 30, 1937*, p. 14.

[35] In 1928, $10,000,000 was appropriated for the purchase of additional I.W.C. stock (45 Stat. 978). By 1937, however, a total of only $12,000,000 had been subscribed for, and Congress then repealed the appropriation of the remaining $3,000,000 (Pub. No. 208 [75th Cong.], sec. 2).

[36] For an intensive study of the purposes, organization, overhead control, and achievements of the Inland Waterways Corporation see Dimock, *Developing America's Waterways* (Chicago: University of Chicago Press, 1935).

line, partly as an experiment to determine after a fair trial the economics and desirability of inland waterway transportation. An indication of the size of the enterprise may be had from its tonnage figures, which indicate transportation of 2,376,336 tons in the peak year of 1936, as compared with 1,605,830 tons in 1933. Net income of $899,769.96 for the fiscal year 1936 was reported by the corporation,[37] although heated discussion of its accounting methods, "government subsidy," and "hidden costs" goes on apace.[38]

By far the largest and most powerful corporation created in the post-war period, yet prior to the Roosevelt administration, is the Reconstruction Finance Corporation, created by act of Congress on January 22, 1932. All of its $500,000,000 of capital stock was subscribed for by the United States, and control is maintained through selection by the President and Senate of six directors in addition to the Secretary of the Treasury (or in his absence, the Under-Secretary of the Treasury), who is a director ex officio. Created to aid in "financing agriculture, commerce, and industry," the R.F.C. was originally empowered to make loans to banks, savings banks, trust companies, building and loan associations, insurance companies, mortgage loan companies, credit unions, federal land banks, joint-stock land banks, federal intermediate credit banks, agricultural credit corporations, livestock credit corporations, and railroads.[39] Although the R.F.C. was conceived as a temporary agency, with activity limited to one year unless extended for another year by the President, Congress has subsequently extended the life of the corporation, while making numerous additions to its lending powers.[40] The immensity of its pro-

---

[37] *Annual Report of the Secretary of War, 1936*, p. 17.

[38] See, e.g., H. G. Moulton, *Waterways versus Railways* (Boston and New York: Houghton Mifflin Co., 1926), and cf. Herbert Corey, "Uncle Sam Finds a Formula for Competing with the Carriers," *Public Utilities Fortnightly*, VIII (1931), 388.

[39] 47 Stat. 5.

[40] The extension of activity under Pub. No. 2 (75th Cong.) is effective until June 30, 1939. For broadening of R.F.C. lending functions see pamphlet en-

gram may be seen in the fact that through March 31, 1937, a total of $6,245,281,775.57 had been disbursed as loans and investments in the ordinary activities of the corporation, while an additional $2,408,200,768.27 had been allocated to other governmental agencies and for direct relief.[41] As of December 31, 1935, earnings of the corporation in interest and dividends exceeded expenses and the interest on its own obligations by $65,175,963.18.[42]

The Federal Home Loan Bank System, set up as a result of the act approved July 22, 1932, presented the next opportunity for governmental participation in the corporate field, and, of the $125,755,025 actually paid in for stock issued by the twelve home loan banks by June 30, 1936, $99,342,000 came from the United States Treasury.[43] In spite of this large majority of stock owned by the federal government, however, and although the home loan banks are subject to regulations of the Federal Home Loan Bank Board, control and management are private rather than governmental, since of the twelve directors constituting the board of each bank only four are appointed in the public interest by the Federal Home Loan Bank Board, while the remaining eight are chosen by the member institutions of each district.[44] Thus, these banks, designed to serve as a central credit reserve system for the thousands of member building and loan associations, mutual savings banks, insurance companies, and similar private thrift and home financing institutions, while offering an interesting example of a large governmental corporate investment, do not present the problems of

---

titled *R.F.C. Act as Amended*, revised currently by the corporation and published at Government Printing Office.

[41] *Report of R.F.C. for the First Quarter of 1937*, pp. 10 and 11.

[42] Summary of activities, published by R.F.C. January, 1936, p. 13.

[43] *Fourth Annual Report of the Federal Home Loan Bank Board, 1936*, p. 15. In addition, an appropriated balance of $23,399,000 was available for further United States subscription.

[44] Prior to January 1, 1936, only two out of eleven members were appointed by the Federal Home Loan Bank Board. The change was made in 49 Stat. 294.

the corporate device used as a governmental administrative agency.

The final step, prior to the Roosevelt administration, in the development which we are tracing was taken under authorization of the Emergency Relief and Construction Act of 1932, when the Reconstruction Finance Corporation chartered a regional agricultural credit corporation in each of the twelve federal land-bank districts. The entire capital stock, amounting to $44,500,000, was subscribed for by the Reconstruction Finance Corporation, which in addition exercised complete control through appointment of the directors, managers, and other officers of the regional corporations.[45] These agencies were designed as emergency institutions to meet the unusual demand for short-term credit through direct loans to farmers and stockmen for agricultural pursuits (including crop production), or for the raising, fattening, or marketing of livestock. From dates of organization through December 31, 1934, loan disbursements totaled $284,796,430.[46] However, since the organization of production credit corporations and production credit associations under the Farm Credit Act of 1933, the emergency need for regional agricultural corporations has disappeared, and since April 30, 1934, the latter have been in the process of liquidation.

Thus, we have reached in our historical survey the threshold of the Roosevelt administration. The widespread use of the corporate device as an agency of governmental administration since March 4, 1933, has provoked an increasing interest on the part of students and observers and, indeed, has made opportune a more careful study of the phenomenon.

THE PERIOD OF THE ROOSEVELT ADMINISTRATION

Curiously enough, the first government corporation created after the inauguration of President Roosevelt in 1933 repre-

[45] See *First Annual Report of F.C.A., 1933*, pp. 44 ff. Administrative supervision of regional agricultural credit corporations was transferred to the F.C.A. as a result of an executive order dated March 27, 1933.

[46] *Ibid.*, p. 158.

sents a new departure not only in that it has no capital stock but also in the uniqueness of its purposes and functions.[47] The Tennessee Valley Authority, created by act of May 18, 1933, has been supported by congressional appropriations and allocations from appropriated funds, and thus, while not a government-owned corporation in the usual sense of the word,[48] it is nevertheless a governmental agency in corporate form.[49] Control is directly exercised by the President through appointment, with advice and consent of the Senate, of the three directors who direct the exercise of all the powers of the corporation. The T.V.A. is a regional planning and development agency charged with the over-all purpose of fostering "an orderly and proper physical, economic, and social development" of the Tennessee River watershed area. More specifically, the corporation is undertaking the development, through construction of a series of dams, of a unified water-control program embracing flood control, navigation, and power production; is engaged in distributing the electricity produced to local governmental units and to co-operative organizations, not organized for profit, but primarily for the purpose of supplying electricity to members; is carrying on programs of agricultural and industrial improvement; and is making studies and plans looking toward the proper use, conservation, and development of the natural resources of the Tennessee Valley area. As of August, 1937, appropriations and allocation of government funds for use by the T.V.A. totaled $191,066,270, of which the major portion has been expended or committed by the corporation.

Less than a month after the birth of the T.V.A., the Home Owners' Loan Corporation was created by congressional act

[47] For a study of the T.V.A. see *Regional Factors in National Planning* (Washington: National Resources Committee, 1935), pp. 83 ff.

[48] I.e., a corporation with stock owned by the government.

[49] The T.V.A. Act clearly establishes the corporate nature of the Authority by naming the incorporators and providing that "incorporation shall be held to have been effected from the date of the first meeting of the board." In addition, the T.V.A. is authorized to have succession in its corporate name and to adopt and use a corporate seal, which shall be judicially noticed.

approved June 13, 1933. All its capital stock of $200,000,000 is subscribed for by the Secretary of the Treasury on behalf of the United States, and the board of directors consists of the five members of the Federal Home Loan Bank Board, who are appointed by the President, with advice and consent of the Senate. The broad purpose of the H.O.L.C. was to make long-term mortgage loans at low interest rates to those who were in urgent need of funds for the protection and preservation of their homes, and who were unable to procure the needed financing through the ordinary channels. It was conceived strictly as an emergency agency and empowered to make loans until June 13, 1936. At the close of the three-year period, 1,021,818 loans, totaling $3,093,424,244, had been granted. Since that time the duties of the H.O.L.C. have been those of collecting and servicing loans and managing acquired property.

The Farm Credit Act of 1933 directed the governor of the Farm Credit Administration to organize and charter twelve corporations to be known as production credit corporations, one of which is located in each of the federal land-bank cities. The total capital stock of $120,000,000 is subscribed by the governor on behalf of the United States Government, and the directors of the several land banks serve also as directors of these corporations, under the general supervision of the Farm Credit Administration. The principal functions of the production credit corporations are to organize, assist in capitalizing, and supervise production credit associations, which are the local lending institutions of the production credit system, and which through combined action with the federal intermediate credit banks provide short-term credit for general agricultural purposes.[50] At the end of 1936, 551 production credit associations had paid-in stock amounting to $85,844,495, of which $75,038,350 was Class A stock owned by the production credit corporations, $51,958 was Class A stock owned by individuals, and the remaining $10,754,187 was Class B stock held by

---

[50] This permanent system is replacing the regional agricultural credit corporations, which are now in liquidation, as noted above, p. 34.

farmer-borrowers.[51] Although the Class A stock is nonvoting, as long as a production credit corporation owns any of that outstanding, the appointment or election of directors, the loan committee, and other employees of the associations is subject to approval of the corporation's president, who also has power of removal. A total of 594,055 loans closed from dates of organization through December 31, 1936, by the production credit associations amounted to $531,639,383.[52]

Created in the same act as agencies of the Farm Credit Administration, a Central Bank for Cooperatives and twelve district banks for co-operatives have issued capital stock almost entirely subscribed for with United States funds controlled by the governor of the Farm Credit Administration. As of December 31, 1936, a total of $57,000,000 for the central bank and $95,000,000 for the district banks had been subscribed in that manner, while the additional stock of less than $3,000,000 was owned by borrowing associations. Control of the Central Bank for Co-operatives is secured through selection by the governor of the F.C.A. of six directors who sit with the Cooperative Bank Commissioner as chairman to direct the operations of the bank. Like the production credit corporations, each district bank for co-operatives operates under the board of directors of the federal land bank in the city in which it is established. The banks for co-operatives have as their purpose the furnishing of credit to national, regional, and local farmers' co-operative buying and selling associations. Large advances and loans to national and regional co-operatives are made by the central bank, while the district banks handle the local needs. Through December, 1936, advances totaling

---

[51] *Fourth Annual Report of F.C.A., 1936*, p. 44.

[52] *Ibid.*, p. 45. It should be noted that the funds loaned to farmers by the production credit associations are obtained from the federal intermediate credit banks principally through the rediscounting of borrowers' notes. Proceeds from the sale of capital stock are invested in government obligations and other approved securities, the major portion of such securities being pledged with the intermediate credit banks as additional collateral for notes rediscounted with the banks.

$215,157,597 had been made, and, while no dividends have been declared, the thirteen banks have reported earned surpluses and reserves for contingencies aggregating $7,719,-859.58.[53]

The Federal Deposit Insurance Corporation was created by act of June 16, 1933, and, out of a total paid-in capital of $289,299,556.99, $150,000,000 has been subscribed by the United States, and the remaining $139,299,556.99 by the federal reserve banks. The stock is nonvoting, but government control is secured by presidential appointment, with Senate advice and consent, of two directors, who together with the Comptroller of the Currency constitute the governing board of three. The purpose of the corporation is to insure to the extent of $5,000 the account of each depositor in all banks which are members of the federal reserve system and in other banks which may become insured upon application to and examination by the corporation and approval by the board of directors. In addition to these examinations and the insurance of bank deposits, the Federal Deposit Insurance Corporation has been authorized to act as receiver for closed banks, and to operate for a limited time new national banks chartered for the purpose of making available to depositors of closed banks the insured portions of their deposits.[54] As of October 31, 1936, out of a total of 15,616 operating banks in the United States, 14,030, or nearly 90 per cent, had their deposits insured by the Federal Deposit Insurance Corporation. The total liability of the corporation has been estimated at $21,000,000,000. For the period from September 11, 1933, to June 30, 1935, income on investments and profit on securities sold exceeded operating expenses and deposit insurance losses and expenses by $4,236,-361.56.[55]

On October 4, 1933, the Federal Surplus Relief Corporation

[53] See *ibid.*, pp. 54 and 144.

[54] See *Annual Report of the Federal Deposit Insurance Corporation, 1934.*

[55] For derivation of this figure, showing items considered and presenting breakdown of income and expenses, see *Report of the F.D.I.C., as of June 30, 1935.*

was incorporated in the state of Delaware as an agency of the Federal Emergency Relief Administration. A nonstock, non-profit organization, the F.S.R.C. was governed by a board of directors consisting of the Federal Emergency Relief Adminis-trator, the Secretary of Agriculture, the Federal Emergency Administrator of Public Works, and the governor of F.C.A. The primary purpose was twofold: first, to purchase, process, and distribute for consumption agricultural products, as a means of removing surpluses and improving prices; second, to supply these surplus products to the needy and destitute on relief rolls throughout the country. The relief function was em-phasized, and operating funds received from the state relief administrations were used for handling large quantities of a wide range of commodities. On November 18, 1935, the title of the F.S.R.C. was changed to "Federal Surplus Commodities Corporation," and emphasis was shifted from the relief to the agricultural aspects of the corporation's functions. By act of June 28, 1937, the F.S.C.C. was continued until June 30, 1939, as an United States agency directly under the Secretary of Agriculture. The latter official was then authorized to use the corporation in administering the funds previously appropriated by Congress for the encouragement of domestic consumption of agricultural commodities and products by diversion from the normal channels of trade.

Almost immediately upon the heels of the Federal Surplus Relief Corporation, the Commodity Credit Corporation was chartered, in pursuance of an executive order,[56] under the laws of Delaware on October 17, 1933. All the original capital stock, amounting to $3,000,000, was subscribed by the Secretary of Agriculture and the governor of the Farm Credit Administra-tion, who hold it jointly for the United States. At congression-al direction in 1936, $97,000,000 of additional stock was issued and subscribed for by the R.F.C. Complete governmental con-trol is exercised through an eleven-member board of directors consisting of officials representing the Department of Agricul-

[56] No. 6340, October 16, 1933.

ture, the Farm Credit Administration, and the Reconstruction Finance Corporation. The Commodity Credit Corporation was designed essentially as a lending institution, for the purpose of making loans to farmers upon agricultural commodities with respect to which the Agricultural Adjustment Administration had a general program of production control. Cotton loans through March, 1937, totaled $459,150,251.87, while corn loans for the same period aggregated $134,418,832.30. Loans have also been made on gum turpentine and gum rosin, and some assistance has been given to tobacco co-operative marketing associations.[57]

One of the ill-fated corporate ventures of the Roosevelt administration was the next to occur. The Public Works Emergency Housing Corporation was incorporated under the laws of Delaware on October 28, 1933, and was designated as a government "agency" under Title II of the National Industrial Recovery Act by an executive order of November 29, 1933. Conceived as an entirely government owned and controlled corporation which should operate as an arm of the Public Works Administration Housing Division in carrying out the low-cost housing and slum-clearance programs authorized by the National Industrial Recovery Act, the Emergency Housing Corporation was for all practical purposes killed by a ruling of the Comptroller-General of the United States, dated January 11, 1934.[58] Since its capital was cut off by the refusal of the Comptroller-General to sign warrants transferring $100,001,000 from "National Industrial Recovery" funds, the corporation was never utilized and has now been liquidated and abolished.

Only slightly more successful has been the history of the Federal Subsistence Homesteads Corporation, incorporated in Delaware on December 2, 1933. The stock was subscribed for the United States by the Secretary of the Interior, and management was vested in a board of directors consisting of the Secretary of the Interior, the Assistant Secretary of the Interior, and

---

[57] *Statement of Commodity Credit Corporation, April 15, 1937*, p. 10.

[58] See below, p. 196.

the director of the Division of Subsistence Homesteads, Department of the Interior. The corporation was designed to serve as the administrative vehicle for carrying out the subsistence homesteads program aimed at the overbalance of population in industrial centers.[59] During the fiscal year 1934, $16,553,970 was allotted by the division and the corporation for use in fifty-nine subsistence homesteads projects.[60] The creation of the Resettlement Administration on April 30, 1935, and the transfer thereto of the functions of the Division of Subsistence Homesteads, resulted in the termination of the activities of the Federal Subsistence Homesteads Corporation.

The incorporation laws of the state of Delaware continued to attract the federal government, and the Electric Home and Farm Authority, Inc., was organized thereunder on January 17, 1934.[61] Capital stock of $1,000,000 was subscribed in behalf of the United States by the three incorporators, who were the three directors of the Tennessee Valley Authority, and who also served as directors of the E.H.F.A. The purpose of the Electric Home and Farm Authority was to make feasible the increase in home and farm use of electricity by seeking to improve the quality, decrease the cost, and finance the consumer purchase of electrical appliances. Operations were originally confined to the Tennessee Valley area and were carried on in connection with the Tennessee Valley Authority electricity program. However, on August 1, 1935, a new corporation was formed under the laws of the District of Columbia and was designated by executive order of August 12, 1935, as a governmental agency to succeed the Delaware corporation and extend the area of activity over the entire United States. Falling heir to the assets of the original E.H.F.A., the second corporation is capitalized at $850,000 and is managed by a board of trustees consisting of eight divisional officers of the Reconstruction

[59] See *Annual Report of the Secretary of the Interior, 1934*, pp. 350 ff.

[60] *Ibid.*, pp. 351 and 352.

[61] See Executive Order No. 5614, December 19, 1933, which authorized the corporation.

Finance Corporation and the administrator of the Rural Electrification Administration.

Another corporation closely associated with the Tennessee Valley Authority is the Tennessee Valley Associated Cooperatives, incorporated by the three directors of the former agency under the laws of Tennessee, January 23, 1934. It is a nonstock corporation, governed by a three-member board of directors, and has operated under an allocation of funds from the Federal Emergency Relief Administration. Its object is to promote, establish, finance, or assist in any other way the development of co-operative enterprises in the Tennessee River basin. By November, 1935, ten co-operatives had been set up, and others were in the process. Activities embraced include fruit, berry, and vegetable canning; seed-potato cultivation; flour-grinding; dairying; and handicraft and textiles.[62]

An important corporate addition to the Farm Credit Administration structure was made by the congressional act approved January 31, 1934, which established the Federal Farm Mortgage Corporation. All the authorized capital of $200,000,000 has been subscribed by the governor of the Farm Credit Administration on behalf of the United States. Control is exercised through a three-member board of directors consisting of the governor of the F.C.A., the Secretary of the Treasury or a Treasury officer designated by him, and the Land Bank Commissioner. The chief purpose of the corporation is to aid in financing the lending operations of the federal land banks and the Land Bank Commissioner, and bonds guaranteed by the United States are issued to supplement the initial capital. As of June 30, 1937, assets (consisting chiefly of land-bank bonds and instruments evidencing real estate, crop, and chattel mortgage loans held by the corporation) totaled $1,680,194,707.71, which gives an indication of the extent of the F.F.M.C.'s participation in the farm loan program.[63] At the same time, a re-

[62] See *Annual Report of the Tennessee Valley Authority, 1934*, p. 46.

[63] *Farm Credit Quarterly, June 30, 1937*, p. 12.

serve fund of $27,368,788.09 representing net earnings since organization was reported.

A final corporate venture during the month of January, 1934, was made with the creation of the Public Works Emergency Leasing Corporation under the laws of the state of Delaware. Only three shares of nonpar stock—to be held by the incorporators in trust for the sole use and benefit of the United States—were authorized in the charter. The purpose of the corporation was to act as an agency of the United States in carrying on the comprehensive program of public works pursuant to the provisions of the National Industrial Recovery Act. However, largely because of the Comptroller-General's ruling in the Emergency Housing Corporation case, a certificate of surrender of corporate rights was filed January 2, 1935, and the leasing corporation was never utilized.[64]

Next to be created was the Export-Import Bank of Washington, incorporated in pursuance of an executive order[65] in the District of Columbia on February 12, 1934. An act of January 31, 1935, gave the bank statutory sanction and continued its existence as a government "agency." Common stock of $1,000,000 is held (save for trustees' qualifying shares) jointly by the Secretary of State and the Secretary of Commerce for the benefit of the United States. Preferred stock amounting to $20,000,000 is held by the R.F.C., which is committed to purchase an additional amount of $15,000,000 on demand of the bank. Control is exercised through a board of eleven trustees elected by the stockholders with the approval of the President.[66] The Export-Import Bank was designed as a financial institution which would be in a position to extend long-term credits to United States exporters desiring to deal with the Soviet Government and, incidentally, was expected to be help-

[64] The late Senator Schall remarked that this dissolution was "under the fear of publicity in my opinion" (*Congressional Record*, LXXIX, 1578).

[65] No. 6581, February 2, 1934.

[66] The original board of five was increased to nine and then to eleven by orders of the President.

ful in connection with any arrangement which might be made for the settlement of debts and claims between the United States and Russia. Since no satisfactory agreement was reached with the Soviet Government, the trade operations of the bank were held up until the trustees and the President of the United States expanded its activities to include all nations except the Soviet Union, and at the present time the bank is engaged in extending credit to exporters and importers in this larger field. As of December 31, 1936, loans aggregating $112,-728,014 had been authorized. Actual disbursements totaled $35,143,244, of which $17,570,616 had been repaid.[67]

Exactly one month later, on March 12, 1934, the Second Export-Import Bank of Washington was incorporated in the District of Columbia, with capital consisting of $250,000 in common stock owned by the United States and $2,500,000 par value of preferred stock subscribed by the R.F.C. This bank operated under a board of trustees composed of nine of the eleven trustees of the first export-import bank and was originally intended to promote trade with Cuba. However, the expansion of the activities of the earlier bank resulted in the retirement of the preferred stock of the second bank, the transfer of its commitments to its predecessor, and its eventual liquidation on June 30, 1936.

A second large governmental insurance corporation made its appearance with the creation by Congress of the Federal Savings and Loan Insurance Corporation, June 27, 1934. The entire capital stock of $100,000,000 was subscribed by the Home Owners' Loan Corporation, and the five members of the Federal Home Loan Bank Board act as the board of trustees which governs operations. The purpose of the corporation is to insure the accounts of solvent home-financing institutions of the building and loan type, and thus its function is comparable to that performed by the Federal Deposit Insurance Corporation

[67] *Annual Report of Export-Import Bank, 1936*, p. 11.

with respect to commercial banks.[68] However, whereas the latter insures the liquidity of deposits, the Federal Savings and Loan Insurance Corporation insures the safety of accounts against losses through default of insured institutions and does not guarantee members any specified return on their investments or the ready convertibility of their securities into cash. By June 30, 1936, 1,099 federal savings and loan associations and 237 state-chartered associations had been accepted for insurance.

A comparatively small corporation, without capital stock, was created by executive order of December 11, 1934,[69] as a corporation of the District of Columbia under the name of Federal Prison Industries, Inc. Its initial capital consisted of cash transferred from the Prison Industries Working Capital Fund on the books of the Treasury and all the assets previously under the jurisdiction of the Industrial Division of the Bureau of Prisons of the Department of Justice. Control is maintained through presidential selection of the board of five directors, one of whom represents industry, one agriculture, one labor, one consumers and retailers, and one the Attorney-General of the United States. The function of the corporation is to manage and operate the industries carried on in the several federal penal and correctional institutions, and it is charged with the duty of diversifying prison industrial operations so as to reduce to a minimum competition with private industries.

More recently, the R.F.C. Mortgage Company was organized under the laws of the state of Maryland, March 14, 1935. Capital stock of $25,000,000 was subscribed by the R.F.C., which controls the operations of the mortgage company

---

[68] See *Second Annual Report of the Federal Home Loan Bank Board, 1934,* pp. 89 ff. Institutions eligible for insurance of their accounts are federal savings and loan associations and state-chartered building and loan associations, savings and loan associations, homestead associations, and co-operative banks. The federal associations are required to insure their accounts, while insurance is optional for the state-chartered institutions.

[69] No. 6917. This order was in pursuance of the specific statutory authorization of June 23, 1934 (48 Stat. 1211).

through the selection of the seven members of the board of directors. The R.F.C. Mortgage Company has as its purpose the re-establishment of a normal market for sound mortgages on urban income-producing property and advances credit to that end. In addition to its capital stock, the company has utilized funds borrowed from the R.F.C. in carrying on its lending activities. The R.F.C. has authorized a total loan of $25,000,000—to be turned over to the mortgage company as needed in its operations. Through July, 1936, the mortgage company in turn had disbursed approximately $16,200,000 in loans.

Ravages of the Ohio River were primarily responsible for the Disaster Loan Corporation, which was created by act of Congress approved February 11, 1937. The R.F.C. was authorized to subscribe up to $20,000,000 of capital stock and to appoint officers and agents to manage the corporation. R.F.C. personnel is utilized entirely. The purpose of the Disaster Loan Corporation is to make loans for the repair of flood damage, although victims of other disasters, such as fire and tornado, may also be assisted. Loans totaling approximately $8,500,000 had been authorized through October, 1937.

To aid in the attack on the farm tenancy problem, the Farmers' Home Corporation was created by the Bankhead-Jones Act of July 22, 1937, as an agency "of and within the Department of Agriculture." Management is vested in a board of three directors, who are employees of the department chosen by the Secretary of Agriculture and operating under his supervision. The United States owns the nominal capital stock, but a 1938 appropriation of $10,000,000 which the secretary may transfer to the corporation as needed is the source of operating capital. Loans are made to farm tenants, farm laborers, and sharecroppers to enable them to acquire farms of their own.

Created by act of September 1, 1937, the United States Housing Authority is a body corporate within the Department of the Interior and under the supervision of its secretary. In contrast to the usual board of directors, a single administrator, appointed for five-year terms by the President with Senate consent, exercises the powers of the corporation. Capital stock of $1,000,000 is subscribed by the United States, and any funds which Congress has appropriated for housing or slum clearance may be allocated to the Authority in the discretion of the President. Designed to remedy unsafe and unsanitary housing conditions, the corporation makes loans and contributions to public housing agencies.

The Agricultural Adjustment Act of February 16, 1938, created the Federal Crop Insurance Corporation as another corporate agency within the Department of Agriculture. Capital stock of $100,000,000 is subscribed by the United States, and control is exercised through the Secretary of Agriculture, who appoints and supervises three directors who also are departmental employees. As a part of the complicated agricultural adjustment program, the corporation insures producers of wheat against loss in yields due to unavoidable causes.

SUMMARY

Upon analysis of the corporate trend sketched above, several significant observations may be made. Government corporations have been created under statutory authorizations of five more or less distinct types. In the first place, incorporation and definition of powers and duties may be directly effected by the act itself. Second, and only one step removed, is that class of corporations whose creation by a certain executive officer or agency is authorized and directed by law. Or Congress may authorize an executive officer or agency to create a certain corporation, or corporations, if deemed necessary or desirable. In the fourth place, corporations have been established by executive officers under general authorization to create "such agencies" as may be necessary for carrying out congressional programs. Finally, Congress may create a government corporation by appropriating money and directing the purchase of stock and other property of an existing private corporation. Eight federal agencies have been incorporated under the laws of Delaware, three in the District of Columbia, two under New York laws, and one each in the states of Washington, Connecticut, Tennessee, and Maryland. The remaining government corporations have been created by statute or have received charters from federal officers.

Of the thirty-eight corporations described,[70] twenty-eight are in existence today; however, of this latter number, three exist only for liquidation purposes and have ceased the major activities for which they were created.[71] Perhaps fifteen may reasonably be described as nontemporary,[72] with the remainder clearly established for emergency purposes, or with a definite limitation of life.

Of primary importance is the extent of government ownership and/or control. Here we find a considerable gradation, ranging from entire ownership and control[73] to part control without ownership and part ownership without control. Most commonly, the corporations in question have had capital stock exclusively held in behalf of the United States and have been governed by directors chosen by officers of the federal government in their official capacity. In some cases capital stock is owned by another government corporation, either the R.F.C. or the H.O.L.C., and occasionally control has been exercised

[70] For purposes of this summary each homogeneous group—e.g., federal land banks, production credit corporations, banks for co-operatives—is regarded as a unit.

[71] War Finance Corporation, United States Housing Corporation, regional agricultural credit corporations.

[72] Panama Railroad Company, federal reserve banks, federal land banks, federal intermediate credit banks, Inland Waterways Corporation, federal home loan banks, T.V.A., production credit corporations, banks for co-operatives, Federal Deposit Insurance Corporation, Federal Savings and Loan Insurance Corporation, Federal Prison Industries, Farmers' Home Corporation, Federal Crop Insurance Corporation, and United States Housing Authority.

[73] A definition of "control" is hazardous. Perhaps the suggestion of Berle and Means is as good as any: "Since direction over the activities of a corporation is exercised through the board of directors, we may say for practical purposes that control lies in the hands of the individual or group who have the actual power to select the board of directors (or its majority)" (*The Modern Corporation and Private Property* [New York: Macmillan Co., 1932], p. 69).

through the purchasing corporation. Government-controlled nonstock corporations, with assets acquired through appropriated or allocated federal funds, are a recent phenomenon.

Also under complete governmental control are the Federal Deposit Insurance Corporation, with almost half of its capital stock privately owned, and the Central Bank for Cooperatives, whose stock is predominantly though not entirely owned by the United States. The federal land banks, whose percentage of governmental stock ownership has varied from overwhelming majority to minority to bare majority, were operated temporarily under complete governmental control and may still be said to be controlled by the government.[74] Under exactly the same control, since governed by the land-bank directors, are the federal intermediate credit banks and production credit corporations, both entirely government owned, and the district banks for co-operatives, which, like the central bank, are predominantly though not completely owned by the United States.

Similar in that in each case a small minority of directors are government appointed, the federal home loan banks, the Second Bank of the United States, and the federal reserve banks are examples of majority government-owned, minority government-owned, and privately owned corporations, respectively. At the bottom of the scale appear two corporations over which the government has exercised no substantial control. Of these, the Bank of North America was under the majority ownership of the United States for a brief period, while the First Bank of the United States is of interest only for the substantial government investment involved.

An attempted classification of purposes and functions reveals that, out of the total of thirty-eight corporations, the appre-

[74] Out of seven directors for each land bank, three are chosen by private interests, one of the other four appointed by the governor of the F.C.A. to represent a private group (national farm loan associations), and the remaining three appointed by the governor to represent the public interest. Together with the general supervision by the Farm Credit Administration, this appointment by the governor of four directors justifies the description "government controlled."

ciable majority of twenty-four have dealt primarily with banking or finance. Seven of these have been a part of the agricultural credit system, and six are now within the Farm Credit Administration structure; two others function in the insurance of deposits and accounts; still another insures producers of wheat against unavoidable crop failures; and the remaining thirteen have been credit agencies for the assistance of industry in general, or for advancing loans to more specific groups.

The nonbanking corporations have enjoyed such varied functions as purchase and distribution of food and other commodities, operation of transportation systems, improvement of housing conditions, administration of a public works program, production of lumber for war use, operation of prison industries, and production and distribution of hydroelectric power as part of a broad regional development program.

In conclusion it may be noted that all of the thirty-eight corporations described have been "federal agencies" in the sense that they are exempt in some or all respects from taxation by the states.

CHAPTER III
SOURCES OF FUNDS

THE first problem which must be faced by a newly born government corporation is that of acquiring capital for the conduct of its operations, whatever the nature of those operations may be. The main sources of such funds have been four in number: direct congressional appropriations, sale of capital stock, borrowings, and operating receipts and earnings. At the outset an undertaking is financed by one of the first two methods, while any or all of the four may be used to supply additional capital after the enterprise is under way.

CONGRESSIONAL APPROPRIATIONS

One of the historic safeguards of public money is the practice of annual legislative appropriation of funds needed for the conduct of governmental services. In the federal government, for example, this means that each regular department or establishment is financed in its work through an appropriation setting forth, often in great detail, the exact amount to be expended for the next year and the particular purposes, objects, and methods of that expenditure. At the close of the period, all surplus reverts to the Treasury,[1] and funds for the following year are supplied by another annual appropriation. Particularly as applied to the regular governmental departments, the principle behind this practice is hardly disputable; annual legislative review and approval of expenditures prevents arbitrary and extravagant use of public funds and retains fiscal control in the hands of representatives of the people. Even here, however, shortcomings of the system have become increasingly apparent. In the first place, the expanding scope

---

[1] "Permanent appropriations," which are sometimes made by Congress, must, of course, be excepted from the general rule.

and complexity of governmental activities place a tremendous burden on legislators, with the result that there is a tendency for Congress either to pass budgetary provisions without careful consideration or else to become enmeshed in a mass of detail in an unfortunate perversion of the important function of broad policy formation. Second, if the details are legislated upon, as they frequently are to an extreme degree, the rigidity which results oftentimes defeats administrative excellence. This is inevitable when an estimate is transformed into a mandate and remains, for all practical purposes, unalterable for the period of a year. Reactions against this rigidity may be seen in the occasional creation by Congress of revolving funds and most strikingly in the appropriation, during the Roosevelt administration, of relief and public works funds, the expenditure of which is almost entirely discretionary and unhampered by legislative prescription.

In spite of the imperfections just mentioned, few would deny that a system of annual appropriations is the best yet conceived for controlling regular governmental expenditures, and certainly the adoption of a federal budgetary plan in 1921 has brought about a great improvement in federal fiscal affairs. The case of the government corporation engaged in the conduct of an economic enterprise, however, is strikingly different and deserves further examination. Examples of such corporations which have been financed by annual appropriations are comparatively few. The three most important have been the Fleet Corporation, the United States Housing Corporation, and the T.V.A. Annual appropriations have been necessary in the case of the Fleet Corporation in order to meet yearly deficits arising out of operation and maintenance since the war period, and following the act of July 19, 1919, which directed the United States Housing Corporation to liquidate, that agency has been supported by annual grants.[2]

[2] Regarding this case, Van Dorn has written: "The Corporation has thus lost one of the chief characteristics which commended it as an efficient agency for carrying on a business function of government. As long as it must look to

Today the T.V.A. affords the chief example of an important governmental corporate enterprise supported by the yearly appropriations of our national legislature. Annually, T.V.A. officials must appear before the congressional committees for testimony regarding the expenditure of previous grants and the feasibility of future financial support. Friends of the corporation can point to four weaknesses in this arrangement. There is always the danger of congressional refusal to appropriate, with the consequence that constructions, developments, and programs may be left half-completed, thereby nullifying the benefits of previous expenditures. Furthermore, the uncertainty surrounding annual congressional action is a handicap to continuity of policy and administrative efficiency.[3] Again, annual appearance before Congress paves the way for political interference in the details of administration. Finally, elaborate preparation for congressional hearings cripples the regular administrative program for from one to three months each year.

Actually, the T.V.A. has had little difficulty in securing funds and in remaining free from congressional interference in management matters. Also, lump-sum grants have obviated the evils of detailed and rigid appropriations.[4] All in all, the annual appropriation system has given Congress regular opportunity to review the work of this experimental corporation without as yet proving to be a serious handicap. The noncommercial nature of many of the T.V.A.'s functions is an important consideration in this connection.

Congress for annual detailed appropriations it is in the same dependent position as a bureau or a board. The camouflage of a corporate name will in no wise protect it from political pressure" (*Government Corporations* [New York: Alfred A. Knopf, 1926], pp. 167–68).

[3] One of the major criticisms made during the first few years of the T.V.A.'s existence involved the failure of the Authority to formulate a complete and long-time planning program.

[4] It should be noted here, however, that T.V.A. expenditures are made with no important departure from the budgetary allotment estimates which have been approved by congressional appropriation committees (see C. H. Pritchett, "The Tennessee Valley Authority" [Doctor's dissertation, University of Chicago, 1937], p. 117).

A more damaging illustration of the practice of annual appropriations may be found in the post-war history of the federally owned barge lines. When operated as the Inland and Coastwise Waterways Service, without corporate status, this enterprise was a great disappointment and the target of scathing criticism. General Ashburn,[5] chief of the Service, when submitting his 1923 report to the Secretary of War, assigned a large share of his difficulties to the dependence upon annual appropriations. One of three fundamental objections to the service as operated he characterized as follows:

Its inability to finance itself in periods of depression, thus necessitating an appeal to Congress for funds, opening the flood gates of criticism with the resultant agitation as to whether or not Congress will, through failure to appropriate, cause the cessation of an operation that is economically sound, the destruction of a solvent transportation agency, the failure of a successful waterway demonstration, because of the law against a Government agency creating a deficit; and under the limits set by such conditions the line is incapable of expansion unless there be a further extension of governmental ownership.[6]

Having reached the conclusion that a corporation was the way out of the difficulty, General Ashburn submitted to the Secretary of War a draft of proposed legislation which would create such an agency. In the 1924 congressional hearings, he expanded his views on the subject and brought out the following points:[7] first, the uncertainty of congressional appropriations to supply a deficiency and to fulfil obligations resulted in the loss of shippers "whose confidence it has taken us years to gain"; second, the inevitable delay in congressional supply of requested funds was a serious handicap; finally, even when the necessary funds were on hand, the absence of express authorization for their use in emergencies and for unforeseen contingencies frequently obstructed efficient conduct of the

---

[5] Then Colonel Ashburn.

[6] *Annual Report of the Chief of Inland and Coastwise Waterways Service, 1923,* p. 11.

[7] *Hearings before the Committee on Interstate and Foreign Commerce, House of Representatives, on H.R. 6647,* pp. 102 ff.

service. In the present connection, perhaps the most significant statement made by General Ashburn throughout the hearings is as follows: "If Congress should appropriate a certain specified sum of money and say that it would be available for a certain number of years, we would get practically the same result as you would get by this corporation, but there are certain notable exceptions."[8] The last clause detracts little from this disclosure.

These contentions by General Ashburn, if isolated, might perhaps be dismissed as representing simply the desire of the chief of the inland waterways service for more power and greater freedom in his work, but today their support is found in the efficient record of the Inland Waterways Corporation, which even its opponents have taken occasion to admire and fear.[9] The 1927 report of the corporation deprecates any attempt to appropriate money for specific objects as an inevitable "throwback" to the same difficulties that "almost throttled the operations" of the service before its incorporation in 1924.[10]

A recent illustration is the case of the Federal Prison Industries, incorporated in 1934 with a permanent appropriation, and thus freed from annual review by Congress. It is significant that the president of the corporation, associated with the work both before and after 1934, looked upon this accomplishment as one of the most hopeful steps on the road to a continuous and progressive policy regarding prison industries.

In general, it may be said that the system of annual appropriations is inapplicable to government corporations carrying on business operations with the requisite flexibility and vigor. To be sure, some critics have characterized permanent appro-

---

[8] *Ibid.*, p. 102.

[9] Herbert Corey, "Uncle Sam Finds a Formula for Competing with the Carriers," *Public Utilities Fortnightly*, VIII (1931), 388.

[10] *Annual Report of Inland Waterways Corporation, 1927*, p. 38. The report further states that "it would be far better to abolish the corporation and the policy of promoting, encouraging, and developing water transportation, and fostering and preserving in full vigor both rail and water transportation, than to appropriate money for specific projects" (*ibid.*).

priations, revolving funds, and initial capitalizations as "back-door treasury hand-outs" that defeat the purpose of democrat-ic government and give the recipients license to extravagance and waste.[11] Their contention that public funds must be ade-quately controlled is incontestable, but, in the case of govern-ment corporate enterprises, that control must be exercised in ways other than by annual appropriations if the maximum benefits of the corporate device are to be realized.[12]

ALLOCATION OF EMERGENCY FUNDS

The relief and public works policies of the Roosevelt ad-ministration brought about a situation unparalleled in our history, which had a significant influence upon the use of gov-ernment corporations. The appropriation of billions of dollars for discretionary allotment and expenditure was followed by the creation of several corporations whose capital funds were to be received not through direct annual appropriations or through a congressional mandate for stock purchase but through the allocation of funds from the emergency reservoirs. Thus, the T.V.A.C., a nonstock corporation, received $300,000 from F.E.R.A.; E.H.F.A. had its capital stock of $1,000,000 subscribed from public works funds; Commodity Credit Cor-poration had $3,000,000 stock paid for out of agricultural ad-justment funds; Federal Surplus Relief Corporation was fi-nanced through allocations from A.A.A. and from the state emergency relief agencies; and even the T.V.A. has been al-located $25,000,000 from P.W.A. funds. The two most striking examples of this trend, however—the Public Works Emergency Housing Corporation and the Public Works Emergency Leas-ing Corporation—were the most short-lived of the group. In-corporated in Delaware with nominal capital stock these agen-

[11] See, e.g., statements of Mr. Blanton and Mr. Taber, *Congressional Record*, LXXVIII, 10157 ff.

[12] Cf. W. F. Willoughby, *The Problem of a National Budget* (New York and London: D. Appleton & Co., 1918), chap. v; Van Dorn, *op. cit.*, chap. xi; Dimock, *Government-operated Enterprises in the Panama Canal Zone* (Chicago: University of Chicago Press, 1934), chap. ix.

cies were conceived as vehicles for carrying out the public works program and were to be financed through the allotment of public works funds. Since they were incorporated by the Federal Emergency Administrator of Public Works himself, they would have suffered no embarrassment in the acquisition of funds and would have been quite free from legislative restrictions. However, as we have noted, both corporations were dissolved without being utilized, as a result of the Comptroller-General's refusal to permit the proposed allotment of funds.

Allocation of annually appropriated funds differs from direct legislative grant in that removal of the corporations from legislative control and interference is further effected. The way is prepared for the application of funds to the best advantage, as indicated by administrative experience, and the rigidity of legislative detail is avoided. The corporations are also a step removed from congressional hearings, and, while the officials responsible for the allocation are held to account, interference in the minutiae of administration is made more difficult. Of course, a continuous policy is dependent upon congressional will and the further supply of funds for allocation. Critics have asserted that corporations of this nature are simply ingenious devices for a veiled extravagance and waste,[13] and potentially there is a measure of truth in the contention. Unfortunately, the flexibility which is necessary for the acme of administrative excellence is also subject to perversion.

Whatever the merits of financing government corporations through such allocations, the phenomenon is hardly to be regarded as of permanent significance. Perhaps the corporation is useful in administering an emergency allotment, but the allotment is not feasible as a source of funds for a corporate enterprise of any permanent nature.

CAPITAL STOCK

Most of the statutes authorizing the formation of United States Government corporations have made provision for the

---

[13] E.g., the late Senator Schall (see *Congressional Record*, LXXIX, 1571 ff.).

issuance by the corporation of capital stock. Frequently the exact amount is prescribed, as, for example, in the case of the War Finance Corporation, the Inland Waterways Corporation, and the Federal Farm Mortgage Corporation, with capital stock of $500,000,000, $15,000,000, and $200,000,000, respectively. In other instances the provision relating to stock is in the form of a maximum limitation. Thus, the First Bank of the United States was to have stock "not to exceed $10,000,-000," while the Emergency Fleet Corporation and the Home Owners' Loan Corporation were limited by statute to not more than $50,000,000 and $200,000,000 of stock, respectively. Yet a third variation is found in the case of such corporations as the federal land banks, with stock of "not less than $750,000 each" and the regional agricultural credit corporations, with stock of "not less than $3,000,000 each." Executive corporations not specifically created by statute may issue stock merely to conform with state incorporation laws, as witness the three no-par shares of the Emergency Housing Corporation.

United States ownership has resulted from an express mandate to a designated federal officer or agency to subscribe all the capital stock of a corporation, from an equally definite order to procure a certain lesser amount of stock, from an *authorization* for United States subscription up to a certain amount, or finally from an authorization for United States subscription to any unsubscribed balance after a certain period of time. The importance that has been given the stock issue is indicated not only in the history of government corporations but also in the literature. Van Dorn defines "government-owned corporations" in terms of government ownership of *the capital stock*, since it "is their most distinguishing characteristic" and indeed it is only of recent date that the use by the federal government of nonstock corporations has been attempted. The sale of capital stock has provided the various corporations with funds which could be applied to operations in a manner free from the difficulties surrounding annually appropriated funds. This fact is in large part responsible for whatever success the corporate agencies have achieved in carrying out their programs.

Where the entire corporate stock is owned by the government, the situation may differ not at all in nature from a permanent appropriation with no stock issue involved. The stock device was designed in private enterprises largely for the purpose of securing capital from a multitude of sources on a scale too great for a single contributor. In the case of the government, however, the necessary amount is concentrated, and the stock purchase becomes a fiction; the same results could be achieved by permanent appropriation. Consider the following examples. The Federal Prison Industries, a nonstock corporation, is empowered to use its initial appropriation and all subsequent earnings as operating capital for its purposes. The T.V.A., also having no capital stock, is empowered to retain from earnings a special continuing and emergency fund in addition to whatever amounts the board deems necessary for operation. The net earnings are to be turned over to the Treasury and may be likened to "dividends." The Inland Waterways Corporation retains its earnings, as does the Prison Industries, and pays no dividends on its government-owned stock. The federal intermediate credit banks, capitalized through government stock purchase, pay all net earnings into the Treasury after reserve requirements have been met. These instances illustrate the fact that the stock issue in itself is immaterial as compared to the particular conditions imposed upon the corporation.[14]

However intriguing the foregoing line of speculation may become, there would appear to be no significant reason for discarding the stock device and, on the other hand, several arguments for its continuance. Where federal corporations are created under state law, its retention will be necessary. Second, dividend payments, in line with traditional business success and efficiency, may prove stimulating and useful, and indeed the whole tradition of private business lends support to the reten-

[14] Cf. General Ashburn's statement, above, p. 55.

tion of analogous features which are at least harmless, and at most beneficial. In the third place, the legal position of the government stock corporation has been somewhat clarified, and perhaps this advantage should not be endangered. Certainly, experience has demonstrated that capitalization through stock issue has been eminently successful in providing government corporations with the necessary funds for carrying out energetically and expeditiously a continuous policy. Not in every case has the initial capitalization been sufficient. The Grain Corporation of the war period had its original $50,000,-000 stock increased to $150,000,000 and later to $500,000,000; the stock of the Inland Waterways Corporation was increased from $5,000,000 to $15,000,000 in 1928; and the United States subscribed to an additional $125,000,000 of federal land-bank stock almost two decades after the creation of those banks. Such additions in the realm of government do not compare with the rapid growth of innumerable successful and expanding corporations in the field of private enterprise, but they do illustrate the fact that enlarged capitalization is sometimes advisable and can be achieved.

Congressional determination of the amount of capital stock to be issued by a government corporation affords a significant measure of control over this phase of corporate finance. It is a proper function of the legislature to consider and to regulate the total outlay, in so far as it can be determined, necessary or advisable for a particular corporate enterprise. In the case of a relatively stable project, such as the Inland Waterways Corporation, statutory prescription of the amount would seem to be desirable. On the other hand, the amounts needed by the production credit corporations and the banks for co-operatives depend so completely upon the interest and participation of co-operative associations that provision has been made for issue of stock as occasion demands and as the governor of the F.C.A. might see fit. In the nonstatutory corporations, such as the Federal Subsistence Homesteads Corporation, the Commodity Credit Corporation, and the Public Works Emergency

Housing Corporation, the only limitation seems to be the amount appropriated for the larger purposes which those agencies serve, and capitalization is determined by the officials responsible for administering those appropriations.

To summarize: The practice of capitalizing government corporations through issuing of stock has been widely followed by the federal government and is an important factor in whatever success they have achieved. Such a practice eliminates the major defects which are inherent in a system of annual appropriations, while at the same time it goes a long way toward providing the necessary funds for the enterprise. This desirable flexibility, on the other hand, augments the necessity for adequate control and assurance that the huge outlays will be utilized for the public good; increased authority must be compensated for by a commensurate responsibility.

BORROWINGS

To supplement their initial capital, most government corporations have been given extensive borrowing powers. Indeed, a number of these agencies, such as the R.F.C., H.O.L.C., R.F.C. Mortgage Company, Commodity Credit Corporation, E.H.F.A., and the various farm credit banks, have financed their operations principally in this manner. The magnitude of the fiscal operations of our leading corporate borrowers is indicated in the following figures: R.F.C. notes totaling $4,011,-749,666.67 were outstanding on September 30, 1936,[15] H.O.L.C. bonds amounting to $3,048,369,550 were outstanding on June 30, 1936,[16] and the total of land-bank bonds outstanding on December 31, 1936, was $1,964,654,440.[17]

Legislative provisions dealing with corporation borrowings naturally vary widely in amounts authorized, methods to be employed, and restrictions and requirements set forth. In practically every case, however, a maximum limit is placed by

---

[15] *Quarterly Report of R.F.C., September 30, 1936*, p. 5.

[16] *Fourth Annual Report of F.H.L.B.B., 1936*, p. 127.

[17] *Fourth Annual Report of F.C.A., 1936*, p. 127.

Congress, regardless of the degree of latitude afforded each particular corporation within that limit. Sometimes the limit will be expressed as an exact figure—as in the case of the federal land banks, authorized in 1933 to issue farm-loan bonds not to exceed $2,000,000,000 in the aggregate;[18] the T.V.A., with power to issue bonds up to $100,000,000;[19] and the H.O.L.C., whose bond limitation has progressed by stages from $2,000,000,000[20] to $4,750,000,000.[21] A unique provision of the act authorizing the creation of the United States Spruce Production Corporation places a single limitation of $100,000,000 upon the total of capital stock, *together* "with any bonds, notes, or debentures or other securities issued."[22] At other times, the limitation will be expressed as a factor of the corporation's paid-in capital stock or total assets. The War Finance Corporation was empowered to have outstanding at any one time its bonds in an amount aggregating not more than six times its paid-in capital.[23] The Inland Waterways Corporation was authorized to incur an indebtedness which "at any time shall not exceed 25 per centum of the value of the assets at such time,"[24] while the limitation placed upon bonds of each federal intermediate credit bank was "ten times the amount of the paid-up capital and surplus of such bank."[25] Also, the Federal Deposit Insurance Corporation can issue notes, bonds, and debentures up to three times the amount of its capital and paid-in assessments,[26] and the Central Bank for Cooperatives was given the power to "issue debentures," the total amount not to exceed five times the paid-in capital and surplus of the bank.[27] No

[18] 48 Stat. 42.

[19] 49 Stat. 1078. The original authorization of $50,000,000 was increased by $50,000,000 in 1935.

[20] 48 Stat. 129 (1933).   [21] 48 Stat. 296 (1935).

[22] 40 Stat. 888 (1918).

[23] 40 Stat. 509. This amount was decreased in 1921 to three times the paid-in capital (42 Stat. 183).

[24] 43 Stat. 362 (1924).   [26] 49 Stat. 699 (1935).

[25] 42 Stat. 1456 (1923).   [27] 48 Stat. 263 (1933).

corporation has had its debt limit so frequently altered as has the Reconstruction Finance Corporation. Originally authorized to have outstanding its notes, bonds, and debentures in an amount aggregating not more than three times its subscribed capital,[28] the corporation has seen this provision altered no less than a dozen times since its formation in 1932. The basic limitation was increased to six and three-fifths times the subscribed capital stock by the Emergency Relief and Construction Act of 1932, and, while the National Industrial Recovery Act decreased this amount by $400,000,000, other changes have all represented additions to the authorized total outstanding, in order to enable the R.F.C. to assist in financing the various projects and purposes with which the particular piece of legislation might be concerned.[29] In the case of the act creating the Federal Savings and Loan Insurance Corporation, there is apparently no limitation upon the amount which may be borrowed, since the provision reads: "For the purposes of this title, the corporation shall have power to borrow money, and to issue notes, bonds and debentures, or other such obligations upon such terms and conditions as the board of trustees may determine."[30] This absence of any limitation upon the borrowing power of a government corporation expressly created by statute is quite unique.

A maximum limitation by Congress need not hamper the government corporation in the conduct of its affairs and is a desirable means of keeping borrowing within reason and under the general control of the legislature. Indiscriminate bond issues are discouraged, yet the acquisition of necessary funds in an emergency is not prevented.[31]

[28] 47 Stat. 9 (1932).

[29] See, e.g., 47 Stat. 729 (1932); 48 Stat. 6, 50, 56, 119, 129, 319, 971, 1056 (1933–34); and 49 Stat. 3 (1935).

[30] 48 Stat. 1256 (1934).

[31] While federal corporations created by legislation have almost invariably been placed under a borrowing limitation, this has not been true of several executive corporations which have been created under the Roosevelt administration. The certificates of incorporation of the Commodity Credit Corporation,

As another measure of control, Congress has, as a rule, required approval of some other governmental officer or agency in the issuing of corporation obligations. Ordinarily, the Secretary of the Treasury must approve, as has been true, for example, in the case of bonds issued by the War Finance Corporation, the T.V.A., the R.F.C., the H.O.L.C., and the Federal Farm Mortgage Corporation. Bonds of the intermediate credit banks and the home-loan banks require approval of the governor of F.C.A. and the Federal Home Loan Bank Board, respectively. This type of control has not brought about the strangulation of corporation borrowings and, when wisely applied, is an advantage. Thus, co-ordination of borrowings by the corporations under the F.C.A. is made possible by the supervision of the governor. Also, the approval of the Secretary of the Treasury insures harmony of R.F.C., H.O.L.C., and F.F.M.C. bond issues with the fiscal policy of the Treasury itself.[32] This approval is doubly valuable and necessary when full guaranty of principal and interest is given by the government. Indeed, the Secretary's approval in the H.O.L.C. instance was required only in the amendatory act which provided full government guaranty.[33]

The question of government guaranty of corporate bonds is in itself one of the perplexing problems which must be faced. Acts creating the War Finance Corporation, the federal intermediate credit banks, and the home-loan banks all expressly state that the United States assumes no obligation, either as to interest or as to principal, in connection with the issuance of

---

the Emergency Housing Corporation, the Federal Surplus Relief Corporation, the Federal Subsistence Homesteads Corporation, the Electric Home and Farm Authority, and the Emergency Leasing Corporation all specified the power to borrow money without limit as to amount.

[32] Mr. Ogden Mills, when testifying as Undersecretary of the Treasury in the hearings on the R.F.C. bill in 1932, spoke of the necessity of controlling the sale of corporation securities "in order to protect the Treasury Department in conducting the financial operations of the Government, so that these debentures would not be offered simultaneously, for instance, with Government issues."

[33] 48 Stat. 643.

bonds or notes by the corporations concerned. In the absence of such an express provision, unless a positive guaranty is included in the act, corporations are nonetheless responsible for their own obligations, and the protection of government credit cannot be implied. Among the corporations falling within this class are the Panama Railroad Company, the Inland Waterways Corporation, the Federal Deposit Insurance Corporation, and the Central Bank for Cooperatives.

It is only in recent years that Congress has followed the practice of guaranteeing corporation bonds, and complete underwriting, as to both principal and interest, has occurred in the case of the R.F.C., the T.V.A., the Federal Farm Mortgage Corporation, the H.O.L.C., and the United States Housing Authority. Only the interest on H.O.L.C. bonds was guaranteed in 1933, but, after the corporation had operated for a year, Congress extended the protection to include both principal and interest on all future bond issues.

Guaranty of bonds by the government profoundly affects one of the features of the government corporation—namely, the power to borrow on its own credit—which has been looked upon with favor as an evidence of desirable independence.[34] The wartime Grain Corporation had borrowed over $385,390,-000 without government guaranty, "in the same way as any other reputable business house."[35] Its success in borrowing over $160,000,000 from commercial banks, although its capitalization was only $150,000,000, has been extolled as follows: "The fact that such large amounts were secured from commercial banks especially on the basis of notes during this period of credit stringency indicates the confidence which the banks felt in the integrity of the corporation and those who were responsible for the management of its affairs."[36]

Guaranty, on the other hand, is an admission either of the

[34] See Dimock, *op. cit.*, p. 205; Van Dorn, *op. cit.*, p. 261.

[35] F. M. Surface, *The Grain Trade during the World War* (New York: Macmillan Co., 1928), p. 437.

[36] *Ibid.*, p. 444.

inability of the corporation to stand upon its own feet financially, or else of the inadvisability of having it do so. Is such a
practice conducive to the best efforts of the corporation? Is it a
necessary or desirable practice? Dr. John Thurston has analyzed
the problem and reaches the conclusion that the disadvantages
are predominant.[37] His reasoning is as follows: The advantage
of lower interest rates and the savings therefrom are easily
overestimated, since the risk of ultimate loss to the government
should be counted and since a compensatory loss will probably
result in the consequent decrease in the rate of interest on
regular government bonds. Guaranty of a large amount of corporation bonds may endanger government credit. Contention
of necessity in a particular case is an admission of the economic
unsoundness of the enterprise. The unconscious effect of guaranty may be inefficiency, arising from the knowledge that the
government will have to foot the bill. Finally, there may be a
tendency toward legislative interference unless financial independence is maintained.

These arguments are persuasive, and it is desirable for
corporate economic enterprises which are of a permanent nature and are conceived as self-sufficing to stand upon their own
feet with respect to their borrowings. Thus the Panama Railroad Company and the Inland Waterways Corporation, the
latter designed as an experiment to test the economy of water
transportation, should be able to utilize their assets and financial position as security for whatever borrowings may become
necessary. This is a discipline which puts a premium on efficient and economic operation and provides a serviceable test
of that efficiency and economy.

However, there are considerations which place government
guaranty in a more favorable light. In an interesting session of
the congressional committee considering the R.F.C. bill in
1932, Mr. Eugene Meyer, governor of the Federal Reserve
Board, made the following statement in answer to a question

[37] "Government Proprietary Corporations in the English-speaking Countries"
(Doctor's dissertation, Harvard University, 1935), chap. iii.

as to the probability that a sale of corporation securities would lower the general market value of government bonds: "If they were sold on a proper basis and distributed and handled properly, they would not. If this corporation's operations are constructive and helpful, as we hope they will be, they should be helpful to the market for Government and all other bonds."[38] True enough, this is an optimistic picture of the effects of a recovery agency, but it indicates the possibility of benefits which might follow an instance of government underwriting. The most striking illustration of the practice under discussion may be found in the history of the H.O.L.C. In the hearings and congressional debates concerning the original bill, the question of guaranty was discussed at length, and opposing views were well aired.[39] The Banking and Currency Committee of each house recommended guaranty of interest only, and Mr. Steagall, chairman of the House committee, stated in the Committee of the Whole that the conclusion had been reached that the corporation's capital of $200,000,000 and the security supporting the mortgages received in exchange would make the bonds attractive. He further said: "It would be a serious thing to have the Treasury undertake to guarantee principal and interest on bonds covering the enormous home mortgage indebtedness of the country, amounting to over $20,000,000,-000."[40] However, many members of Congress felt that the bonds were doomed to a dead market and predicted that the purpose of the bill—namely, to give relief to mortgage-distressed homeowners—would be defeated through inability to secure funds. Thus, Mr. McGugin asked how a sale could be expected on 4 per cent bonds secured with collateral taken upon distressed-mortgage property when fully guaranteed government bonds could be bought at the same or even a higher inter-

---

[38] "Reconstruction Finance Corporation," *Hearings before the House Committee on Banking and Currency*, January, 1932, pp. 34-35.

[39] "Home Owners' Loan Act," *Hearings before Subcommittee of the Senate Committee on Banking and Currency*, April, 1933.

[40] *Congressional Record*, LXXVII, 2478.

est figure.[41] Mr. Steagall pointed out that the act contemplated not so much sale of the bonds to the public as their exchange for mortgages, and the act as approved by the President on June 13, 1933, contained a guaranty of interest only. In less than a year, however, the question was again brought before Congress in the form of an amendatory act which had as its prime purpose the guaranty by the United States of both principal and interest of H.O.L.C. bonds. The pessimistic predictions of the previous session had largely come true, and the relief program of the H.O.L.C. was seriously hampered. Presenting the committee report to the Senate and recommending passage of the amendatory provision, Senator Bulkley gave the following four reasons which had arisen out of the corporation's experience: (1) Many mortgagees had refused to accept the H.O.L.C. bonds in exchange for their mortgages, and the result was an arbitrary distinction against some homeowners through no fault of their own. (2) A saving of a considerable sum in interest was contemplated by the amendment. Whereas H.O.L.C. 4 per cent bonds had been selling considerably below par, the result of guaranty should be sale at around par even with lower interest rates. (3) An "educational campaign" had been necessary in connection with the early bonds, and negotiations with mortgagees had been frequently tedious and costly. Guaranty would facilitate the relief activities of the corporation. (4) Federal Farm Mortgage Corporation bonds had been fully guaranteed by act of January 31, 1934, and Congress should not put H.O.L.C. bonds in a different class.[42]

Mr. Steagall had also changed his views on the matter, as is evidenced by the following statement: "Experience has shown that there is great difficulty in persuading mortgagees to accept these bonds even at the present rate. We had to resort to this method of securing the principal, or having the Government secure the principal, in order to make the law effective."[43]

[41] Ibid., p. 2488.   [42] Ibid., LXXVIII, 4805.

[43] Hearings before the House Committee on Banking and Currency, on H.R. 8403 (S. 2999), March, 1934, p. 133; see also report of this committee, House Report 1075 (73d Cong., 2d sess.), pp. 4 and 5.

In fact, by 1934 it had become the consensus of those who were sympathetic with, or had some hope for, the work undertaken by the H.O.L.C., that full guaranty was necessary if the purpose of granting relief to distressed homeowners was to be successfully realized.[44] Clearly, this is quite a different picture from that presented, for example, by the Inland Waterways Corporation, with its mandate to test the economy of water transportation. An undertaking in which the relief motive is predominant will inevitably suffer in a profits and loss appraisal, and it is difficult to apply the criteria which are utilized in the testing of private businesses and government enterprises of a primarily commercial nature. Judgment on the operations of the H.O.L.C. is premature, but it is contended by some critics that approximately 30 per cent of the collateral held by the corporation is worthless, and that ultimate payment on the bonds must fall upon the taxpayers. Would such an eventuality prove that the operations of the corporation have been without qualification unsuccessful? The answer is at least debatable.

The increasing credit activities of the federal government under the Roosevelt administration have had an important influence on the whole question of government corporation borrowing. Thus, if the needed credit will be supplied by another government agency, the problem is solved without raising the issue of bond guaranty by the United States. For example, the act of June 16, 1934, provides that the R.F.C. shall purchase at par debentures of the F.D.I.C. up to $250,000,000 when

[44] In this connection it is interesting to note that the first report of operations submitted by the Federal Deposit Insurance Corporation, March 31, 1934, called attention to the fact that the act creating the corporation provides no guaranty of bonds. It further stated: "It is believed that in the absence of such a provision difficulty would be experienced in marketing obligations of this Corporation for the purpose of financing any extensive operations such as would be entailed in making liquidation purchases or loans. The directors, therefore, recommend that the subsections above referred to be amended by providing for a guaranty by the United States Government of such obligations of the Corporation as may be issued with the approval of the Secretary of the Treasury and that the Secretary of the Treasury may purchase and sell such obligations" (p. 6).

requested to do so by the directors of the latter corporation. Other R.F.C. loans have been made to federal land banks, regional agricultural credit corporations, and federal intermediate credit banks, while the Commodity Credit Corporation, the R.F.C. Mortgage Company, and the E.H.F.A. are almost entirely dependent on R.F.C. credit. The R.F.C., in turn, has secured the great majority of its funds through sale of its notes directly to the Secretary of the Treasury. Within the F.C.A., the Federal Farm Mortgage Corporation was created for the primary purpose of providing a market for farm-loan bonds and became for a time the principal agency for the financing of the agricultural credits program.[45]

Thus, one observer, after contrasting government corporations with departmental agencies because of their freedom in normal times to borrow from the banks and sell securities on the open market, remarked in 1934: "At the present time, however, this is not of much importance, for to an ever-increasing extent governmental financial agencies are dominating the credit field, and the President has at his disposal large sums which may be made available either to department or corporation."[46]

OPERATING RECEIPTS AND EARNINGS

The fifth main source of funds for the government corporation is to be found in its receipts and earnings from goods and services rendered. Presumably, in an economic enterprise this is to be the fountainhead of funds once the business is under way. Thurston has spoken of the practice of meeting expenses primarily by sale of goods and services rather than taxation in the following terms: "Indeed this characteristic seems of sufficient importance that it may be regarded as the *prima facie* determinant of whether a government corporation is engaged

[45] See *Second Annual Report of F.C.A.*, pp. 9 and 31.

[46] Joel I. Seidman, "Business Operations of the Federal Government," *Editorial Research Reports*, Vol. II, No. 11 (1934).

in an economic as distinguished from a governmental enterprise and therefore properly called proprietary."[47]

Unquestionably, the best illustration of this phenomenon in the federal sphere is the history of the Panama Railroad Company. From the time of the original government investment of $7,000,000 in 1904, the Panama Railroad Company has carried on and operated its many and varied services on a pay-as-you-go basis, and receipts have been sufficient to pay the costs of operation, to pay approximately $12,000,000 in dividends to the United States, to build up reserves for depreciation and construction amounting to over $13,000,000, and to make many capital improvements. Gross receipts from sales and services furnished during the fiscal year 1933, for example, amounted to $11,135,557.90.[48] Naturally, in the case of the huge fiscal corporations, funds from this source are much greater in amount. Thus a statement of cash receipts of the R.F.C. during the first six months of 1935 included the following large items:[49]

Interest and discount collected................ $28,710,169.57
Dividends collected on preferred stock purchased   10,229,738.47
Interest collected on capital notes and debentures.....................................   5,290,571.39

It is the hope of every government economic enterprise that it will be able to finance itself through operating receipts and earnings.[50] The realization of that hope depends upon many factors of which the more important are: (1) The nature of the enterprise itself. Clearly, if the government is operating a necessary or desirable service which is too unprofitable for private business to undertake, earnings will be affected accordingly.[51] (2) The price placed upon goods and services rendered. This is

---

[47] Op. cit., pp. 123–24.

[48] Annual Report of the Panama Railroad Company, 1933, p. 8.

[49] Quarterly Report of the R.F.C., June 30, 1935, p. 98.

[50] The question as to availability of such funds for corporate use without further appropriation is discussed in succeeding chapters.

[51] This would, of course, be equally true in the case of uneconomic ventures which are unnecessary and undesirable.

a controllable factor particularly where government monopoly exists. (3) The general efficiency and vigor with which the enterprise is managed.

SUMMARY

Generally speaking, annual appropriations for the financing of government corporate enterprises are unsatisfactory. This is not to deny the desirability of such a system for the old-line departments and establishments. However, the flexibility and freedom which have been among the primary reasons for the use of the corporate device when government wants quick and energetic action in the conduct of certain of its services, would be to a large degree counteracted by the necessity of annual grants from the legislature. This is, of course, most true when such appropriations are made in detail. With the passing of annual appearances before the legislature, other means must be found for insuring the responsibility and accountability of the corporation.

In line with the foregoing observations, the corporate enterprises of the federal government have been with only a few exceptions relieved of annual appropriations and financed through an initial capitalization resulting from the issue of capital stock which has been purchased in whole or in part by the government itself. This method provides the corporation with a lump sum which may be permanently employed, subject always to statutory regulation, in the operations for which it was created. From the administrative point of view it has proved generally successful in ridding the corporation of the annual legislative financial strait-jacket.

Exercise of its borrowing power has been the third main source of funds for the government corporation. Frequently, the original capitalization proves inadequate; sometimes expansion of activities becomes desirable; perhaps an emergency arises which requires additional funds—in all these instances the power to borrow additional funds provides a possible solution, and the record testifies to its frequent utilization. Ordinarily, a statutory limit is placed upon borrowings, and often the approval of an outside governmental official, usually the Secretary of the Treasury, is required; both of these devices, when wisely applied, are desirable means of control. While the government corporation has historically been commended for its power to borrow on its own credit, recent developments have brought into the spotlight the question of government guaranty of corporation bonds. The R.F.C. and the H.O.L.C. have raised in opposition to the advantages of financial independence and self-sufficiency the necessity of securing funds at favorable rates in order to carry on emergency programs believed by Congress to be vital to national recovery. Aside from these huge financial transactions, the power of the government corporation to borrow from commercial banks in order to meet emergencies or for other short-term purposes is undoubtedly conducive to successful administration.

Lastly, the corporation secures capital through the sale of goods and services, and while the adequacy of this source is not the *sine qua non* as in the case of the private enterprise, nevertheless it assumes major importance where government economic enterprise is most successful. Where the corporate device is used purely for the administration of relief, as, for example, in the case of the Federal Surplus Relief Corporation, funds must be otherwise secured.

CHAPTER IV
EARLY GOVERNMENT CORPORATIONS
THE PANAMA RAILROAD COMPANY

THE Panama Railroad Company is of particular interest to the student of public administration for several reasons: it affords the earliest example of a business enterprise administered through a corporation entirely owned and controlled by the federal government; it is one of the minority of such corporations which may reasonably be considered permanent agencies; and its previous history as a private corporation, together with the manner in which government ownership was effected, offers a unique approach to the question of freedom from ordinary governmental regulations.

The problem of what to do with the railroad company was one of many which arose in 1904 when the United States Government acquired rights and property in the Canal Zone. This question particularly perplexed the Isthmian Canal Commission and Secretary of War Taft, since, at the end of 1904, 1,013 out of 70,000 shares of the capital stock were still in private hands.

In a letter to the President, Mr. Taft called attention to the consequences of mixed ownership in the following words:

It is, of course, obvious that as long as there is private ownership of any of the shares of the railroad company, the railroad must be operated for the benefit of all the stockholders to secure the greatest profit to the owners of the stock; and that directors elected by the stockholders are trustees not for the United States only but also for the private persons owning the stock, and that the policy of the directors must be that which will inure to the greatest benefit of all the stockholders.[1]

[1] See "Letter of the Secretary of War Transmitting the First Annual Report of the Isthmian Canal Commission, 1904," *House Document 226* (58th Cong., 3d sess.), p. 14.

However, as he further pointed out:

The United States purchased the shares in the company for the purpose of using the railroad to assist it in the construction of the canal, and it is quite evident that this purpose will be largely defeated unless the representatives of the United States may use the railroad without let or hindrance in canal construction.

Happily, this particular question was soon settled, since in 1905 the remaining shares of capital stock were acquired by the government, and since that time the railroad company has been operated as an adjunct of the canal, although still performing its commercial functions as a common carrier. Inaugurated by an executive order of President Roosevelt in 1904, this policy of subordination to canal interests has gathered momentum, and today plays a large part in the management of the many services operated by the railroad company. Professor Dimock, after his study of Canal Zone activities, concluded that "the complete separation of the functions of the Railroad from those of the Canal would probably improve the Railroad and would probably make of it a better experiment in government-owned corporations, but the larger interests of the United States on the Isthmus would be served less efficiently."[2]

As a New York State corporation, the Panama Railroad Company has enjoyed all the freedom in financial matters which would characterize any private corporation chartered in that state, except in so far as Congress has limited that freedom by statute. Thus, the capitalization of $7,000,000, represented by stock owned by the government, has been employed by the directors in maintaining and expanding the various services without any such minute directions and restrictions as might appear in appropriations for a regular government department. No danger of the reverting of unexpended surpluses to the federal Treasury exists. No annual appropria-

[2] M. E. Dimock, *Government-operated Enterprises in the Panama Canal Zone* (Chicago, 1934), p. 41.

tion is necessary for the meeting of operating and maintenance expenses.

The capitalization of the Panama Railroad Company has not been increased since 1905, in accordance with the general policy of the stockholders, that is, the United States Government, that the corporation must pay its own way. The success of this policy is evidenced by the increase of capital assets from $11,421,117.93, in 1904, to $34,600,660.12, in 1935; by the payment of dividends totaling $12,144,905; and by the accumulation of reserves for the construction of steamships and for replacements totaling $13,103,901.65.[3]

The ability to borrow money on its own credit is one of the attributes of the Panama Railroad Company, as distinguished from a government department, but, in addition to the policy

---

[3] *Annual Report of the Panama Railroad Company, 1935*, p. 18. This record has not been achieved entirely without the help of congressional appropriations. From 1906 to 1909, canal appropriations included items to the railroad company for new equipment and improvements totaling in all $4,835,000 (34 Stat. 33, 34 Stat. 761, 34 Stat. 1369, 35 Stat. 317, 35 Stat. 1025). These appropriations were conceived as loans to the corporation and were not to be expended "until the obligation of the Panama Railroad Company for the full amount thereof and drawing four per cent interest payable to the United States shall have been delivered to the Secretary of the Treasury of the United States and by him accepted" (34 Stat. 761). Actually $2,786,829.53 of the total was expended by the corporation, and this sum, together with an additional $2,298,367.50 appropriated by Congress for retirement of outstanding bonds (34 Stat. 1369), was carried on the company books as a capital liability due the United States Government. By 1911, $1,687,714.92 had been repaid when Congress provided that the corporation should make no "further payment on the principal or interest on notes heretofore given by it to the United States for moneys appropriated for its use" (36 Stat. 1450). The obligation, however, was recorded in each annual balance sheet until 1928, in which year Congress directed the Treasurer of the United States to cancel and surrender to the Panama Railroad Company its notes (45 Stat. 532). Thus, the profit and loss statement for 1928 records the writing-off of indebtedness to the United States amounting to $3,247,332.11 (*Annual Report, 1928*, p. 32).

A further beneficence of Congress occurred in 1910, when the Panama Railroad Company was relieved of the payment of the annual subsidy of $250,000 which had been required under the concession granted by Colombia (36 Stat. 772).

It may be conceded that the foregoing subsidies, while worthy of note, do not seriously mar the Panama Railroad Company's record in "paying its own way."

not to issue bonds already referred to, the financial success of the enterprise has made borrowings of any kind almost negligible. In an emergency, certainly, the power would be of value.

Another distinguishing feature is freedom from government regulations in the making of purchases.[4] The peculiar work of the Commissary Division of the corporation, through which merchandise worth over $5,000,000 is purchased annually for resale to the government, to the Canal, and to individuals and companies in the Canal Zone makes this flexibility in purchasing operations extremely significant.[5] Purchases are for the most part made from the New York offices, and the methods of the purchasing agent are those of a private corporation rather than a governmental agency. Such iron-clad rules as advertisement for bids and inevitable acceptance of the lowest bid, with attendant delays and disadvantages, do not apply. Rather are purchases made through the invitation of bids when competition is considered desirable, the negotiation of prices with bidders and suppliers in order to save money for the corporation, and the buying of proprietary articles without competition when speed or economy so dictates. In purchasing articles for resale, the Panama Railroad Company must consider their attractiveness to its customers and must satisfy the whims and desires of such prospective purchasers rather than any bare requirements of a detailed specification. The competition of other merchants in Panama must be met, and only through the exercise of judgment and even ingenuity can the most favorable results be achieved. Consequently, corporation officials feel that governmental restrictions, designed to prevent misuse of appropriated funds, would prove an insuperable handicap.

[4] For a discussion of Panama Railroad Company purchases see Dimock, *op. cit.*, pp. 118 ff.

[5] During the fiscal year 1935 gross revenues from sales totaled $7,453,501.67, from which the deduction of total cost of purchases and expenses left a net profit of $220,574 (*Annual Report of the Panama Railroad Company, 1935*, p. 31).

In securing machinery and materials required in physical operation, and not for resale, the Panama Railroad Company makes its purchases through the Washington office of the Panama Canal. Government regulations are applicable, and results have apparently been satisfactory enough to warrant continued use of the services of the canal office, although mandatory acceptance of the lowest bid has at times seemed less efficient to corporation officials than the free exercise of engineering judgment.

Of great significance in the management of the Panama Railroad Company has been the power to utilize capital and earnings without annual congressional appropriations, and without deposit of such funds in the federal Treasury. Capital improvements have been undertaken by the directors from corporation earnings, and, as mentioned above, this practice of purchasing rolling stock, equipment, and otherwise improving the property, has resulted in the increase of capital assets from $11,421,117.93 in 1904 to $34,600,660.12 in 1935. Operating and maintenance expenses have, of course, been met from earnings, and $700,000 in dividends is annually paid into the United States Treasury.

The investment of reserve funds has been entirely in the hands of the directors, who act upon the advice of a finance committee. Recently, losses due to depreciation of securities held by the corporation have been criticized in Congress, and Mr. Collins, in 1933, proposed an amendment to the War Appropriation Bill which would prohibit investment in securities and demand deposit of earnings in a special Treasury fund.[6] A point of order defeating the amendment was sustained, but the subject reappeared in the hearings before the House Appropriations Subcommittee in 1935.[7] President Schley testified that a recent policy of the Panama Railroad Company Board had been to get rid "of the private corporation bonds as

---

[6] See *Congressional Record*, LXXVI, 2438.

[7] "War Department Appropriation Bill for 1936," *Hearings before the Subcommittee of House Committee on Appropriations*, Part II, p. 59.

fast as we could, without taking a heavy loss," and to transfer the funds into United States securities. While asserting
that officials of the Treasury Department were consulted before the purchase of government bonds, President Schley
stated that they had no control over, and had made no com-
ments on, the investment policy of the railroad company, as
determined by the directors. An examination of the 1935 report of the Panama Railroad Company reveals a substantial
decrease in private securities and a corresponding increase in
United States bonds, as compared with earlier years.

An interesting ruling of the United States Attorney-General,
dated November 24, 1915, gives an insight into the financial
position of the Panama Railroad Company. In holding that
the executive officers of the government had no authority under
existing law to fix rates over the Panama Railroad below the
cost of service, with the purpose of reimbursing the losses of
private shippers resulting from the closing of the Panama
Canal, the opinion stated:

> If we observe the fiction and treat the railroad as a wholly independent
> corporation—which has been the course pursued in past dealings with it
> (25 Op. Atty. Gen. 466; MS Opinion of Attorney General McReynolds,
> August 16, 1914)—the question turns upon the power of the directors.
> No federal statute exists by which their power is defined. It must be de-
> termined, therefore, by reference to the ordinary principles of corporation
> law.[8]

Pointing out the fundamental principle of corporation law
that assets cannot be given away by directors without unanimous consent of the stockholders, the Attorney-General stated
that Congress must speak for the United States in that regard.
On the other hand, he continued, if the corporate fiction be
disregarded, giving money from the treasury of the railroad
company would really be giving money from the Treasury of
the United States, "which is not permissible, of course, except
in consequence of specific appropriation by Congress."

There is little question that Congress can determine finan-

[8] 30 Op. Atty. Gen. 508.

cial policies of the Panama Railroad Company whenever it so desires. Thus, the corporation is prohibited from carrying any insurance to cover marine or fire losses.[9] A recent and more drastic example of congressional action is the War Department Appropriation Act of July 14, 1932, in which a special dividend of $2,800,000, to be expended in constructing the Madden Dam, was demanded from the corporation. This sum of necessity came from reserves and surplus, and Governor Schley was moved to remark in his *Annual Report* that "it is important that its [Panama Railroad Company's] capital be not so depleted by further detachments for unrelated uses as seriously to weaken the Company and render it less capable of performing its services for the Panama Canal and the Government of the United States."[10]

Finally, the Panama Railroad Company has been free from auditing and accounting control of the General Accounting Office. In 1905 the Isthmian Canal Commission prescribed a system of auditing whereby local auditors of the Panama Railroad Company in New York and on the isthmus would be subject to the jurisdiction of a general auditor in Washington, who would have full control and authority over all Canal Zone activities.[11] By the act of August 1, 1914, Congress directed the consolidation of the functions of receiving, disbursing, and accounting for funds of the railroad with similar functions of the Canal "*provided*, that separate accounts shall be kept of the transactions under each fund."[12] While this consolidation has been both censured[13] and upheld[14] by investigators, the fact remains that accounts of the railroad company have been kept along business lines, and without submission to control of the General Accounting Office. Haskins and Sells, certified public accountants of New York, have been employed annually to

[9] 36 Stat. 1451.   [10] *Annual Report, 1933*, p. 5.

[11] *Annual Report of the Isthmian Canal Commission, 1905*, p. 179.

[12] 38 Stat. 679.

[13] See *Report of Special Panama Canal Commission, 1921*, p. 13.

[14] See Dimock, *op. cit.*, p. 146.

verify the cash and securities held in New York in the custody of the officers, the Committee on Securities of the Board of Directors, and the Trustees of the Pension Fund; and to audit the general books and accounts that are kept in the New York office. This firm accepts the verification of the auditor of the Panama Canal of the company's cash on hand at the isthmus, and accepts the accounts of the company covering operations on the isthmus, as rendered by monthly reports of the auditor of the Panama Canal. In 1935 Haskins and Sells were directed by the board to make a complete audit of all accounts of the company in New York and on the isthmus, and to make a complete check of all the company's cash and securities.

The Comptroller-General of the United States has recognized the corporate status of the Panama Railroad Company in various decisions[15] and has taken the position that under present law company accounts are not subject to audit and control by his office. However, he has not been satisfied with this arrangement and in addition to general recommendations that all government corporations be made accountable to him, he proposed in 1935 that the Panama Railroad Company as a separate entity be dissolved; that its activities be transferred to the Panama Canal; that a complete accounting be rendered to the General Accounting Office of all transactions; and that all funds be deposited subject to provisions of existing law relating to the deposit of other public funds of the United States.[16] Some concession was made by the Comptroller-General in recommending at the same time the establishment on the books of the government of a capital (revolving) fund "in a specified amount for the business activities of the Panama Canal," but it is hardly surprising that officials of the railroad company vigorously opposed Mr. McCarl's suggested changes in the existing setup. President Schley submitted to a congressional committee a memorandum summarizing his reasons

[15] Unpublished MS of August 17, 1928; unpublished MS of March 6, 1930; 11 C.G. 38 (1931).

[16] See *House Document 115* (74th Cong.), pp. 5 ff.

for not adopting "the proposal to require the Panama Railroad Company to render accounts to the General Accounting Office" as follows:[17]

1. No useful purpose would be served, in view of the present careful audits made by the comptroller of the Panama Canal on the Isthmus and by a nationally recognized accounting firm in New York.

2. A complete change of procedure, increased operating expense, and the hampering of business transactions would result.

3. It would impose upon the railroad company the "artificial, unsatisfactory, and legalistic rules and procedure in reference to contracting, purchasing, suspensions, and disallowances that have no place in the conduct of a commercial business, and the business of a common carrier."

4. The accounts of a common carrier could not reasonably be rendered so as to constitute a proper basis for audit under government laws and regulations.

5. Other governments, notably, Great Britain, have had success in freeing commercial activities of their corporate agencies from accounting rules "of a restrictive nature."

6. The fact that the accounts are not now rendered for audit to the General Accounting Office is no evidence that the affairs of the company are not conducted honestly, efficiently, and economically in the best interests of the United States.

7. Investigations of administrative officers, legislative officials, and outside scholars[18] have confirmed the merit of existing methods.

8. Under present methods, the company is "the outstanding example of an activity of our Government which has consistently returned a profit to our Treasury."

Finally, in explaining his position, President Schley was careful to point out that no lack of responsibility in accounting for activities and finances was contended for. This is clearly revealed in his concluding statement:

In setting forth these reasons against subjecting the accounts of the Panama Railroad Company to audit by the General Accounting Office, *as the term audit is understood in governmental procedure*, this must not be taken as an objection to granting the Comptroller General the authority to examine the accounts of the Panama Railroad Company in its various offices and to investigate its methods of doing business in conformity with ordinary business practices of well-recognized public accounting

---

[17] "War Department Appropriation Bill for 1936," *op. cit.*, pp. 104–5.

[18] Specific reference was made to Professor Dimock's study.

firms and *to make reports of his findings to Congress.* While no necessity for such procedure is seen, in view of the elaborate auditing requirements now imposed by the officers having supervision of Panama Railroad Company activities, certainly no objection whatever is intended to be made thereto. *All that is desired is that no procedure shall be imposed upon the Panama Railroad Company which will reduce the value of the continued use of the company as an adjunct of the Panama Canal.*[19]

Congressional debates reveal some interest in the question, but at the present time no legislation has been enacted which would change the status of the corporation. In July, 1935, however, Mr. Blanton made the following statement on the floor of the House: "General McCarl audits all the funds that Congress appropriates for the Panama Canal, but he does not audit the receipts of the Panama Railroad Company and the Panama Steamship Company, although he should audit them, *and the time is going to come when he will audit them before we get through.*"[20] It should be noted that Mr. Blanton had reference not merely to an audit, but that he spoke of placing the Panama Railroad Company "under the same jurisdiction of the General Accounting Office as other offices and departments of the Government."

WARTIME CORPORATIONS

Whereas the Panama Railroad Company had been in existence as a private corporation prior to government ownership, and has since that time retained much of its freedom in financial matters, the World War crisis saw the creation of seven government corporations specifically for the purpose of administering expeditiously and vigorously various functions which the government undertook to perform. Each of these agencies enjoyed a much greater freedom in financial matters than do regular departments and establishments, but particularly in the comparatively long and active life of the United States Shipping Board Emergency Fleet Corporation

---

[19] "War Department Appropriation Bill for 1936," *op. cit.*, p. 105. (Italics ours.)

[20] *Congressional Record*, LXXIX, 10978. (Italics ours.)

have the various questions been laid open in operation, in controversy with the Comptroller-General, and in judicial decisions. The other wartime corporations performed their emergency duties with a flexibility and vigor that had hardly time to be questioned before liquidation was begun. It should perhaps be noted that, after 1919, the Housing Corporation in effect lost its corporate status through statutory provision for the covering of its receipts into the Treasury.[21] Since that time expenses have been met through annual appropriations, and accounts have been handled through the regular government accounting officers.[22]

The Emergency Fleet Corporation began operations in 1917 under the theory that its capital constituted a revolving fund without further congressional action, that its officers were free to utilize all funds in the manner of a private corporation without the application of ordinary governmental restrictions, and that its accounting should follow regular commercial practice. While in addition to its capital stock the Fleet Corporation received over $3,000,000,000 from congressional appropriations into the Emergency Shipping Fund, these subsequent advances did not alter the status of the corporation, since the first act in which such an appropriation appears specifically provided that the moneys were to be expended "as other moneys of said corporation are now expended."[23] It is significant that this language was inserted in the bill at the suggestion of the general manager of the Fleet Corporation, who explained to the chairman of the Senate committee concerned that he would thus have a broader latitude in utilizing the funds, and would not be tied "in any way by technicalities."[24]

---

[21] See 41 Stat. 55–56; 41 Stat. 222; 42 Stat. 640, etc.

[22] See 26 C.D. 673 (1920), holding the Housing Corporation to regular governmental procedure in the purchase of supplies, since it was a "Government establishment in Washington," and since "funds for the operations of the corporation are appropriated by law in like manner as are funds for other operations of the Government."

[23] Act of June 15, 1917 (40 Stat. 183).

[24] See *Congressional Record*, LV, 3549.

This argument was presented to the Senate by the committee chairman, and the language was accepted in a manner clearly indicating the intention of Congress to recognize the need for vigorous and unhampered administration of the corporation's functions.[25]

While the intention of Congress thus seems clear, the final authority on the subject is to be found in the decision of the United States Supreme Court in *Skinner and Eddy Corporation* v. *McCarl*, October 10, 1927.[26] This case involved several claims arising out of contracts with the Fleet Corporation, and, in holding that such claims were not within the jurisdiction of the Comptroller-General of the United States, the Court used the following language:

> The accounts of the Fleet Corporation, like those of each of the other corporations named[27] . . . . have been audited, and the control over their financial transactions has been exercised, in accordance with commercial practice by the board or the officer charged with the responsibilities of administration. Indeed, an important if not the chief reason for employing these incorporated agencies was to enable them to employ commercial methods and to conduct their operations *with a freedom supposed to be inconsistent with accountability to the Treasury under its established procedure of audit and control over the financial transactions of the United States.*[28]

Thus, the court concluded that "the Fleet Corporation is an entity distinct from the United States and from any of its departments or boards; and the audit and control of its financial transactions is, under the general rules of law and the administrative practice, committed to its own corporate officers except so far as control may be exerted by the Shipping Board."[29]

While this Supreme Court decision would seem at first glance

---

[25] Said Mr. Lodge: "General Goethals is a great administrator. . . . . Nothing is more important at this moment than the building of ships as rapidly as possible for the transportation of supplies to the allies" (*ibid.*).

[26] 275 U.S. 1.

[27] Reference had been made in an earlier part of the opinion to the Grain Corporation, the Spruce Corporation, the Housing Corporation, the War Finance Corporation, the Panama Railroad Company, the Inland Waterways Corporation, and the federal intermediate credit banks.

[28] 275 U.S. 7–8. (Italics ours.)   [29] *Ibid.*, p. 11.

to settle the matter, and to confirm the views of corporation officials, the actual relations of the Fleet Corporation to the accounting officers of the government, both before and after 1927, provide ample material for a lengthy study. We can only hope, within the scope of this chapter, to review some of the highlights.

The first important development occurred in August, 1917, when the Comptroller of the Treasury decided, in reply to a query from the Secretary of the Treasury, that appropriated funds to be expended by the Fleet Corporation should be issued on a pay warrant, *under which there was no accounting to the treasury*.[30] In so deciding, the Comptroller declared that the corporation was not required to account for expenditure of its original capital; that the appropriation act of June 15, 1917, had provided for expenditure of additional funds "as other moneys of said corporation are now expended"; that prior to that act moneys were expended as the officers of the corporation directed; and that "the intent of Congress in authorizing it to receive the public moneys to expend as its other money, can mean nothing else than to relieve it of accounting for the use of public moneys as such moneys are usually accounted for."

This early ruling was entirely in accord with the views of corporation officials, and they proceeded to operate as a private business enterprise. Notwithstanding that fact, the trustees, after a unanimous resolution, requested Treasury Department supervision through an audit conducted in the ordinary manner of a private corporation audit,[31] and, supposedly in pursuance of this request, Congress on July 1, 1918, passed a law providing that "the Secretary of the Treasury is authorized and directed to cause an audit to be made of the financial transactions of the United States Shipping Board Emergency Fleet Corporation, under such rules and regulations as he shall prescribe."

[30] 24 C.D. 118, August 16, 1917.

[31] Resolution of May 23, 1918 (see *House Document 695* [71st Cong.], p. 31).

In spite of the obvious desire of the Fleet Corporation, and the apparent intent of Congress, the Secretary of the Treasury proceeded to issue rules and regulations which the corporation considered "practically in accord with government standards," and the result was that compliance was not given.[32] Again, the view of the Fleet Corporation was upheld in a decision of the Comptroller, addressed to the Secretary of the Treasury, and describing the effect of the act of July 1, 1918, as follows:

> This statute directs that an audit of the financial transactions of this corporation be made. . . . . It does not declare that funds of the corporation are public moneys, nor does it in terms require that the accounts of the corporation shall be settled in the same manner as public accounts. It is a special statute requirement that transactions of a corporation shall be audited, and does not divest a corporation of its corporate power to handle its own funds free of other general laws governing public moneys.[33]

Specifically, this decision held that funds of the Fleet Corporation in the form of working capital, allotments from the Emergency Shipping Fund, or net proceeds derived from operation were not moneys of the United States which were required to be deposited in the Treasury or in a designated depository as public moneys.

In 1922, after the creation of the General Accounting Office, Secretary of the Treasury Mellon recommended that Congress specifically transfer the duty of auditing the Fleet Corporation transactions to this new agency.[34] In making this request, Mr. Mellon declared that although further definition of the nature of the audit to be made was a matter affecting the corporation and the General Accounting Office, yet

> . . . . as a matter of fact, the nature of the audit *has already been determined*, in effect, by the legislation under which the United States Shipping Board Emergency Fleet Corporation was authorized to be created

[32] See 25 C.D. 702.

[33] Decision of December 12, 1919 (see *House Document 695* [71st Cong.], p. 32).

[34] Apparently the Comptroller-General did not agree with the view that such duties had already been transferred in the Budget and Accounting Act (see *Senate Document 105* [67th Cong., 2d sess.], p. 2).

and to spend the moneys appropriated by Congress for emergency shipping purposes. If it is desired to define in the law the character of the audit, this could be done by adding a clause to the effect *that it should be in accordance with the generally accepted principles of accounting which govern the accounts of large business corporations.*[35]

Thus, in 1922, Congress directed the Comptroller-General to continue the audit "in accordance with the usual methods of steamship or corporation accounting."[36] By his own interpretation the power therein granted was not that ordinarily exercised over public funds, nor did the act vest any "authority in the General Accounting Office to prescribe the accounting procedure or to enforce its findings."[37] This view of the effect of the statute was also held by the Supreme Court in the Skinner and Eddy Corporation case, referred to above.

It is difficult to reconcile the foregoing opinions with many of the decisions that have been rendered by the Comptroller of the Treasury, and his successor, the Comptroller-General, since 1918. An early ruling held that the act of March 29, 1920, placing certain restrictions and limitations on the purchase of typewriters by the "various branches of the Government of the United States" was applicable to the Fleet Corporation, and consequently purchases in the open market were illegal.[38] A contract with an American marine insurance syndicate whereby the Fleet Corporation advanced funds for working capital in return for surveys performed on Shipping Board vessels, was objected to on the ground that "funds of the Emergency Fleet Corporation are sufficiently public moneys as to be subject to statutory restrictions and audit requirements, including section 3639, R.S., requiring custodians of public moneys to keep them safely without loaning, and section 3648, R.S., requiring that no payment under an appropria-

[35] *Senate Document 105* (67th Cong.), p. 3. (Italics ours.)

[36] Act of March 20, 1922 (42 Stat. 444).

[37] Unpublished MS of January 5, 1923; also *House Document 217* (72d Cong.), p. 2.

[38] 27 C.D. 140 (1920); see also similar decisions of Comptroller-General, April 18, 1924, and September 10, 1930.

tion shall be made in advance of the service rendered."[39] An act of 1916, prohibiting the use of any appropriation for payment to the same person of more than one salary from the government when the combined amount exceeded $2,000 per year, was held applicable to funds of the Fleet Corporation.[40] Also, the act of June 20, 1874, which directs the Secretary of the Treasury to cover into the Treasury all unexpended balances of appropriations which remain on Treasury books for two fiscal years, was held applicable to the emergency shipping fund.[41]

A decision of March 1, 1924, held that the payment of judgment against corporation vessels rendered by foreign courts prior to authorization by the General Accounting Office, was contrary to an act of March 9, 1920,[42] and hence illegal, in spite of the fact that the purpose be "to prevent the arrest of the vessels or to save interest charges."[43] Expenditures for entertainment of several ladies not connected with the corporation and for expenses of the brother of former Secretary of the Navy Denby on a long trip to the Orient were objected to by the Comptroller-General as "not legally authorized charges against the funds of the United States."[44] In 1926 it was held that interest derived from funds appropriated annually under the emergency shipping fund and deposited in various banks should be covered into the Treasury as miscellaneous receipts, "there being no provision in the Appropriation Act (43 Stat. 1209) for crediting such interest to the appropriation or using the same for purposes for which the appropriation was made."[45]

---

[39] 27 C. D. 311 (1920); see also subsequent decisions of Comptroller-General affirming, cited in *House Document 217* (72d Cong.), p. 52.

[40] 1 C.G. 14 (1921).   [41] Unpublished MS of December 20, 1922.

[42] 41 Stat. 527. This act, while recognizing the legality of suits against the corporation, provided that judgments should be paid "by the proper accounting officers of the United States." There would seem to be little argument with the Comptroller-General's interpretation of this statute.

[43] 3 C.G. 566.

[44] Unpublished MS, October 9, 1924.   [45] 5 C.G. 1004.

The purchase and storage of automobiles, as well as carrying insurance thereon, were declared illegal by the Comptroller-General in an interesting decision of June 2, 1928. In answering the contention that, since the Fleet Corporation was not a regular government department or establishment, such expenditures were legal, Mr. McCarl admitted that certain unusual powers were enjoyed, but added:

Yet such powers have to do particularly with the operations of the corporation as a shipping concern and the administration of its affairs relating to transactions with outsiders. In such matters the corporation may proceed as a private corporation rather than as a Government department. But in the relations of the personnel to the corporation, not connected with outside transactions, such personnel is primarily to be considered as subject to the lawful limitations and regulations applicable to Government personnel, unless specifically exempted by law.[46]

With particular reference to expenditures for insurance, the opinion reads as follows:

It long has been the established policy of the Government not to carry insurance on public property, and any change in such policy should be made by Congress when and where deemed advisable. The automobiles of the Merchant Fleet Corporation must be regarded as public property belonging to the United States and, as such, subject to the policy of the Government in that respect.

Compensatory grants to employees who had failed to have their claims recognized by the Employee's Compensation Commission were declared illegal by the Comptroller-General, in spite of authorization of the board of trustees of the Fleet Corporation, and in spite of the contention that such action was "within corporate powers."[47] A contract with the Radio Marine Corporation was objected to on the grounds that collection, deposit, and disbursement by the private corporation of funds acknowledged to be the property of the United States was contrary to law, in spite of assurance on the part of the

[46] Unpublished MS, June 2, 1928.

[47] Unpublished MSS of June 8, 1929, September 19, 1929, and April 16, 1931. Statutory provisions upon the interpretation of which the Comptroller based his decision are 39 Stat. 749, as amended by 42 Stat. 650, secs. 20, 32, and 36.

Fleet Corporation that the radio company acted only as its bonded agent, with definitely limited powers, and under adequate safeguards.[48] Similarly, the practice of the Fleet Corporation in contracting for supplies and services ("which is tantamount to advancing public funds") for account of operators performing under lump-sum agreements, was declared illegal as contrary to section 3648 R.S., which provides that "no advances shall be made in any case whatever," and in addition was censured because the "Government is deprived of the use of moneys so advanced for a considerable time, and as there is also some administrative expense involved in such transactions, full reimbursement for the expenditure is not received by the United States."[49] Exception was taken to stevedoring contracts on the grounds that the corporation had violated section 3709, R.S., in not accepting the lowest bid offered.[50] More recently, the corporation's practice of depositing funds in private banks was declared contrary to law in a ruling of February 8, 1932. Said the Comptroller-General: "Inasmuch as it is admitted that the funds in the hands of the Merchant Fleet Corporation are public moneys, it is held that the general statutes applicable to the safeguarding of such public moneys are applicable in the absence of specific legislation to the contrary."

In several instances the Comptroller-General's rulings have been more favorably inclined toward administrative freedom of the Fleet Corporation. Thus, when the vice-president borrowed in behalf of the corporation $54,000 in order to save one day's crew expenses in making settlement with a ship's crew, the question of payment of a voucher covering documentary stamps and one day's interest on the note was decided as follows:

It is obvious that the propriety of this official action is now primarily for administrative consideration—the thing having been done and the

[48] Unpublished MS, October 29, 1930.

[49] Unpublished MS, February 16, 1931.

[50] See *Annual Report of the Comptroller General, 1931*, pp. 8-9.

expenses incurred—and it is not for an advance decision by this office, the effect of which would be mainly upon whether administrative approval should be given.

I am constrained then, having regard also to the accounting relation of the corporation to this office, to consider the matter as an administrative one and not requiring my decision.[51]

In a similar vein, the finality of the corporation's jurisdiction, when denying a claim against itself, was affirmed by the General Accounting Office, and disappointed claimants were so informed.[52]

Meanwhile, the audit authorized by the act of March 20, 1922, was being conducted by the General Accounting Office with a small force and a scarcity of funds.[53] Its progress may be traced through the annual reports of the Comptroller-General.[54] Not always were relations with the corporation strained, and in many instances voluntary conformity with suggestions was given. Thus the 1927 report states: "It is gratifying to report that many exceptions taken by the General Accounting Office to certain financial transactions have met with cooperative action on the part of the Merchant Fleet Corporation, with the result that the accounts are submitted in much better condition than during the early years of operations, and there is a more general following of the laws and decisions governing the use of public funds."[55] A concrete example of such co-operation may be found in the collection and recovery by the corporation of items to which exception had

[51] Unpublished MS, October 5, 1921.

[52] Unpublished MSS of June 30, and December 6, 1923.

[53] In 1923 the Comptroller-General requested additional funds and stated that "regardless of what may be thought of the wisdom of the enactment approved March 20, 1922, providing for the audit, while the duty remains upon this office to do the work it is respectfully suggested that adequate means should be provided" (unpublished MS, February 24, 1923).

[54] E.g., see *Annual Report of the Comptroller General, 1925:* "The work of auditing the accounts of the Emergency Fleet Corporation has continued throughout the year. One hundred and fifty-two accounts, 96,793 vouchers, aggregating $188,000,000 were audited" (p. 13).

[55] *Ibid., 1927*, p. 37.

been taken by the General Accounting Office. Such collections in 1928, for example, totaled $317,525.58,[56] and in 1929 amounted to $744,880.14.[57]

Nevertheless, Mr. McCarl was convinced that congressional surrender of "its legislative control over accounting for public money" through the use of the corporate device was dangerous, and in 1928 he "earnestly recommended that full and adequate provision be made for publicity in the financial transaction of such corporations by the requirement that they account through the General Accounting Office to the Congress for their expenditure of public money, and that, with the exceptions stated in the law as being necessary for their operation, they be required to observe the sound principles stated in the law as of general application for the expenditure and accounting for public money."[58] A bill recommended by the Comptroller-General for these purposes was introduced into Congress and considered in committee but never passed.[59]

In the absence of such express legislation, the position recently taken by the Comptroller-General is hard to reconcile with early decisions of the Comptroller of the Treasury, with the opinion of the Supreme Court, and indeed with some of his own prior rulings.[60] In his 1931 report, to illustrate, he cites the divergence of views between the corporation and his office as to whether or not the general statutes, particularly section 3709, R.S., apply to the financial transactions of the corporation.[61] As for his own view: "It is believed that it was not the

[56] Ibid., 1928, p. 92.   [57] Ibid., 1929, p. 109.   [58] Ibid., 1928, p. 12.

[59] H.R. 12180 (70th Cong.). See Annual Report of the Comptroller General, 1929, pp. 2 and 16; ibid., 1930, p. 8.

[60] See, e.g., decision of June 2, 1928 (above, p. 149), wherein it is stated that in transactions with outsiders, the "corporation may proceed as a private corporation rather than as a Government department."

[61] Other regulatory statutes concerned in this "divergence of views" include 27 Stat. 591, prohibiting the employment of private detectives or guards by a government service; 37 Stat. 184, prohibiting expenditure of appropriated money for membership fees of any employee of the United States in any society or association without express statutory authorization; 37 Stat. 414, prohibit-

intent of the Congress to so single out this particular activity and thereby render the audit a mere formality; or, in other words, to grant to the Fleet Corporation and/or Shipping Board entire immunity from accountability within the purview of such general safeguarding statutes."[62]

One point, however, in which Mr. McCarl had been entirely consistent, was also brought out clearly in the 1931 report:

> The result of these differing viewpoints is the taking in the audit of exceptions to financial transactions of the Fleet Corporation in cases of palpable losses of Federal moneys, *without the requisite power here to make such audit findings effective.* As a result, they are only being carried into effect to the very limited extent to which the Fleet Corporation and/or Shipping Board, through their various channels, admit the irregularities disclosed and *voluntarily recede from their administrative positions.*[63]

The voluntary co-operation referred to by the Comptroller-General grew largely out of the policy of the Fleet Corporation to comply with all regulatory statutes in so far "as they are not in conflict with and do not, when applied, act as obstacles to the efficient operation and maintenance of Government-owned vessels which are engaged in a commercial enterprise of a highly competitive nature."[64] On the other hand, as has been intimated, officials of the corporation did not hesitate to refuse compliance with general laws and rulings which they considered obstructive to efficient administration. Some illustrative examples are cases involving purchase and storage of

---

ing the use of appropriated money for telephone service installed in any private residence; sec. 192, R.S., prohibiting expenditure of over $100 per year for newspapers by departments other than Department of State; sec. 3648, R.S., prohibiting any advance of public money except as authorized by the President of the United States to disbursing officers and to the military and naval service (see *House Document 321* [72d Cong.], pp. 1–2).

[62] *Annual Report of the Comptroller General, 1931*, pp. 8–9.

[63] *Ibid.*, pp. 9–10. (Italics ours.)

[64] See *House Document 321* (72d Cong.), p. 3.

automobiles and purchase of insurance thereon,[65] contracts
with marine insurance syndicates and the Radio Marine Corporation, compensatory grants to employees, deposits in
private banks, rejection of lowest bids, and the employing of
private guards to watch warehouses, piers, and other properties. In most cases the facts surrounding and justifying the
action taken, in the opinion of the corporation officials, had
been presented at length either to Congress or to the Comptroller-General.[66]

As to the merits of proposals by the Comptroller-General for
a stricter control of financial transactions through his office,
Fleet Corporation officials, both in 1924 and as recently as
1932, took the position that regular governmental accounting
control would defeat successful operation, would increase expenses, would place the Fleet Corporation at a decided dis-
advantage in a competitive business, would discourage
managing operators of Shipping Board vessels, and in general
would be impracticable and inadvisable.[67] However, in exact
accord with the views of Panama Railroad Company officials,
it was clearly pointed out that no objection would be had to a
thorough audit by government accounting officers, which
would rather be welcomed if conducted along commercial
rather than governmental lines.

All of the foregoing questions were brought out into the open
after 1929, with the publication of the Comptroller-General's
first audit report to Congress, and with the subsequent publication of the Fleet Corporation's reply, a second audit report,

[65] Incidentally, Congress sustained the Shipping Board's position in these two
respects by express statutory authorization in the independent offices act of
1930 (45 Stat. 1244) and subsequent appropriation acts.

[66] See especially *Hearings before Select Committee on Shipping Board and
Emergency Fleet Corporation, Pursuant to House Resolution 186* (68th Cong., 1st
sess. [1924]), 4,709 pages; also reports to Congress analyzing audit reports of the
Comptroller-General, *House Document 695* (71st Cong.) and *House Document 321*
(72d Cong.).

[67] See *House Document 695* (71st Cong.), p. 33.

and a second reply.[68] Some of the exceptions taken in the first
audit report were under the following headings: settlement of
claims, liquidated damages, sale of vessels, sale of surplus
property, sale of securities and failure to hold sureties for de-
falcation of principals, traveling expenses, use of "commitment" accounts, and deposits in banks. "Divergent views" as
to the application of general regulations were cited, the inability of the General Accounting Office to enforce its rulings
was reiterated, and, finally, the "futility" and danger of conducting public business through corporations not subject to
regular governmental accounting control was asserted.

The corporation's "analysis" of this audit report questioned
the qualifications of the auditors for "steamship auditing" and
the value of an audit admittedly incomplete; explained some
of the acts to which exception had been taken, and pointed out
that practically all the disputed questions had been thrashed
out before a special congressional investigating committee;[69]
reiterated a belief in the corporation's freedom under its
present legal status; and expressed a serious objection to the
changes in that status proposed by the Comptroller-General.

The second audit report contained exceptions similar to
those in the first, with additions under the headings: lump-
sum agreements, variance between the offer and acceptance
and the contract of sale, inventories, stationery and advertising matter, payment of bonuses to employees, repairs subsequent to sale of vessels, and irregular accounting procedures.
It is interesting to note that this time, while expressly recog-

[68] *House Document 111* (71st Cong.), *House Document 695* (71st Cong.), *House Document 217* (72d Cong.), *House Document 321* (72d Cong.). These reports, totaling almost 250 pages, contain a wealth of material bearing upon the financial powers of the Fleet Corporation, including objections both legal and administrative on the part of the Comptroller-General, explanations and attempted justification by the corporation, and proposals for remedying the existing relationship, which was unsatisfactory to both.

[69] *Hearings before Special House Committee, Pursuant to House Resolution 186* (68th Cong., 1st sess.).

nizing the need for a measure of corporate freedom,[70] the Comptroller-General proposed legislation requiring accounting in the manner of ordinary public moneys, *yet granting to the accounting officers authority to allow credit for expenditures not otherwise allowable under the law but shown to be necessary to the conduct of corporate business.*[71]

Again, the Fleet Corporation replied in an exhaustive analysis, and, while much old ground was covered, a few illustrative arguments may be noted. The lump-sum agreement[72] was justified in a long section which indicates that, whatever the merits of the plan may actually be, it was adopted after careful administrative consideration and fourteen years of experience and in full confidence that it represented the best plan for safeguarding the interests of the government in the liquidation of the Fleet Corporation.[73] Regarding the payment of bonuses, it was declared that, while the Fleet Corporation had recognized unusual efficiency and meritorious services rendered by employees, it did "not often give such rewards and when it does they are well deserved. As a corporate agency of the Government it has the power to make such payments which, as hereinbefore stated, are in line with commercial custom." With regard to the Comptroller-General's statement that many members of Congress evidently thought his

[70] "It is appreciated that when the Government undertakes the conduct of a business, commercial in nature, such as the operation of vessels in commerce, a railroad, etc., there may frequently be required expenditures, because of the nature of the business undertaken, that could not properly be allowed by the accounting officers under existing law if made in connection with the conduct of the Government" (*ibid.*, p. 2).

[71] *Ibid.*, pp. 2-3.

[72] Under the lump-sum agreement, vessels were delivered over to an operator for operation over agreed routes; said operator was to receive and retain all voyage revenues and assume voyage losses, and in addition to receive a lump-sum compensation from the corporation. This latter sum was calculated in each case on the basis of losses per voyage experienced by the corporation immediately prior to the agreement and also by considering other factors in anticipation of future costs of operation.

[73] See *House Document 321* (72d Cong.), pp. 6 ff.

control to be complete, contrary to the facts, the Fleet Corporation's reply was as follows:

It is believed that the Congress has been and is fully informed as to our activities and methods of operation and particularly, that it has full knowledge of the fact that the United States Shipping Board Merchant Fleet Corporation functions, so far as efficiency requires, as would a privately owned organization engaged in the same line of commercial activities.[74]

Finally, it was contended that the Comptroller-General "can not or will not recognize the powers and authorities granted by statute" to the corporation; that he had substituted an audit "of his own convenience that is neither commercial nor governmental in its nature" for the audit "in accordance with the usual methods of steamship or corporation accounting" required by statute; and that he was depriving the corporation of the benefits to be derived from the type of audit contemplated by Congress whereas such an audit "would be of real value to the Congress and to the United States Shipping Board."[75]

In summarizing the experience of the Fleet Corporation, several observations might be made. Aside from express statutory guides and restrictions,[76] the corporation, in practice, was its own judge as to the best manner of utilizing its funds for

[74] *Ibid.*, p. 102.

[75] *Ibid.*, p. 5. "It is the opinion of the Shipping Board that such an audit would generally include a verification of the accuracy of the Fleet Corporation's financial statement, including its semiannual balance sheet and monthly financial statements as well as all financial reports which are submitted both to the Shipping Board and to any branch of the United States Government." It should be noted that Congress in appropriation acts regularly prohibited expenditures for the services of certified public accountants, which makes the corporation's claim of "deprivation" more easily understandable (see, e.g., act of August 24, 1921 [42 Stat. 192], and act of June 12, 1922 [42 Stat. 647]).

[76] A number of such restrictions appear in the various appropriation acts. Thus, the corporation was prohibited from using appropriated funds in paying certain kinds of claims, in hiring attorneys or accountants, in paying actual subsistence expenses of over $5.00 per day (42 Stat. 192), and in the preparation, printing, publication, or distribution of newspapers, magazines, journals, or other periodicals (42 Stat. 647).

the major purposes set down by Congress. The policy of con-
forming to standard governmental procedures and regulations
where practicable was asserted, but in other cases the corporation did not hesitate to refuse compliance with regulations of
the governmental accounting officers where such regulations
were considered handicaps to efficient operation. The audit
performed by the General Accounting Office was unsatisfactory to both parties: to the   corporation because an interference in matters properly administrative was felt; to the
General Accounting Office because of its inability to enforce its
rulings; and to both because of the incomplete nature of the
audit due to meager facilities and funds. It is extremely difficult to evaluate all the charges made by the Comptroller;
certainly some extravagances and some extremely dubious
transactions were pointed out.[77] On the other hand, acceptance
of all the exceptions and proposals would undoubtedly have
handicapped effective administration. Few impartial observers would question the efficiency of transactions such as
the following: payment of judgments rendered by foreign
courts in order to prevent arrest and detention of corporation
vessels while the General Accounting Office considered the
claims; purchase and storage of automobiles deemed necessary
for the use of corporation officials; payment of premiums on insurance of corporation property; hiring of watchmen to guard
warehouses, piers, and other properties; deposit of funds in
private banks to insure easy access; and the making of lump-
sum agreements after long experience and careful administrative consideration had resulted in the conviction that such a
plan best safeguarded the interests of the government in the
liquidation of the corporation. Yet, all these transactions were
objected to by Mr. McCarl.

Taken as a whole, the relations between the Fleet Corporation and the General Accounting Office could hardly be called

---

[77] E.g., entertainment and expenses of persons not connected with the corporation. See also figures in sales of vessels, *House Document 111* (71st Cong.),
pp. 12 ff., and *House Document 215* (72d Cong.), pp. 14 ff., 30.

a model for the government corporation. A more satisfactory arrangement must be sought.

THE INLAND WATERWAYS CORPORATION[78]

Of all the government agencies which have been incorporated by federal statute, the Inland Waterways Corporation has, in financial matters, enjoyed the most complete freedom from specific legislative restrictions, from statutory regulations of general application, and from the control of regular governmental accounting officers. The incorporating act in effect subscribes for the capital stock on behalf of the United States, sets forth the general purposes of operation, and then turns the corporation loose to operate as a private business under the direction of the Secretary of War.[79] No yearly report is required, although actually a report has annually been made to the Secretary of War; no accounting for finances is mentioned; the power to borrow money is expressly granted; no restriction is placed on expenditures; and the corporation is authorized to "conduct the business of a common carrier by water" and to exercise "such powers as may be necessary or incidental to fulfill the purposes of its creation."

Mention has already been made of the part played by General Ashburn in the creation of the Inland Waterways Corporation and particularly his desire to be freed from the necessity of annual appropriations.[80] Writing in 1933, General Ashburn declared that the "main idea in the creation of a corporation was to create a body independent of the Comptroller, and with funds available before exhausted."[81] This is in line with his statement before the House committee in 1924, at which time he asserted that no business organization could function successfully under government departmental re-

---

[78] Chronologically, the Inland Waterways Corporation was preceded by the federal land banks, created in 1917, and the federal intermediate credit banks, created in 1923. However, these banks are now part of the Farm Credit Administration structure and will be considered in the following chapter.

[79] 43 Stat. 360 (1924).   [80] Above, pp. 54-55.

[81] *Military Engineer*, XXV (May–June, 1933), 251.

strictions, and pointed out that the purpose behind the creation of a corporation was a freedom from the red tape usually surrounding governmental operations.[82]

How well General Ashburn succeeded in his plan may be illustrated in three ways. In the first place, the Comptroller-General of the United States has followed a strict policy of "hands off." His *Annual Report* for 1929 states that the "Inland Waterways Corporation is an example of an existing corporation in which the legislation creating it omitted to confer on the General Accounting Office jurisdiction to require an accounting to be rendered to it of receipts and expenditures."[83] A decision of April 10, 1928, held that, although the General Accounting Office exercised jurisdiction over the appropriations made by Congress for purchase of capital stock to the extent of paying the funds to the corporation, it "exercises no jurisdiction over funds received and expended by the corporation in its operation as a corporate body."[84] This position is affirmed in later decisions, the Comptroller-General protesting that Congress had, in effect, turned over public moneys for expenditure "without any requirement that such expenditures be subject to the statutory restrictions or safeguards which experience has taught are necessary in the expenditure of public funds, or that they be accounted for through the General Accounting Office to Congress."[85]

Second, an avowed opponent of government operation, writing in 1931, viewed "with alarm the very smart device by which the Inland Waterways Corporation has been freed from any form of governmental control whatever."[86] He praised General Ashburn's "shrewdness" in securing this free-

---

[82] *Hearing before the House Committee on Interstate and Foreign Commerce, on H.R. 6647* (68th Cong., 1st sess. [1924]), p. 103.

[83] *Annual Report of the Comptroller General, 1929*, p. 12.

[84] Unpublished MS, April 10, 1928.

[85] Unpublished MSS of January 25, 1929, and August 2, 1930.

[86] Herbert Corey, "Uncle Sam Finds a Formula for Competing with the Carriers," *Public Utilities Fortnightly*, VIII, No. 7 (1931), 389.

dom from the necessity of asking for appropriations and "explaining fifty cent pieces to the Comptroller of the Treasury," and declared that a new formula had been found by which government could be successful in business—that is, "form a company and give it the money needed and then cut every string that ties it to the clumsy governmental structure."[87]

In the third place, a recent, thorough study of the overhead control and management of the Inland Waterways Corporation reveals its financial operations as those of a private company engaged in the carrier business.[88] It is significant that in this monograph no mention is made of the Comptroller-General or the General Accounting Office; and the freedom of the corporation from ordinary governmental restrictions as to expenditures, earnings, and accounting is taken for granted.

Whereas the Inland Waterways Corporation is not subject in financial matters to general governmental regulations,[89] the by-laws promulgated by the Secretary of War contain certain pertinent provisions. Thus, the approval of the Secretary of War is necessary for the making of contracts relating to the purchase or sale of real estate, contracts involving $10,000 or more, contracts with states, municipalities, or other public bodies; for the employment of attorneys; and for the borrowing of money or the issuance of notes.[90] In practice, the secretaries of war have been sympathetic to the management, and the foregoing restrictions have tended in most cases to become

[87] Mr. Corey concludes: "Those who do not like the idea—and I am one of them—are offered one morsel of comfort. There are few Ashburn's" (*ibid.*, p. 304).

[88] Dimock, *Developing America's Waterways* (Chicago, 1935).

[89] E.g., purchases may be made on the open market, without advertising, if deemed desirable. However, the corporation has developed its own regulations for purchasing; e.g., contracts involving $1,000 or more must be made after advertising except in emergencies. Corporation by-laws provide for the payment of premiums on employee bonds by the corporation, contrary to governmental practice.

[90] Inland Waterways Corporation by-laws, revised March 1, 1932.

formalities.[91] As for the borrowing of money, the corporation for years had $3,000,000 on the books of the Treasury for capital stock unissued,[92] and the issuance of bonds has not been resorted to. Only current debts have been contracted.

Other pertinent provisions of the by-laws provide that the secretary-treasurer shall be the accountable officer for all corporation funds and securities; that he shall collect, hold, and deposit funds in "such depositories, under such conditions as may be approved by the Secretary of War"; that he shall be responsible for the formation and administration of the general accounting policy of the corporation; and that he shall submit monthly and annually financial statements showing the financial condition of the corporation to the Secretary of War. As a common carrier, the Inland Waterways Corporation keeps its books in accordance with the classification of accounts prescribed by the Interstate Commerce Commission. Following ordinary commercial practice, corporation accounts are audited annually by a firm of certified public accountants.[93]

While the Inland Waterways Corporation has operated with the flexibility of a private business, several attempts have been made to curtail that freedom. Mr. McCarl recommended for passage by the Sixty-ninth and Seventieth congresses a bill "to require the prompt rendition of accounts," in which the Comptroller-General would be given power to fix the time for rendition of accounts and to refuse requisitions for further funds in cases of delinquency.[94] The terms of the bill were to apply to "all officers and persons in the service of the United States, its corporate or other agencies," and in committee

[91] See Dimock, *Developing America's Waterways*, p. 46; cf. Corey's statement that, "unless I have learned nothing of the practical operations of politics, the Inland Waterways Corporation is as independent of actual control by President Hoover and Secretary of War Pat Hurley and the Committees of Congress as I am" (*op. cit.*, p. 390).

[92] This $3,000,000 was repealed by Congress in Pub. No. 208 (75th Cong. [1937]).

[93] See, e.g., *Annual Report of the Inland Waterways Corporation, 1934*, p. 1.

[94] H.R. 12180 (70th Cong.).

hearings (1928) some doubt appeared as to whether or not the bill would place the Inland Waterways Corporation under the jurisdiction of the General Accounting Office. Mr. Lurtin R. Ginn, Assistant Comptroller-General, was uncertain when questioned but later submitted a memorandum answering in the affirmative.[95] Also, a letter of the Comptroller-General referred to the proposed bill as follows: "Such language would appear to require an accounting to the General Accounting Office by the Inland Waterways Corporation for all funds within its jurisdiction, unless the Committee should deem it necessary to amend the act so as to exclude corporations not now required by law to render an accounting to this office from doing so."[96]

Needless to say, officials of the Inland Waterways Corporation strenuously opposed the passage of the bill, and letters from General Ashburn and Secretary of War Davis arguing at length for preservation of the *status quo* were received by the committee.[97] Despite repeated recommendations of the Comptroller-General,[98] such a bill has not received the sanction of the legislature.

A more recent and more direct attempt to curtail the financial freedom of the Inland Waterways Corporation occurred in 1932. Attention of the House Appropriations Committee had been called to the acceptance by the corporation of a diesel engine bid of $112,000, to the exclusion of a low bid, "apparently on the specifications and submitted by a responsible bidder," of $86,000. The committee report on the war appropriation bill for 1933 declared that "the Corporation authorities may feel that they acted in the best interest of the Government, and perhaps they did, though the information in the

[95] *Hearings before House Committee on Expenditures in the Executive Departments, on H.R. 12180* (70th Cong. [March 28 and 31, 1928]).

[96] Unpublished MS, May 3, 1928.

[97] See printed hearings (above, n. 95), appendixes.

[98] *Annual Report* for 1926, 1927, 1928, 1929, 1930, 1931, 1932.

possession of the committee would not appear so."[99] Consequently, the matter had been referred to the Comptroller-
General, and upon his recommendation the following provision was reported favorably by the committee:

Hereafter, all expenditures by or on behalf of the Inland Waterways
Corporation shall be accounted for and audited as are expenditures by
the executive departments and establishments generally, but in such
connection the Comptroller General of the United States is hereby
authorized to sanction the use of moneys provided for the operations of
the corporation, and to allow credit accordingly for expenditures not
otherwise allowable, if and when established to be reasonably necessary
to a proper functioning of the legal activities of the corporation.

In the debate on the floor of the House,[100] Mr. Britten dep-
recated the rejection of the lowest responsible bid and declared that "good business, fair competition, economy in
government, all demand that this Inland Waterways Corporation accept the language of General McCarl and carry on in
an open, dignified, orderly procedure." On the other hand,
Mr. McDuffie defended the corporation:

Now if the gentleman knows anything about steamboats—I do not
know whether he does or not—he knows that there are times when it
might be absolutely necessary for the man who operates this Corporation
to turn down the lowest bid because the bidder did not meet the specifications for a particular engine for a particular kind of boat. That is all
that happened in the case mentioned by the gentleman from Illinois.

In making a point of order against legislation on an appropriation bill, Mr. McDuffie maintained that "there is nothing
here to show that any economy will be effected under this
provision; on the other hand, it might have the opposite
effect." The chairman of the Committee of the Whole sustained the point of order, and this, like other efforts to curtail
the Inland Waterways Corporation's financial powers, failed
of consummation.

[99] *House Report 1215* (72d Cong.), p. 25.

[100] See *Congressional Record*, LXXV, 10703.

SUMMARY

As the first business corporation to be completely owned and controlled by the United States Government, the Panama Railroad Company affords an interesting study. Largely because its prior existence as a private enterprise conditioned its later development under government control, the P.R.C. has enjoyed a degree of freedom and flexibility in management which makes it resemble more closely a private company than a government department. Characteristic features are: permanent use of its capital and hence freedom from the necessity of annual appropriations; the power to borrow money; freedom from regular governmental procedures in matters of expenditure; availability of earnings for operating expenses, reserves, and improvements; and an annual audit by a private accounting firm. Recent attempts to place the company under the accounting and auditing control of the General Accounting Office have been successfully resisted, and at the present time the Comptroller-General has no jurisdiction over P.R.C. affairs.

The wartime corporations were frankly conceived as emergency agencies and were given wide powers and great managerial flexibility. Whereas the brief duration of the war crisis gave little opportunity for the contesting of this freedom, the continued existence of the Fleet Corporation afforded time for more leisurely consideration of financial powers and limitations. In 1927 the Supreme Court upheld the freedom which had been exercised in practice and declared that control of financial transactions rested within the Fleet Corporation itself and was not meant to be exercised by the Comptroller-General and his office. In spite of this decision, however, the next five years were characterized by bitter disputes between the corporation and Comptroller-General McCarl with respect to the latter's audit reports to Congress. While he unquestionably disclosed some extravagances and improper financial transactions, the Comptroller-General's exceptions were on the whole based upon a legalistic and technical approach which seemed to corporation officials to represent an unwarranted interference in administrative affairs. Lacking the power to enforce his rulings, the Comptroller-General appealed to Congress for coercive powers over Fleet Corporation transactions, but his efforts in this direction met with no success.

Perhaps of all the government corporations directly created by congressional act, the Inland Waterways Corporation has been most effectively isolated from the regular governmental financial controls and restrictions. Operated along business lines, the I.W.C. has unrestricted use of its capital and earnings, may borrow money, may regulate its own expenditures, and may determine its own accounting and auditing procedures. Comptroller-General McCarl repeatedly called attention to this condition and recommended placing the I.W.C. under his audit and control, but here again his attempts were unsuccessful.

CHAPTER V
THE FARM CREDIT ADMINISTRATION
ORGANIZATION

THE Farm Credit Administration represents a unique development in the federal use of corporations for administrative purposes. Although not itself in corporate form, the F.C.A. is the overhead organization which coordinates and supervises the activities of the several corporations and agencies which are concerned with the extension of agricultural credit. It provides a centralized system of control designed to make unnecessary any direct supervision of the individual corporations by the central financial and accounting agencies of the federal government. The Farm Credit Administration is responsible to Congress and the President; the subsidiary corporations are responsible to the F.C.A.

The creation of the Farm Credit Administration by an executive order of March 27, 1933, was in pursuance of a congressional mandate given the President to investigate, coordinate, and consolidate executive and administrative agencies of the federal government with a view to increased efficiency and greater economy in administration.[1] The executive order consolidated within the new organization the powers and functions of the various federal agencies already operating in the agricultural credit field. Transferred to the F.C.A. were the functions of the Federal Farm Loan Bureau, the Federal Farm Loan Board, the Farm Loan Commissioner, and the crop production and seed loan offices of the United States Department of Agriculture. The Federal Farm Board's functions with regard to winding up its stabilization activities and the functions of the R.F.C. pertaining to the management of the regional agricultural credit corporations were also taken over.

[1] 47 Stat. 1517.

By act of June 16, 1933, the Farm Credit Administration was given direct statutory basis and new credit facilities in the form of banks for co-operatives, and production credit corporations and associations were established. Thus was completed a "permanent cooperative credit system designed to meet at minimum cost the entire range of needs of farmers for mortgage loan accommodation and for financing their production, marketing, and purchasing operations."[2]

The importance of the corporate device in the administration of farm credit activities becomes apparent upon even a cursory examination of the operating units within the F.C.A. Constituting the permanent agricultural credits system are four groups of corporations—namely, the federal land banks, the federal intermediate credit banks, the banks for co-operatives, and the production credit corporations and associations. As has been pointed out above, these agencies operate in each of twelve districts covering the United States and provide credits ranging from long-term mortgage loans to short-term loans for general agricultural purposes. In operation long before the Farm Credit Administration was established, the land banks and intermediate credit banks have administered their affairs in the manner of private banking corporations, following ordinary business principles and methods. Operations have, of course, been subject to statutory and supervisory limits, and the primary purpose has been the provision of credit on favorable terms rather than the making of unlimited profits. It might be noted that while production credit corporation stock is entirely government-owned, and cooperative bank stock predominantly so, provision is made in each case for the retirement of such stock in favor of that owned by farmer and association borrowers. The ultimate desire of Congress and F.C.A. officials in each case is a farmer-financed and farmer-controlled system.

In addition to the four groups of permanent corporations, there are other corporate agencies within the F.C.A. which

[2] *Farm Credit Administration Statement, September 30, 1935,* p. 2.

should be mentioned. Most important is the Federal Farm Mortgage Corporation, which, though technically an independent corporation, is managed by a three-member board of directors, two of whom are F.C.A. officials. The twelve regional agricultural credit corporations created by the R.F.C. in 1932 have been transferred to the Farm Credit Administration for liquidation purposes. In addition, the F.C.A. also charters and supervises federal credit unions, which are co-operative thrift and lending organizations supported entirely by members' purchases of capital stock and limited borrowings. No capital is supplied these unions by the government. National farm loan associations are also chartered by, and under the supervision of, the F.C.A., although their capital is supplied by farmer members. These farm loan associations have been the medium through which federal land-bank loans are made to farmers.

For the co-ordination and supervision of this widespread family of farm credit agencies, the Farm Credit Administration Washington office is organized as shown in Chart I on page 111. The governor is appointed by the President, with the advice and consent of the Senate, and is assisted by two deputy governors. Four commissioners, also appointed by the President and Senate, supervise separate fields of activity within the organization. Thus, the Land Bank Commissioner regulates the federal land banks and the national farm loan associations and also directs the liquidation of the joint-stock land banks. The Intermediate Credit Commissioner has charge of the work of the twelve intermediate credit banks. The Co-operative Bank Commissioner is the chairman of the board of the Central Bank for Co-operatives and in addition is responsible for the supervision of the twelve district banks for co-operatives. Finally, the Production Credit Commissioner is the supervisor of the production credit system which embraces both the twelve production credit corporations and the local production credit associations.

Within this larger framework the operating units in each of

CHART I*

FARM CREDIT ADMINISTRATION
WASHINGTON OFFICE

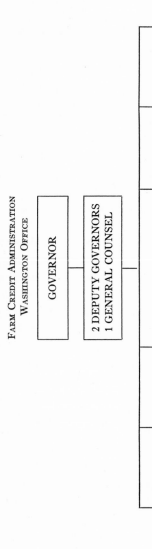
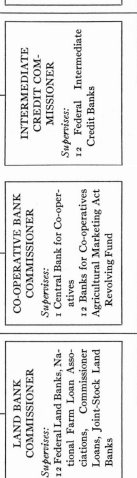

GOVERNOR

2 DEPUTY GOVERNORS
1 GENERAL COUNSEL

LAND BANK COMMISSIONER
Supervises:
12 Federal Land Banks, National Farm Loan Associations, Commissioner Loans, Joint-Stock Land Banks

12 Regional Agricultural Credit Corporations

CO-OPERATIVE BANK COMMISSIONER
Supervises:
1 Central Bank for Co-operatives
12 Banks for Cooperatives
Agricultural Marketing Act Revolving Fund

INTERMEDIATE CREDIT COMMISSIONER
Supervises:
12 Federal Intermediate Credit Banks

PRODUCTION CREDIT COMMISSIONER
Supervises:
12 Production Credit Corporations
Production Credit Associations

Crop Production and Seed Loan Offices

*First Annual Report of the F.C.A., 1933, p. 5.

the twelve districts are co-ordinated in several ways. As we have noted, a single board of directors serves the land bank, the intermediate credit bank, the production credit corporation, and the bank for co-operatives, all of which are located in a central city of the district. Sitting as a co-ordinating body, the single board of directors is called the "Council of the Farm Credit Administration" of the district. A "general agent" for each district is nominated by the governor of the F.C.A. and appointed by this district council as a co-ordinating executive officer. The district "advisory committee" is composed of the general agent and the presidents of the four major corporations within the area. A typical district organization is shown in Chart II on page 113.

This elaborate overhead organization which exists for the supervision of the many corporations dealing with agricultural credit has no parallel in other branches of the federal service. A measure of control is provided which makes the problem of the financial powers of the subsidiary corporations quite different from that which arises in the instances where an individual corporation, as, for example, the T.V.A. or the R.F.C., is independent of overhead administrative control.

FINANCING THE SYSTEM

The capital investment of the United States in the farm credit corporations, as of December 31, 1936, is shown in the table on page 114. In addition to capital stock, the government has supplied paid-in surplus to the land banks in pursuance of the Emergency Farm Mortgage Act of 1933, which provided for the granting of extensions and deferments to borrowers, and has also supplied paid-in surplus to the intermediate credit banks in order to meet the credit requirements of eligible borrowers. While these extraordinary grants have been made from time to time, the farm credit banks and corporations are set up to operate on their own funds and do not require annual appropriations for the making of loans and the meeting of administrative expenses. In addition to capital stock and paid-in

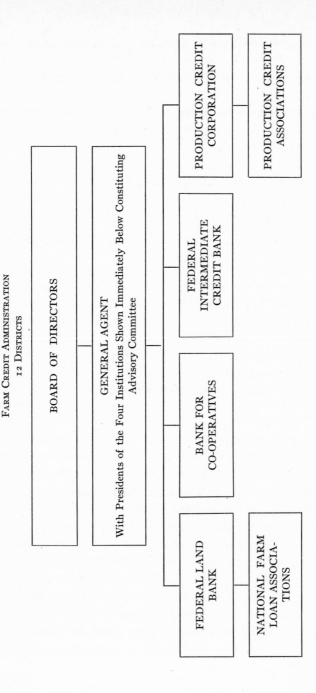

CHART II*

FARM CREDIT ADMINISTRATION
12 DISTRICTS

BOARD OF DIRECTORS

GENERAL AGENT

With Presidents of the Four Institutions Shown Immediately Below Constituting
Advisory Committee

FEDERAL LAND BANK

NATIONAL FARM LOAN ASSOCIA-TIONS

BANK FOR CO-OPERATIVES

FEDERAL INTERMEDIATE CREDIT BANK

PRODUCTION CREDIT CORPORATION

PRODUCTION CREDIT ASSOCIATIONS

* *First Annual Report of the F.C.A., 1933*, p. 6.

surplus, the federal land banks have secured loan funds from the sale of bonds to the investing public and to the Federal Farm Mortgage Corporation, from the sale of notes to the R.F.C., and to a lesser extent, from the sale of notes to commercial institutions. As of December 31, 1936 land-bank

FARM CREDIT ADMINISTRATION
Amount of Capital Stock and Paid-in Surplus Owned by the United States Government as of December 31, 1936

Federal Farm Mortgage Corporation:
Capital stock........................... $200,000,000
Federal land banks:
Capital stock........................... 124,066,135
Paid-in surplus......................... 128,016,019
Federal intermediate credit banks:
Capital stock........................... 70,000,000
Paid-in surplus......................... 30,000,000
Production credit corporations:
Capital stock........................... 120,000,000
Central Bank for Co-operatives:
Capital stock........................... 57,000,000*
District banks for co-operatives:
Capital stock........................... 95,000,000*
Regional agricultural credit corporations:
Capital stock........................... 15,000,000†
Paid-in surplus......................... 14,138,909†

Grand total......................... $853,221,063

* From Agricultural Marketing Act revolving fund.
† From Reconstruction Finance Corporation.

bonds outstanding totaled $1,964,654,440, while on the same date notes payable to the R.F.C. amounted to $24,636,146.74.

The issue of farm-loan bonds is subject to the approval of the Farm Credit Administration and, as may be seen, forms the most important source of land-bank loan funds. During the depression years 1934 and 1935, the bond market was such that farm-loan bonds could not be marketed on favorable terms and were hence exchanged with the Farm Mortgage Corporation for fully guaranteed bonds of that corporation or cash. In December, 1935, however, the land banks again entered the investment market, and $100,000,000 in bonds was heavily oversubscribed.[3] It is hoped that new loan funds may be supplied in that manner in the future.

Supplementing their capital and surplus, the intermediate credit banks have obtained loan funds through the sale of debentures to the investing public, subject to the approval of the F.C.A., and occasionally through rediscount of paper with federal reserve banks. Short-term commercial loans are also within the corporate powers of the banks and have sometimes been resorted to.

Loans of the co-operative banks have been made from capital funds, but their authority to rediscount paper with the intermediate credit banks has been used to a certain extent, $22,294,211 being outstanding as of December 31, 1936. The power of the Central Bank to issue debentures has not yet been exercised.

The production credit corporations are not engaged in lending activities but have used their capital in financing and supervising the production credit associations, which may secure additional loan funds through borrowings, subject to approval of the governor of the F.C.A., or through rediscounting with the intermediate credit banks.

In reviewing the sources of funds with which the farm credit corporations operate, the following facts are impressive:

1. The government's investment is large. This is in spite of the ultimate desideratum, expressed by Governor Myers as follows: "It is intended that the permanent system will not use Government funds, but will enable farmers to reach the investment market. It is expected that these institutions will be self-supporting, subject only to Government regulation and examination."[4]

2. There is great flexibility with the F.C.A., so that additional funds may be obtained from other agencies in the organization, as through sale of bonds, rediscounting of loans, and similar interagency transactions.

3. Annual appropriations are required only for administrative ex-

---

[3] See *Statement of F.C.A., before Subcommittee of House Committee on Appropriations, January 31, 1936, and February 1, 1936,* p. 971.

[4] *Ibid.,* p. 945.

penses of the overhead organization, not by the operating corporations themselves.

4. The governor of the F.C.A. has wide powers of control, such as the determination of capital stock issues, approval of borrowings and general supervision of interagency financial transactions.

EXPENDITURES

In the making of loans, the various corporations operate within statutory limits prescribing the types of loans which may be made, maximum and minimum individual loans, maximum interest rates, and other similar conditions. Illustrative are land-bank loans, which are to be secured by first mortgages on farm real estate, must be in amounts not in excess of 50 per cent of the appraised normal value of the land plus 20 per cent of the appraised value of the permanent improvements, must be within the limits of $100 and $50,000 to individual borrowers, and must be made at interest rates which ordinarily may not exceed by more than 1 per cent the interest rate on the latest issue of farm-loan bonds by the bank. With the approval of the governor, this interest rate on loans may be raised, but it is in no case to exceed 6 per cent.[5] This outside limit also exists in the case of co-operative bank loans, the exact interest rate for which is determined by the governor of the F.C.A. in accordance with guiding principles outlined in the law.[6]

Individual loans are made by the district agencies, under general regulations of the Farm Credit Administration in Washington. The F.C.A. has recognized the importance of decentralization of authority and follows the policy of allowing the district directors and officials a large measure of discretion in conducting operations. These local officials are familiar with the local situation and are able to adjust their operations to meet peculiar needs. As Governor Myers stated before a congressional committee early in 1936: "We are decentralizing responsibility; confining the Washington operations to supervision, examination, and assistance, believing that the officers

---

[5] See 12 U.S.C.A. sec. 771.   [6] 49 Stat. 316.

and directors in the district can run the district institutions under supervision more effectively than they can be run from here."[7] With specific reference to loans, Governor Myers declared: "We do not make the loans, but if we thought a mistake had been made we would ask them to review it, and if we thought their policies were unsound we would ask them to review those policies."

In other matters of expenditure, the district corporations of the F.C.A. have enjoyed a measure of freedom comparable to that of private business enterprises. Thus, in the matter of purchasing, they are not bound by regular government regulations and forms, but determine their own procedure. "Suggestions" regarding good purchasing procedure have been sent out from the Washington office, but not by way of regulations, and a maximum of freedom and dispatch has been retained. Obviously, the problem of purchasing supplies and materials has been a minor one for the credit agencies, and the percentage of total operations comprised by such expenditures is very small. The freedom enjoyed, however, does indicate an absence of red tape in business operations.

Also comparable to private business practice is the use of corporation funds for insurance purposes. Protection of collateral by an appropriate form of property insurance is deemed necessary and is resorted to as within the general corporate powers granted by law. This is in spite of the fact that the expenditure of public funds for insurance purposes is prohibited in the case of ordinary governmental departments and establishments.

The district boards of directors employ the personnel of the four permanent units and fix their salaries, subject to approval of the F.C.A. In the case of the Farm Mortgage Corporation, the administrative and clerical work has been supplied by the F.C.A. for reasons of economy. Beginning in 1935, the same service has been rendered the Central Bank for Co-operatives,

---

[7] *Statement before Subcommittee of House Committee on Appropriations, January 31 and February 1, 1936,* p. 946.

which had originally set up its own administrative organization under the control of its board of directors.

One of the important problems with which the land banks are confronted is the handling and disposition of real estate acquired through foreclosure or deeds in lieu of foreclosure. Farms owned outright on December 31, 1936, numbered 22,589, with a carrying value of $73,864,656. In addition, 6,486 sheriffs' certificates, judgments, and similar items, with carrying value of $26,622,397, were held by the banks. During 1936, 15,013 farms and parts of farms had been sold or otherwise disposed of.[8] Efficient handling of these farms along business lines would be impossible under general governmental rules regarding real estate, and the F.C.A. has set up its own procedures, with a special real estate unit designed to study and improve existing practices. Express sanction of the F.C.A. position in this matter may be found in the Farm Credit Act of 1937. Congress in that statute specifically exempted the Farm Credit corporations from all provisions of law "relative to the acquisition or disposal of property . . . . or relative to the making of contracts or leases by or for the United States."[9]

Unlike the corporate agencies in the four permanent groups, the Federal Farm Mortgage Corporation's use of funds for operating expenses has not gone entirely unrestricted. An executive order of August 5, 1935[10] required the F.F.M.C., along with other New Deal agencies, to limit its administrative expenses to amounts approved at the beginning of each fiscal year by the director of the Budget Bureau. Almost a year later, Congress prohibited the incurring of any obligations for administrative expenses, "except pursuant to an annual appropriation specifically therefor."[11] This latter provision had been vigorously opposed by F.C.A. officials, who pointed out the difficulty of forecasting the factors—for example, rate of new mortgages and drought damages—which would vitally

[8] See *Fourth Annual Report of F.C.A., 1936*, p. 26.

[9] Pub. No. 323 (75th Cong.), sec. 6b.

[10] Executive Order No. 7126.   [11] Pub. No. 739 (74th Cong.).

affect expenditures of the Farm Mortgage Corporation.[12] It was also conceivable that the use of appropriated funds would subject the corporation to all the governmental expenditure regulations. The latter danger was not realized, however, since the first "appropriation" under the new plan was rather an "authorization" for the F.F.M.C. to use $15,000,000 of its own funds for administrative expenses during 1938.[13] Limitations on travel and purchase of periodicals were imposed, but expenses for real estate operations were specifically declared "nonadministrative." In addition, the original authorization for the corporation to "determine and prescribe the manner in which its obligations shall be incurred and its expenses allowed and paid"[14] was reaffirmed.

EARNINGS

In the case of each of the four permanent units of the F.C.A., operating expenses are paid out of earnings. There is no question of turning such funds over to the United States Treasury as miscellaneous receipts. Earnings of the land banks result from the 1 per cent interest spread between the rate on farm-loan bonds and the rate on land-bank loans. A similar interest spread creates earnings of the intermediate credit banks; the co-operative banks derive their earnings from interest on loans of their capital funds; and the production credit corporations meet operating expenses from the interest earned on their investments in approved securities.

Statutory provisions in each case prescribe the application of earnings in excess of operating expenses (1) to the making-up of losses; (2) to the restoration of impairment, if any, of capital and paid-in surplus; and (3) to the building-up of reserves and surpluses. From the date of their organization to December 31, 1931, the intermediate credit banks paid franchise taxes to the

---

[12] See "First Deficiency Appropriation Bill for 1936," *Hearings before Subcommittee of the Committee on Appropriations, U.S. Senate, on H.R. 12624* (74th Cong., 2d sess.), pp. 293 ff.

[13] Pub. No. 173 (75th Cong.), Title II (1937).   [14] Cf. 48 Stat. 345.

government totaling $2,496,779, which represented one-half of
net earnings above expenses and reserves for contingencies.
However, in 1932, 100 per cent of earnings was required to be
carried to surplus until a fund equivalent to capital stock was
built up,[15] and in pursuance of this provision no further franchise taxes have been paid the government. The other banks
and corporations are also occupied with building up the required reserves and surpluses, after which the land banks may
declare dividends on non-government-owned stock, and the co-
operative banks may declare dividends not to exceed 7 per
cent per annum.

Surplus funds are invested in the manner prescribed by law,
usually under the direction of the governor of the F.C.A. Thus,
the latter may direct the investment of surplus funds of the
production credit corporations in direct obligations of the
United States or in Class A stock of production credit associations, or both.[16]

ACCOUNTABILITY

It is in the field of accounting and auditing, however, that
the Farm Credit Administration offers its most striking variation from the general pattern of government corporations. As
Governor Myers indicated before the congressional committee,
the function of the Washington office has increasingly become
that of supervision and examination, and careful controls have
been set up in order to detect and rectify financial abuses which
might appear in the operation of the banks and corporations.

Uniform accounting procedures for all units operating under
the F.C.A. have been set up by a special division of the organization, and field men of the F.C.A. have assisted the district
banks and corporations in attaining this uniformity. Monthly
financial reports are made by the banks and corporations to the
Washington office, and these are reviewed by the Financial
Analysis and Statistical Section of the Division of Finance and
Research as a means of keeping in close touch with operating
conditions. Suggestions for improvement, frequently resulting

[15] 47 Stat. 159.   [16] 48 Stat. 259.

from a comparison of the reports of other similar units, are often forwarded to the banks and corporations for their guidance.

Supplementing these monthly reports, examiners of the F.C.A. make examination of each bank, corporation, and production credit association twice annually. In addition to checking to see that the prescribed accounting procedure is followed, these examiners make a thorough audit and examination of accounts and records for the six-months period. Frequently shortages and errors are found and adjusted on the spot. This is a significant characteristic of the F.C.A. examiners; they have administrative powers and are not simply auditors. However, in discharging the legal obligation of the F.C.A. with regard to the examination of accounts, they do take the place of any further independent audit. According to Governor Myers: "We have an examination division that is intended to give all these institutions the equivalent of a certified public accountant's audit in order to be sure that their accounts are in proper order and that everything is handled in the best business-like manner."[17]

The position of the General Accounting Office with reference to Farm Credit Administration activities is a peculiar one. Auditing control is exercised by that office over (1) appropriated funds used for administrative expenses of the F.C.A. itself; (2) the transactions of the F.C.A. field offices which are engaged in making emergency crop and feed loans from federal funds; and (3) the accounts of the Federal Farm Mortgage Corporation. In the case of the latter agency, since its loan funds are obtained from the sale of bonds fully guaranteed by the government, the F.C.A. has taken the position that its transactions are made with federal funds and consequently should be subject to General Accounting Office audit. Since the function of the corporation is to aid in financing loans of the land banks and the Land Bank Commissioner, since its

[17] *Statement before Subcommittee of House Committee on Appropriations, January 31 and February 1, 1936, p. 938.*

authority to furnish such funds is clearly set out in the statutes, and since freedom in the manner of expenditures is expressly guaranteed by law, the audit has not raised any serious problems.

On the other hand, the General Accounting Office has not exercised any functions in connection with the accounts of the F.C.A. district banks and corporations. Warrants issued in connection with the purchase of capital stock by the United States Government must, of course, be countersigned by the Comptroller-General, but, once the capital is received, the banks become accountable only to their private stockholders and to the F.C.A. Several factors have undoubtedly contributed to the failure of the General Accounting Office to audit these accounts. In the first place, as has been indicated, periodical examinations have been required by law of the supervising agencies—the Federal Farm Loan Board and its successor, the Farm Credit Administration. Second, the nature of the business transacted would make an audit along governmental lines expensive and impracticable; the prospect of having each bank submit to the General Accounting Office regular accounts together with every check and supporting document is illustrative. In the third place, all the permanent units, with the exception of the intermediate credit banks, are co-operative—that is, supported by private as well as public capital—and by design they are presumed to be in a transition period prior to continuous operation under private ownership and management.

SUMMARY

The Farm Credit Administration, as an overhead organization for the co-ordination and control of some fifty-odd banking corporations in which the government is vitally interested, offers a possible solution to several of the problems which are raised by governmental use of the corporate device. One question which will undoubtedly assume growing importance if the number of government corporations continues to increase is that of achieving some co-ordination and co-operation between the many independent agencies. The Farm Credit Administration, it will be remembered, was established as a co-ordinating body, and took from various departments and establishments the control of all units operating in a related field, that of supplying agricultural credit. The result has been a unified attack on the problem through the uniform application of major principles and policies and an exchange of services and experience between the operating units to an extent not possible under a less integrated system.

With respect to the actual administration of the district units, the problem of the Farm Credit Administration has been to exercise supervision without too much dictation and without interference in policies and practices developed by the local directors to meet local needs. The F.C.A. has met this problem by decentralizing responsibility "as much as possible," and officials of the central organization have repeatedly stated their belief that the most efficient operation can be achieved only if the district officials are given a large measure of discretion free from restrictive orders and regulations. Governor Myers has said of the district directors that "they formulate the policies, employ the personnel, and fix the salaries, subject to supervision from here." The Washington office has had a decided preference for "suggestions" to the local units, rather than "regulations." In spite of the recognition of the importance of decentralized responsibility, however, the power of the governor of the F.C.A. over the subsidiary corporations is quite extensive. Four out of seven directors in each district are appointed by the governor, and his approval is required for innumerable major transactions.

Several observations may be made regarding the accounting and examination system as set up within the F.C.A. Uniform accounting procedures facilitate comparison and improvement in individual cases, and yet because of the relatedness of the field in which all the units operate do not impose an obstructive rigidity. Monthly reports keep the Washington office in touch with financial operations, and thorough examinations are made frequently enough to detect abuses and encourage efficient administration. The examiners are outsiders in the sense of giving each bank an independent audit, and yet are familiar with the purposes and policies of the entire system and with the problems confronting the operating units. They are thus not subject to the criticism frequently made against General Accounting Office auditors, as by Fleet Corporation and T.V.A. officials, to the effect that they are unfamiliar with operating problems and not qualified to testify as to the efficiency of business transactions. Furthermore, F.C.A. examinations have tended more and more toward efficiency audits in that such factors as credit position, service rendered, and general efficiency are emphasized. For corporations engaged in business enterprise such an emphasis would seem much more valuable than an audit based on legalistic and rigid details, as audits by the General Accounting Office have tended to become. Under the latter plan legal and regularized procedures must be followed even though the cost be several times the claim or transaction involved. For the Farm Credit banks, attempting to operate on a small interest spread and on a basis of self-sufficiency, the burden of such unbusiness-like methods would be too heavy to bear. Imposition of the government's $10,000 limit on salaries would mean the loss of some of the executives and specialists whose abilities and experience add to the efficiency of the Farm Credit Administration banking system. Again, whereas hundreds of inevitable ten-cent errors are written off under the present arrangement, General Accounting Office control would result in frequent exorbitantly expensive attempts at collection. Finally, F.C.A. corporations would be seriously hampered if forced to follow governmental rules in the expenditure of money to put their enormous real estate holdings in shape for rental or sale.

On the whole, the Farm Credit Administration represents a

system of control and supervision over the subsidiary corporations which has supplanted the regular controls usually applied to transactions of governmental agencies. Adequate safeguards have been set up, and, if F.C.A. officials continue in their avowed determination to allow the corporations a maximum of freedom and flexibility within broad limits, the example may be helpful in solving the problems arising in connection with the financial powers of other government corporations.

CHAPTER VI

THE TENNESSEE VALLEY AUTHORITY

EARLY DEVELOPMENTS

SINCE the inauguration of President Roosevelt, the question of the extent to which a government corporation shall exercise freedom in financial matters has been most acutely and dramatically debated in the case of the Tennessee Valley Authority. The roots of the problem extend back through the evolution of the government corporation as an administrative agency, but may be found more immediately in the oft-quoted words of President Roosevelt, who proposed to Congress the creation of a "Tennessee Valley Authority—a corporation clothed with the power of government but possessed of the flexibility and initiative of a private enterprise." In accordance with this request, bills introduced into the Seventy-third Congress by Senator Norris, and by Representatives Hill, McSwain, and Rankin, authorized the creation of a corporate authority, and committee hearings were begun. Large questions of power policy, fertilizer production, flood control, and navigation—which were examined at length—overshadowed the problems of financial freedom and accountability. The section providing for a General Accounting Office audit which was finally passed[1] had been offered as an amend-

---

[1] The complete text of sec. 9(b) was as follows:

"The Comptroller General of the United States shall audit the transactions of the Corporation at such times as he shall determine, but not less frequently than once each governmental fiscal year, with personnel of his selection. In such connection he and his representatives shall have free and open access to all papers, books, records, files, accounts, plants, warehouses, offices, and all other things, property and places belonging to or under the control of or used or employed by the Corporation, and shall be afforded full facilities for counting all cash and verifying transactions with and balances in depositaries. He shall make report of each such audit in quadruplicate, one copy for the President of the United States, one for the chairman of the board, one for public inspection at the

ment by Senator Norris, who said in explanation: "I had a conference on the subject with the Comptroller-General, and this amendment is the result of that conference. . . . . I think the amendment provides a very complete method of auditing the operations of this corporation." Little was Senator Norris aware of the prolonged controversy which was to ensue! No specific reference to the manner of expenditures was contained in the act. However, as managers on the part of the House, Representatives McSwain and Hill submitted the following statement to accompany the report of the Conference Committee:

We have sought to set up a legislative framework but not to encase it in a legislative straitjacket. We intend that the corporation shall have much of the essential freedom and elasticity of a private business corporation. We have indicated the course it shall take, but have not directed the particular steps it shall make.[2]

As to receipts and earnings, the T.V.A. Act contained the following provisions, which would seem to allow the board considerable discretion:

The net proceeds derived by the board from the sale of power and any of the products manufactured by the Corporation, after deducting the cost of operation, maintenance, depreciation, amortization, and *an amount deemed by the board as necessary to withhold as operating capital, or devoted by the board to new construction*, shall be paid into the Treasury of the United States at the end of each calendar year.[3]

With this background, the T.V.A. began its operations. Almost immediately contact was made with the Comptroller-

---

principal office of the corporation, and the other to be retained by him for the uses of the Congress. The expenses for each such audit may be paid from moneys advanced therefor by the Corporation, or from any appropriation or appropriations for the General Accounting Office, and appropriations so used shall be reimbursed promptly by the Corporation as billed by the Comptroller General. All such audit expenses shall be charged to operating expenses of the Corporation. The Comptroller General shall make special report to the President of the United States and to the Congress of any transaction or condition found by him to be in conflict with the powers or duties intrusted to the Corporation by law."

[2] *House Report 130* (73d Cong., 1st sess.), p. 19.

[3] Sec. 26. (Italics ours.)

General, and upon his recommendation the Authority appointed to its staff a man who had formerly been employed in the General Accounting Office, and who was familiar with governmental accounting procedure. The Authority early expressed a desire to co-operate with the Comptroller-General and to facilitate the audit required by the T.V.A. Act.

The beginning of serious disagreement occurred in October, 1933, when the Comptroller-General made a formal request for the submission by the T.V.A. of monthly accounts current and prescribed in some detail the accounting classifications and procedures which should be followed by the treasurer of the corporation. After quoting section 9(b) of the act,[4] the Comptroller-General specified that "in order to facilitate the audit required by the provision of law, *supra*, all paid checks and an executed copy of each contract, and monthly accounts current with supporting schedules should be submitted to this office in connection with all funds received and/or disbursed by the Treasurer of the Tennessee Valley Authority."[5] While the T.V.A. officials interpreted the act as requiring an annual audit at their offices and not the submission of accounts and schedules as demanded by the Comptroller-General, they began, as a conciliatory measure, to render skeleton accounts without original contracts or supporting documents. According to the Comptroller's view, this did not meet legal requirements, and on January 29, 1934, he ruled that the T.V.A. must deposit original signed copies of contracts in the General Accounting Office, and that the furnishing of photostatic copies was not a compliance with section 3743, Revised Statutes.[6]

Meanwhile, President Roosevelt had issued on January 3,

[4] See above, n. 1.

[5] Unpublished MS, October 21, 1933.

[6] "All contracts to be made, by virtue of any law, and requiring the advance of money, or in any manner connected with the settlement of public accounts, shall be deposited promptly in the offices of the Auditors of the Treasury." The Treasury auditors had, of course, been succeeded by the General Accounting Office.

1934, the following executive order, familiarly known as No. 6549:

By virtue of the authority vested in me as President of the United States, it is hereby ordered and directed that accounts of all receipts and expenditures by governmental agencies, including corporations, created after March 3, 1933, the accounting procedure for which is not otherwise prescribed by law, shall be rendered to the General Accounting Office in such manner, to such extent, and at such times as the Comptroller General of the United States may prescribe, for settlement and adjustment pursuant to Title III of the Act of June 10, 1921, 42 Stat. 23.

In the view of the Authority, this executive order did not affect the status of the T.V.A., since its accounting procedure was "otherwise prescribed by law," and consequently compliance was not given. When, however, the Deficiency Act of June 19, 1934, appropriated $1,000,000 "to enable the General Accounting Office to employ personnel to examine and settle claims and to audit and settle the accounts of receipts and expenditures of governmental agencies, including governmental corporations created after March 3, 1933," the Comptroller-General again demanded the submission by the T.V.A. of monthly accounts of all receipts and expenditures, together with supporting papers, for "audit and settlement" in the General Accounting Office. Mr. McCarl took the position that the procedure should be the same as that applicable to departments and establishments generally, and that the smooth working of this procedure should in the future render unnecessary, at least with respect to receipts and expenditures, the audit as contemplated by the T.V.A. Act of 1933.[7] The T.V.A. board, however, again disagreed with the Comptroller-General's legal interpretation and maintained that the fundamental freedom originally intended by the President and Congress had not been destroyed by the language of the Appropriation Act. The latter, according to this view, had merely provided funds for the audits required in the executive order of January 3, and thus in no way affected the T.V.A. However, the desire for co-operation was again expressed, and a con-

[7] Unpublished MS, June 26, 1934.

ference was held between the chairman of the T.V.A. board and the Comptroller-General for discussion of the points in disagreement. As a result, Mr. McCarl proposed the establishment, at T.V.A. headquarters, of an office for continuous pre-audit of T.V.A. accounts, and set forth his program, which included among other details deposit into the Treasury of all receipts and other funds of the T.V.A.[8] While the Authority officials agreed to the establishment of an office for a continuous audit, and indeed had frequently asserted their consent to such a plan, they steadfastly maintained that a pre-audit was not contemplated by law, and would seriously impair the freedom and efficiency desired in the conduct of corporation affairs. Objection was also made to the covering of receipts and other funds into the Treasury, whereas the T.V.A. Act had provided for such a disposition only of "net proceeds."

Several opinions on specific points had meanwhile been given by the Comptroller-General. In August, 1933, he ruled that the act of August 5, 1909, which prohibits payment by the United States of the premium upon any bond required by law or otherwise of any officer or employee of the United States, was applicable to officers and employees of the T.V.A.[9] He further declared that T.V.A. funds could not be expended for insurance premiums, since nothing in the T.V.A. Act excepts the Authority from the established policy of the United States to assume its own risks of lost or damaged public property.[10] A point of major importance was raised in connection with the solicitation and acceptance of bids during the development of the construction plant for Norris Dam. The T.V.A. contended that, while in most cases the low bid received gave a sufficient margin of capacity over the minimum required in the specifications, occasionally equipment represented in a low bid was so poor, although meeting minimum specifications, that the purchase of superior equipment at a

[8] Unpublished MS, September 26, 1934.

[9] Unpublished MS, August 25, 1933.　　　　　[10] Ibid.

slightly higher price was advisable. The desirability of developing a well-balanced plant justified this policy, according to the Authority, and in support of this contention was cited the fact that the Norris plant was running at about 25 per cent capacity above the maximum specified, representing a saving estimated at between $50,000 and $100,000 per month. In the words of Chairman Morgan:

The low costs being achieved on the Norris Dam are being generally recognized by contractors as unusual. Those costs could not have been achieved without the exercise of expert judgment on the part of the men in charge, nor without a certain amount of freedom of action in the purchase of equipment. In our opinion, the freedom of action conferred by the Tennessee Valley Authority Act is essential if such economies are to be achieved.[11]

In answering these arguments, the Comptroller-General declared that, when the peculiar nature of a project demands superior equipment, that fact should be contained in the specifications, or the invitation to bidders. "Specifications should reflect the need. . . . . any other procedure would be unfair and out of harmony with the law governing the uses of public moneys—and to buy in excess of the actual need is extravagance." Thus, he decided that the T.V.A., as well as other government agencies, should not issue specifications and request bids thereon, and then undertake to accept a bid, or to make a contract, not with relation to the low bid meeting such specifications, but with relation to what some bidder might offer which was considered superior to that so specified.[12]

The climax of the entire dispute was reached in April, 1935, at which time the first annual audit report of T.V.A. transactions was published. This report, which covered the fiscal year 1934, had been prepared at T.V.A. headquarters by personnel of the General Accounting Office, and its publication was like a bombshell in its effect. Three hundred ninety-four pages were filled with detailed exceptions to expenditures

[11] Quoted in unpublished decision of Comptroller-General, February 20, 1935.
[12] Ibid.

by the T.V.A., and the grand total to which exception was taken was $2,013,326.51. This revelation was the signal for spirited attacks by T.V.A. opponents, and Senator Austin's vituperative denunciation of "these defalcations, these excess expenditures, these violations of the law"[13] was front-page news for the press of the country. According to Senator Austin, the General Accounting Office had found the "most astounding state of affairs that has ever occurred in the handling of the public money of the United States."

The audit report is an interesting document. The exceptions taken to T.V.A. expenditures were broadly classified as follows:[14]

Travel and subsistence..................... $	29,371.29
Purchase of utility company property........	850,743.00
Contracts, formal, less formal, and miscellaneous.................................	1,001,928.87
Newspapers, magazines, and books...........	10,078.00
Disbursements for other governmental departments.................................	71,045.39
Repairs to steam plant.....................	50,159.96
Grand total...........................	$2,013,326.51

While the items were considered in detail, a summary showing the nature of the various exceptions taken was given on page 134 of the report.[15] This list evidenced the fundamental

[13] *Congressional Record*, LXXIX (May 8 and 9, 1935), 7134 ff.

[14] *Report of Audit of the Transactions of the Tennessee Valley Authority, from June 16, 1933, to June 30, 1934, Made by Personnel of the General Accounting Office*, p. 134.

[15] "The nature of exceptions established consists of purchases without competition, in volation of sec. 3709, R.S.; emergency purchases unsupported by showing of emergency; modifications of specifications; awards on basis of personal preference; dual compensation; excessive allowances and reimbursement of traveling expenses of prospective employees; payment of per diem at designated posts of duty; allowance for overtime to annual employees; allowance of charge for use of personally-owned motor vehicles without prior authorization; overpayments on pay rolls; payment of pay rolls without administrative approval; subscription to newspapers and periodicals in excess of statutory limitation; payments for rented office equipment lost or stolen; payments for power plants, transmission lines, and real estate acquired without having clear title

disagreement between the Comptroller-General and the T.V.A. regarding the legitimate powers of the corporation, and embraced, as well, minor and technical criticisms and queries. What Senator Austin either failed to recognize or omitted to mention in his speech to the Senate was the fact that the report was entirely tentative, subject to complete or partial explanation by the T.V.A., and that doubtful items were included in anticipation of such explanation. As Mr. McCarl himself stated before the House Military Affairs Committee, almost two weeks later:

I think it is premature for you to question me with respect to these exceptions. I think it is unfair to the Authority, and I think it is unfair to me. I think that the Authority should have an opportunity and must be given an opportunity, to answer them.[16]

In the Senate, Senator Norris rose to the defense of the T.V.A. against Senator Austin's accusations and declared that, while the Comptroller-General had found fault with many things, "in no place that I know is there an insinuation or a charge that one penny was stolen or misappropriated."[17] He cited one case in which the board "saved a considerable amount

---

thereto; rent for land occupied by CCC camps paid at rates higher than for land purchased outright; lump-sum payments under cost-plus contracts and fees without original invoices and in excess of reported progress of work; claims paid for loss and damage to property; apparent overpayments on electrical equipment under annual agreements; cost of reconditioning plant agreed by contract to be for account of lessee; rent for building without evidence showing that payments are not in excess of 15 per cent of fair market value; preaudited certified vouchers increased and payments made to vendors in excess of amounts shown on invoices; allowances in expense accounts for bridge toll ticket books before such books have been used; loans to cooperative associations without security; hire of special conveyances such as busses and aeroplanes for visitors and students; and noncompliance with contractual provisions for insurance protection covering personal injury."

[16] "Tennessee Valley Authority," *Hearings before the Committee on Military Affairs, House of Representatives* (74th Cong., 1st sess. [May, 1935]), p. 656.

[17] *Congressional Record*, LXXIX, 7229. The correspondence which took place between Senator Norris and Comptroller-General McCarl with regard to the audit report outlines in detail the position of each in the matter and provides interesting reading as well. The letters are printed in *ibid.*, pp. 8342 ff.

of money" by rejecting a low bid contrary to the Comptroller's view; he effectively answered Senator Austin's intimation that the members of the T.V.A. board had been dishonest in making overpayment on their own salaries; and finally he stated his opinion that, if the cases cited in the report were run down, it would be found in a great many instances that the Comptroller-General was merely saying, in effect, "What does this mean? What does that mean? I reject this or that."

In any event, the many factors involved were poorly, if at all, understood by the general public, and the impression that T.V.A. had been guilty of wasteful and fraudulent practices in its expenditure of public funds undoubtedly gained currency. Also, the House Committee on Military Affairs, which had for its consideration a series of amendments to the T.V.A. Act, was moved to reconvene for further hearings as a result of the audit report.[18] The printed report of these hearings in which both Dr. Morgan and Mr. McCarl testified not only throws light upon the audit report and upon T.V.A. expenditures but lays open the fundamental questions at issue between the advocates of corporate freedom and those favoring close supervision and control by the Comptroller-General.

COMMITTEE HEARINGS, MAY, 1935

Dr. Morgan was the first witness, and in an extended statement he undertook to explain the T.V.A.'s position on the question of financial freedom and to answer the major exceptions contained in the audit report. The first group of objections considered had to do with the purchase of equipment from other than the lowest bidder. Dr. Morgan pointed out in convincing manner the complexity of a huge construction project such as the Norris Dam, the necessity for developing a well-balanced and sturdy plant, the value of a reasonable exer-

[18] Chairman McSwain, in calling upon Dr. Morgan for testimony, said: "I presume that you have gathered from what was said that this hearing is set, perhaps, largely in response to certain statements made in the audit—annual report of the audit by the Comptroller General" ("Tennessee Valley Authority," *op. cit.*, pp. 554-55).

cise of discretion and judgment by expert builders in the interest of economy and efficiency, the seriousness of delay in such a program, and the high degree of efficiency achieved at the Norris Dam plant, which had operated 90 per cent of the full working time for five months, at about 120 per cent of its rated efficiency. He cited two instances where protests of low bidders to the Comptroller-General had been decided in the T.V.A.'s favor after delays of seventy and one hundred eleven days, respectively, and stated that, "if we had held that job up for one hundred eleven days, until the argument was settled, our work for the season would have been wrecked."[19] He asserted the desirability in some cases of making general specifications in order to bring about greater competition and to secure superior equipment through the exercise of expert judgment by the purchaser. The best illustration of this practice may be seen in the case of the cableways which were to span the Norris chasm. A complete unit, composed of a complex mechanism of towers, hoisting machinery, electrical controls, track, carrying cable, hoisting cable, sheaves, and buckets, was needed, and an attempt to draw up rigid specifications would have been obviously foolhardy. On the other hand, it would be just as uneconomical to accept a design which technically qualified under the general specifications yet which was clearly inferior to another, perhaps slightly more expensive, but considerably more dependable unit. In such a case, as Dr. Morgan said, "any well-managed private contractor" would have been able to exercise his judgment without fear of violating the Comptroller's rule requiring acceptance of the lowest bid meeting the specifications.

Dr. Morgan next considered two groups of exceptions listed under the heading "awards on the basis of personal preference" and "purchases without competition in violation of Section 3709, Revised Statutes." Both groups totaled less than 1 per cent of total purchases, and Dr. Morgan emphasized the impracticability of delay in some instances and the nature of cer-

[19] *Ibid.*, p. 565.

tain proprietary items on which no competition could be secured in others. "Personal preference" he declared to be a misnomer for engineering judgment. With reference to the whole question of open competition Dr. Morgan pointed out that 98 per cent of all T.V.A. purchases had been through competitive bidding and that in over 95 per cent of the cases the lowest bid had been accepted.

Other groups of exceptions, such as "dual compensation," "allowance for overtime to annual employees," "overpayment on payrolls," "pre-audited certified vouchers increased," and "subscription to newspapers and periodicals in excess of limitation" were answered by Dr. Morgan in a manner that tempts one to applaud administrative excellence rather than to condemn "fraudulent" use of public funds. Thus, the purchase of toll-bridge coupon books at a discount, representing a saving of 50 per cent in the cost of toll services, was objected to in the audit as "allowances in expense accounts for bridge toll ticket books before such books have been used." Dr. Morgan aptly observed, "It should not require a special act of Congress to permit such economy." Another criticism referred to the exercise of discretion upon receipt of identical bids, whereas the Comptroller-General had ruled that in such cases the T.V.A. must draw lots among the identical bidders. Said Dr. Morgan, "This seems to us to be inefficient as it destroys the last vestige of competition. If price is identical then we should concern ourselves with selecting the best quality so as to maintain actual competition to the highest possible degree."

Particularly in reservoir clearance work, the T.V.A. has met with small damage claims, and the Authority's policy of settling most of such claims on the spot had incurred the objection of the General Accounting Office. Dr. Morgan pointed out the expediency and economy of this policy as contrasted with the adjudication and settlement of each such claim by the General Accounting Office at a cost amounting to "several hundred per cent of the actual claim."

In conclusion Dr. Morgan summarized his position. He

maintained that Congress in the T.V.A. Act had decided that
the engineers on the job, rather than the auditors, should exercise judgment in operating and construction methods. "The
wisdom of that determination of Congress is illustrated by
the auditor's criticisms found in this report." He expressed his
high regard for the services of the Comptroller-General in
keeping Congress and the public fully informed, in demon-
strating more economical accounting methods, and in maintaining a system of public accounting superior, in many respects, to private accounting. His objection was not to a pure
audit by the Comptroller-General[20] but to a serious limitation
of administrative discretion and flexibility. Finally, he offered
a substitute for compliance with all the regulatory statutes and
"settlement of accounts" by the Comptroller-General:

> But in my opinion, if this freedom of discretion and judgment can be
> exercised on the one hand, and if we can have his [Comptroller-General's]
> cooperation on the other and if, in addition to what he is doing, he could
> furnish competent engineers at our expense to go over that job, to keep
> track of it, in any field that he wants to explore, to see whether it has a
> good honest tone to it, to see whether anything ought to be looked into
> further—if the Comptroller General can furnish us that kind of service, so
> that we can have a degree of freedom of judgment along with his careful
> analysis of costs, I believe there is a possibility that the TVA can make
> a contribution to the practice of construction by the Government. We
> may raise it to a new level of economy and still keep all the reasonable
> precaution that the Government exercises in its expenditures.[21]

Comptroller-General McCarl's testimony before the same
committee, though comparatively brief, is also exceedingly
interesting. Mr. McCarl had apparently receded from his former position regarding the submission of accounts, since
he stated that in "this particular instance of the Tennessee
Valley Authority, the law provided that the audit should be
made as it was made, and that instead of accounts being
rendered, there should be an audit report."[22] He then testified

---

[20] "If the opportunity should come to us to dispense with those services we
would not do it" (*ibid.*, p. 573).

[21] *Ibid.*, p. 574.   [22] *Ibid.*, p. 654.

to the tentativeness of the audit report and declared his opinion
to be that he should hear the Authority's side of the case before
submitting his final report to the President and Congress. In
reply to the question "whether you have any evidence whatever in your judgment of any fraud on the part of any of the
directors of the T.V.A.?" Mr. McCarl answered, "You are
dealing with a public trust, and I do want to say this, that I
certainly have found no fraud."

Proceeding to the major disagreement between himself and
the T.V.A. Mr. McCarl declared:

> I think that there is a fundamental difference involved here, and I
> think you should resolve it in fairness to the Authority, in fairness to the
> Government, and in fairness to the accounting officers of the Government.
> You have created a corporation; that is, you have given it a corporate
> entity, and then you have specifically and quite minutely enumerated by
> law what it may do. It is exempt from this law and that law, but it has
> not been so exempted from all regulatory statutes, statutes that have
> been recognized from the beginning as essential and necessary in public
> transactions.
>
> I will not call it a dispute, but a difference of opinion exists as to
> whether or not this Authority is amenable to any law with reference to
> the uses of public money because it is a corporation.
>
> My view is that the regulatory statutes from which it has not been ex-
> empted are applicable—applicable first because they are applicable, and
> applicable secondly because they are good and wholesome.[23]

Mr. McCarl then discussed section 3709, Revised Statutes,
delaring its purpose to be the securing of open competition,
economy in governmental purchases, and fairness to all involved. He declared it to be, in his judgment, "one of the most
wholesome statutes ever written." He reiterated his contention that the T.V.A. had not been exempted from this statute
and that hence it was applicable to transactions of the Authority. However, he recognized that T.V.A. officials confidently believed that section 3709 would greatly handicap their
work and that they were not required by law to observe its
provisions. "I think that they will so tell you very frankly, and

[23] *Ibid.*, p. 658.

it may be that there is a basis for their contention, but if there is a true basis for the corporation being exempted from such law then you should exempt it by law."

This, then, was the major point made by the Comptroller-General: while favoring close regulation, he desired statutory clarification in any event. "If you give them [T.V.A.] work to do, and that work cannot be done under section 3709, and there must be a deviation from it, for the success of the Tennessee Valley undertaking, then the Congress should grant the exemption by law and not expect me to do so." He mentioned other laws, such as that relating to the regulations issued by the President governing what may be paid for travel, and the "Buy American" law, and intimated that their application to the T.V.A. was also debatable. In conclusion, he declared:

I think that we have gone long enough under this haphazard arrangement. If there is a regulatory law applicable to the doing of a thing, it should be observed unless an exemption has been granted by law, and these are matters that I hope you will act upon in the near future.

In the presence of the Comptroller-General, Dr. Morgan was allowed to re-emphasize his suggestion that competent men, not necessarily auditors, be sent to the scene of activity, at T.V.A. expense, in order to keep constant check upon operations for the General Accounting Office.

It is my honest belief that the difference between the method that the Comptroller General suggests and the method that I suggest represents millions of dollars; . . . . by the combination that I suggest, of his having complete exploratory powers, which should be complete, and in that connection putting engineers on that job, and judging it from an engineering standpoint, and at the same time giving us that freedom of action, I believe that we can raise government operation to a very high level of efficiency, and I believe further that by that method we could do Government work as cheaply as private work is done.[24]

With this variety of evidence before them the committee members retired into executive session. Some desired to "bind the Board to some business principles" and have rigid control

[24] *Ibid.*, p. 660.

by the Comptroller-General; others were more sympathetic to the Authority's position and could "see difficulty in operating under competitive bidding in certain cases"; Chairman McSwain felt that "all Government expenditures should pass through the hands of the Comptroller General" but that immediate change in the operating methods of the Authority would be confusing and inadvisable. Hence he thought it best to let the T.V.A. operate as it had been for a year or so until present projects were completed, and "then as to future business, subject them by proper legislation to the direct control of the Comptroller General."[25]

DISCUSSIONS IN CONGRESS

While the House Military Affairs Committee was thus pondering the general problem as to the extent of T.V.A.'s financial freedom, the Senate was itself involved in a similar discussion. The occasion was the introduction by Senator Barbour of a bill "to regulate the expenditure of public moneys heretofore and hereafter available for expenditure in carrying out the act of May 18, 1933, known as the 'Tennessee Valley Authority Act of 1933,' and for other purposes."[26] Consisting of four sections, this bill would provide, first, that all T.V.A. funds should be deposited in the Treasury and withdrawn only pursuant to accountable warrants; second, that except in the case of an immediate public emergency all payments on contracts in excess of $100 must be after advertisement and acceptance of the lowest bid; third, that except in emergency no bid should be accepted for seven days after being opened nor while any protest was still undecided by the Comptroller-General; and, finally, that the Comptroller-General should have discretion to allow payments otherwise unallowable when

[25] *Ibid.*, p. 838.

[26] *Congressional Record*, LXXIX, 7298. Senator Barbour had introduced this bill into the previous session of Congress as S. 3274, but it had died in the Committee on Finance. The matter was first brought to his attention, as he himself relates, by one of his constituents whose low bid had been turned down by the T.V.A.

such payments were shown to be reasonably necessary for the accomplishment of the corporation's work, as authorized by law.

In defense of his proposal, Senator Barbour cited T.V.A. rejection of low bids, and declared his conviction that no valid reason existed why the Authority should not be subject to the same laws as government departments. He argued that any out-of-the-ordinary conditions could be properly cared for under the fourth section of his bill.[27]

Senator Norris rose to the defense of the T.V.A.'s position and declared that if Senator Barbour's proposal were adopted, "to a very great extent it would nullify all the benefits which can come from the proper administration of the T.V.A. Act."[28] He attacked each section in turn, saying, for example, of the section which would provide for a delay in the acceptance of bids, that "it would be disastrous. It would cost the Government of the United States, through this instrumentality, millions of dollars, if that kind of a provision were in the law."[29] Upon the conclusion of Senator Norris' speech, Senator Barbour pressed for a vote upon his amendment, and it was rejected.

While waiting for Congress to act, the Comptroller-General handed down an official ruling to the effect that a resolution of the T.V.A. board of directors authorizing the purchase of supplies without advertising when the amount did not exceed $500 per unit purchase would not be accepted in his audit as waiving the provisions of section 3709, Revised Statutes.[30]

[27] *Ibid.*, pp. 7298–99. Senator Barbour further said regarding his bill: "I may add, for it is no secret, that in its preparation I consulted with the Comptroller General and have been aided by his suggestions and advice in respect to this matter, as it would affect the Tennessee Valley Authority, though I, of course, take full responsibility for my proposition."

[28] *Ibid.*, p. 7467.

[29] Senator Norris also read into the *Record* a statement by the T.V.A. which opposed Senator Barbour's bill with reasons along the lines of those brought out in the Military Affairs Committee hearings.

[30] Unpublished MS, June 18, 1935. The resolution referred to had been adopted by the board on August 6, 1934, as a result of information that ap-

In his words:

The TVA, though a body corporate . . . . is, nevertheless, a governmental agency operating under appropriations made by the Congress (48 Stat. 275; 1055).

Expenditures of public moneys—appropriations made by the Congress —unless otherwise specifically provided by statute, are subject to the provisions of the statutes of the United States and in the instant case there is for consideration and application Section 3709, R.S.

On June 26, 1935, the House Committee on Military Affairs reported favorably its product of a bill amending the T.V.A. Act. Section 13, dealing with the questions of expenditures and accounts, represented the views expressed by the Comptroller-General in committee hearings and would, if passed, have drastically curtailed the freedom for which the Authority contended. Its provisions had been drafted by the Comptroller-General himself upon the request of Mr. Buchanan, and authorized withdrawal of funds only on accountable warrants, the application of all laws regulating expenditure of public funds, the rendition of all accounts to the General Accounting Office for settlement and adjustment, and disapproval by the Comptroller-General of requisitions for funds "should there by any administrative delinquency in the rendering of accounts as directed." The committee report stated:

This section speaks for itself, and is based upon the simple proposition that the Tennessee Valley Authority is the agent, the creature and the arm of the Federal Government. . . . . The other arms and agencies of the Federal Government, such as the executive departments, must and do function efficiently under the system of accounting to and through the General Accounting Office proposed by Sec. 13.[31]

However, this was by no means the unanimous position of the committee members, of whom five, while voting to report the bill for discussion and amendment by the House, felt that

---

proximately 75 per cent of the Authority's purchases of materials, stores, equipment, machinery, and supplies involved expenditure of less than $500 per unit purchase, and in the belief that much time and money could be saved.

[31] *House Report 1372* (74th Cong.), pp. 10–12.

passage in the reported form would "retard rather than advance the great program now under way."

The promised struggle on the floor of the House was realized.
Mr. Hill, one of the committee's five minority members, became the champion of the T.V.A.'s viewpoint and offered an
amendment to strike out all of section 13 and substitute language much more agreeable to the Authority. Mr. Hill's
amendment provided for purchases by competition and after
advertising, with three important exceptions: first, in case of
immediate need; second, in the case of repair or supplemental
parts and repair services; third, in case of purchases involving
less than $500. Furthermore, the board was expressly author-
ized to consider, in the awarding of contracts, such factors as
the bidder's financial responsibility, skill, experience, record of
integrity, ability to furnish repairs and maintenance services,
and the time of delivery or performance offered. On the auditing side, this amendment substantially retained the audit provisions of the original T.V.A. Act, but provided that the audit
report should not be made until after the Authority had had
reasonable opportunity to answer exceptions therein, and to
file a statement for submission by the Comptroller-General
with his report.

In defense of his amendment, Mr. Hill submitted a printed
statement, of which the following is an extract:

It was the clear hope of the President and the intent of the Congress
that the Tennessee Valley Authority should be free from that extra cost
of doing Government business which results from routine Government
procedure. . . . . The amendment which I am proposing in lieu of this
provision of the bill [sec. 13] meets all reasonable requirements and at the
same time preserves the policy of the original TVA Act. The chief com-
plaint of the Comptroller General has been that the Authority has not
conformed as rigidly as he believes it should to the law requiring competitive bidding in purchases by Government departments. In view of the
somewhat unique character of the Authority, as described above, it
would be impracticable to apply the existing law to its transactions.
However, the amendment which I propose is modeled after this law and

other existing laws with such slight changes as are necessary to meet the special requirements of the Authority.[32]

In the ensuing debate, Mr. Hill emphasized the thorough and searching nature of the audit provided in his amendment,[33] the modern and near-perfect bookkeeping system of the T.V.A., the handicaps of securing permission for every purchase,[34] and the dangers of red tape in accounting. A spirited discussion followed, and both sides of the question were thoroughly aired by members of the House. On the opposing side, the wholesomeness of government regulations was cited;[35] the T.V.A. contention for preferential treatment was denounced; and Mr. Hill's amendment was declared to be an open door to partiality, waste, and extravagance.[36] However, with a few minor changes, the proposal of Mr. Hill was approved by the House—162 ayes and 120 noes—and when the amendatory act was finally passed by both houses and approved by the President on August 31, 1935, a substantial victory had been won by the Tennessee Valley Authority. Important exceptions to acceptance of low bids had been authorized, the board's

[32] *Congressional Record*, LXXIX, 10792–93.

[33] "In other words, my amendment provides that we shall have the Comptroller General make the most thorough and searching audit possible of the fiscal affairs of the Tennessee Valley Authority at least once a year. In doing this we are proceeding just as ordinary private business does. It carries on its business and then from time to time it has an audit made. The only difference is that we will have a much more thorough, complete, and searching audit from the Comptroller General than ordinary business has of its affairs" (*ibid.*, p. 10973).

[34] "We have the Inland Waterways Corporation and we ask that the Tennessee Valley Authority be treated in the same way as the Inland Waterways Corporation" (*ibid.*, p. 10974).

[35] "No scandal has ever attached to Government departments and agencies so guided" (Mr. Harter, *ibid.*, p. 10974).

[36] Mr. May said of "this wild, extravagant, money-spending, riotous-living bureau" that "when the Congress of the United States puts itself in the attitude of not making this extravagant monster conform to practices required of all other bureaus and Government agencies, it puts itself in a position to be criticized, and justly criticized by the country" (*ibid.*, p. 10891). A much more dispassionate, reasoned and convincing argument in favor of rigid control over expenditures is that of Mr. Plumley (*ibid.*, pp. 10776–78).

resolution to make purchases under $500 on the open market had been ratified, an opportunity to answer General Accounting Office exceptions before their publication had been guaranteed, and the expense of the audit, except in so far as it dealt with power operations, had been shifted to the General Accounting Office.[37] No mention was made of the extent to which other laws governing the expenditure of government funds should or should not be applicable to the Authority. In view of this fact, the "difference of opinion" between the Comptroller-General and the T.V.A. as to the proper status of the corporation was by no means dispelled. With reference to earnings, the amendatory act expressly provided that a continuing fund of $1,000,000 may be withheld "to defray emergency expenses and to insure continuous operation." This fund was to be in addition to regular operating capital already authorized to be withheld before the covering of proceeds into the United States Treasury.

Before tracing further developments, it is necessary to take notice of a provision of the Second Deficiency Appropriation Act, approved August 12, 1936, which had also projected itself into the picture. After appropriating $36,000,000 to the T.V.A., this act provided that these and all other funds of the Authority should be "covered into and accounted for as one fund to be known as the 'Tennessee Valley Authority Fund' and shall remain available until June 30, 1936." It will be noted that the T.V.A. was hereby subjected to a fiscal-year limitation in the use of appropriated funds not hitherto imposed.

LATER DEVELOPMENTS

Taking the view that by the appropriation act provision together with the pertinent sections of the amendatory T.V.A. Act, Congress had "now definitely prescribed the breadth and limit of authority to be exercised by the Tennessee Valley Authority in its uses of public moneys," the Comptroller-Gen-

[37] For the complete text of sec. 9(b), as amended, see 16 U.S.C.A. sec. 831h (Supp. 1936).

eral again demanded from the T.V.A. the regular submission
of monthly accounts to his Washington office.[38] According to
his interpretation, the effect of the appropriation act was to
require that withdrawals from the "Tennessee Valley Authority Fund" for disbursements be only on accountable warrants,
and the combined effect of the two acts was to require submission of accounts as he should direct.

When the officials of the T.V.A. contended that no change
had been intended or effected by Congress in the place and
manner of audit, the Comptroller-General remained adamant.
He first repeated his view that the appropriation act had
made mandatory the submission of accounts because of the
"accountability of the receiving and disbursing officer (or officers) of the Tennessee Valley Authority for all moneys received from the Federal Treasury on accountable warrants or
from other sources."[39] But he also expressed his dissatisfaction
with the field audit as tried in 1934, saying that "there is no
accounting, in the true sense where the accounting officers of
the Government must search out and find, if possible, documents and facts essential to show the legality of payments
made by an accountable officer" and concluding that, "under
any procedure where responsibility for accounting is relaxed
there is always a tendency toward carelessness—payments
without proper documentary support, and too often improper
or illegal—while enforced accountability makes for carefulness
and the resolving of all doubts as to correctness and legality
before payments are actually made."[40]

Expressing a desire to co-operate, T.V.A. officials agreed to
submit accounts to Washington, provided the Comptroller-
General would concede the rightness of their contention that
the law, as amended, gave him powers of post-auditing and
reporting without the power to "settle and adjust accounts,"
and provided also that he would agree that under the law the
T.V.A. treasurer was an officer of the Authority, responsible

[38] Unpublished MS, September 11, 1935.
[39] Unpublished MS, October 22, 1935.   [40] Ibid.

to it, and not an officer directly accountable to the Comptroller-General.

Mr. McCarl's reply of November 6, 1935, denied both contentions, and reaffirmed his previous interpretation of the appropriation act and its effect, the accountability of the T.V.A. disbursing officer, and the duty of the General Accounting Office to apply regular governmental procedure.[41] Furthermore, he intimated that further noncompliance on the part of the T.V.A. might result in his refusal to approve requisitions of the Authority for funds from the Treasury.[42] Finally, he said of the amendatory T.V.A. Act:

> While enlarging the responsibilities of the Directors of the Authority through giving them wider discretion in connection with certain uses of public moneys,[43] [it] is further *legislative emphasis of the fact of the applicability to Authority transactions of all laws controlling the uses of public moneys from which it has not specifically been exempted by statute.*[44]

Thus, the dawn of the year 1936 saw the deadlock unbroken. The detailed reply of the T.V.A. to the exceptions taken in the first annual audit report was sent to the Comptroller-General in December. It remained to be seen how convincingly, in his eyes, the Authority had vindicated itself, and consequently what would be the nature of his final report to the President and Congress.[45] The major dispute over expenditure methods is still unsettled, but on March 3, 1936, the T.V.A. submitted to the General Accounting Office its first detailed account

[41] Unpublished MS, November 6, 1935.

[42] "While this office desires to be cooperative, it can not as you must realize, continue indefinitely to approve advances from the Treasury with no proper accounting for uses of prior advances."

[43] In an interesting decision of September 9, 1935, the Comptroller-General had ruled that the discretion conferred in the act of August 31, 1935, "is a legal one which must be based upon record facts reasonably supporting the conclusion reached with respect to any particular transaction."

[44] Italics ours.

[45] Since this chapter was written, the Comptroller-General's office has accepted the T.V.A.'s explanation of all but $89,585.70 of the $2,013,326.51 of expenditures originally challenged (see *Congressional Record*, LXXXIII [March 9, 1938], 4137).

current, with supporting documents. The filing of this account, covering the month of July, 1935, and involving some seven thousand separate documents weighing approximately two thousand pounds, was undertaken by the Authority as a conciliatory measure, and did not signify any change in the T.V.A.'s position as to the basic principles at issue. The Comptroller-General continued to take exception to the Authority's transactions, such exceptions to transactions during July, 1935, for example, totaling approximately $2,000,000. They were based largely upon "insufficient supporting documents" and failure to have land titles approved by the Attorney-General before purchase.[46]

SUMMARY AND CONCLUSIONS

The record of the Tennessee Valley Authority, in its struggle for freedom from red tape[47] in financial matters, has been a stormy and exciting one. Unique in its purposes, its structure, its authorized duties—this government corporation adds a vivid chapter to the historical development of the corporate device as an agency of governmental administration and unquestionably has offered a wealth of experience for future utilization. It combines within the wide scope of its powers and functions activities that have long been recognized as "governmental" with those more often described as "economic." From the former, as for example, afforestation and educational work, no cash return is expected; from the latter, as in the case of electric-power sales, receipts are confidently expected

[46] Said the Comptroller-General: "In the audit of accounts this office is required by law to determine the legality of expenditures of appropriated funds independently of the administrative office, and may not, therefore, accept the unsupported conclusions of the administrative auditors as to the correctness or legality of payments. . . . . With the accounts so far received from the Tennessee Valley Authority there has not always been furnished sufficient information to authorize allowance of credit for the payments involved and the letter from the Comptroller of the Tennessee Valley Authority would seem to indicate either a misunderstanding of the audit functions of this office or a failure to comprehend the nature of the detailed information necessary to determine credit for payments from appropriated funds" (16 C.G. 239).

[47] Some would say "freedom from responsibility."

to bring about complete self-liquidation, and in any event will approach that objective. While these two aspects of the work have not been and perhaps cannot be entirely segregated, most of the discussion over financial freedom has centered around the construction program, which is comparable in many respects to private enterprise. True it is that some have suggested isolation of the power program and its operation on a purely "business" basis, but the difficulties inherent in such a scheme are practical as well as constitutional. Otherwise, a "Tennessee Valley Power Corporation" might offer a better comparison with government-operated "economic" enterprises in the stricter sense of the term[48] than does the present T.V.A.

Reviewing the development sketched in the present chapter, one is impressed by the following facts: the President and the congressional leaders sponsoring the creation of the T.V.A. desired a large measure of freedom and flexibility in order to circumvent red tape and to make possible progressive administration; Congress on the whole has had no clear idea either of the present financial status under law of its corporate creation or of the financial position which would best serve the public interest; neither the original T.V.A. Act nor the supplementary statutes settle unequivocally the major accounting and expenditure questions involved; consequently, an apparently insoluble dispute has arisen between the Comptroller-General and the Authority.

With specific reference to the T.V.A.–Comptroller-General controversy, two significant questions arise. Under existing statutes, which position has been legally sound? Second, and more important, which contention, regardless of existing law, represents the better administrative solution?

On the first count, the T.V.A. officials have presented the stronger case. Behind their contention rests the record of the Fleet Corporation, and consequently the weight of the only Supreme Court decision bearing upon the question. An examination of the original T.V.A. Act, especially with the clear

[48] E.g., Inland Waterways Corporation and Panama Railroad Co.

intent of the President and congressional leaders kept in mind, does not reveal the power of the Comptroller-General to "settle and adjust accounts" or otherwise to exercise regulatory supervision, except through a post-audit. This view is strengthened by the testimony of Mr. McCarl before the Military Affairs Committee. There is good reason to believe that the act of June 19, 1934, which appropriated money for expenses of the General Accounting Office, was not intended to, and did not actually, change the fundamental nature of T.V.A. freedom as previously granted; this provision was utterly ignored in subsequent congressional debates dealing with the existing and desired status of the T.V.A. in relation to the General Accounting Office. As for the amendatory act of August 31, 1935, the Comptroller-General's contention that Congress inferentially subjected the T.V.A. to all regulatory laws in the absence of express exemption is not convincing in view of the following facts: first, the express changes in the act *support* arguments advanced in committee by the T.V.A.; second, no *additional* language is included which imposes further limitations upon the Authority in accounting and expenditure matters; and, finally, and of great importance, language which *expressly* and *unequivocally* embodied the restrictions desired by the Comptroller-General was before the House of Representatives but was rejected in favor of the language of Mr. Hill, an ardent T.V.A. supporter, which ultimately became law. There remains, then, the language of the Second Deficiency Appropriation Act of 1935, creating the "Tennessee Valley Authority Fund" and, according to Mr. McCarl, subjecting the T.V.A. to regular governmental accounting and adjustment procedure. This act, peculiarly within the province of the Comptroller-General, is difficult to interpret, but the following considerations are persuasive: First, committee hearings reveal that the language in question was *desired* by the T.V.A. as a bookkeeping and custodial measure;[49] second, letters of

---

[49] *Hearings, Subcommittee of House Committee on Appropriations, June 4, 1935,* pp. 594–95.

the President and the Director of the Budget pertaining to the contested provision are in apparent agreement with this interpretation;[50] and, in the third place, Congress, in considering at length the T.V.A. amendatory Act, rejected *express* provisions designed to accomplish what Mr. McCarl contended the appropriation act had effected by implication—this despite the fact that all congressmen, including those bitterly opposed to restrictive measures, ignored in the debates such an interpretation.[51]

It will be noted that the foregoing analysis, while in our view quite persuasive, is not entirely conclusive. The T.V.A. differs from other corporations, as, for example the Fleet Corporation (whose freedom had been upheld by the Supreme Court), in that it has operated under annual congressional appropriations rather than a stock capitalization; the Comptroller-General bases many of his arguments on his power of control over "the expenditure of appropriated moneys." Then, too, the legal effect of the provisions of the appropriation act requiring that funds be "covered into and accounted for as one fund to be known as the 'Tennessee Valley Authority Fund,' " is to say the least debatable.

Finally, there remains the question as to the extent of financial freedom for the T.V.A. which will best serve the public interest. Let us examine several concrete examples of the

[50] *House Document 181* (74th Cong.). The President declared that the reasons for the proposed provision are set forth in the Budget Director's letter, which reads in part as follows:

"The purpose of this proposed provision is to establish the 'Tennessee Valley Authority Fund' and to authorize the Authority to include therein all funds from whatever source derived. This procedure will simplify control accounting, cost finding, and financial reporting by consolidating the separate accounts of appropriations, allotments, and receipts and permitting the authority to function in this respect like other large construction agencies of the Federal Government."

[51] On the contrary, Mr. McLean offered as an *amendment* to the Appropriation Act a section expressly accomplishing all of Mr. McCarl's objectives, but this amendment was stricken out on a point of order as legislation on an appropriation bill (*Congressional Record*, LXXIX, 9853).

effect of regular governmental procedures upon Authority transactions. In May, 1935, a railroad company had been paid 57 cents too little, and, after examining the records, the Comptroller-General required further evidence concerning the claim. Photostatic copies which he demanded cost $1.27; the cost of the Authority's time was estimated at $4.00, and expense to the General Accounting Office was probably several dollars. In short, between $5.00 and $10.00 was spent to settle a claim of 57 cents, resulting from an oversight, and the major part of the expense was charge to the T.V.A. In another instance, a low bid was accepted on an item of construction equipment against the judgment of T.V.A. engineers, yet in the attempt to conform to governmental regulations. This equipment, cheapest by about $1,000, was only one unit in a complicated installation, and, when it failed to function properly, the direct result was a ten-day delay on the Norris Dam project, while the more expensive unit was being contracted for, manufactured, and delivered.[52]

Cases in which the T.V.A proceeded to adopt economical measures only to have them objected to by the Comptroller-General are numerous. The saving of 50 per cent on bridge-toll charges by purchase of coupon books has already been mentioned. In another instance, a certain amount of steel for the erection of the T.V.A. concrete mixing plant was contracted for; yet, when construction was under way, it was found necessary to locate the plant lower down the hill, and hence to have a higher structure for which additional steel would be required. Rather than hold up the work to call for bids and arrange for a second contract, the T.V.A. required the original contractor to furnish the additional steel at the same price. The General Accounting Office, however, took exception to this action as an award on the basis of "personal preference."

A final illustration is the Comptroller-General's objection to the "improper use of automobiles." A case in which a

[52] See *Annual Report of the Tennessee Valley Authority, 1934*, p. 52.

T.V.A. employee traveled 4,765 miles at a cost of 2 cents per mile was compared to a case of "mismanagement" in which another employee traveled only 268 miles at a cost of 56 cents per mile, most of which was set depreciation. According to the Comptroller-General, the latter employee should not have had a car of his own, but should have been assigned a car from a central pool, whenever one was needed. The facts in the case are interesting. The case of "bad management" concerned the construction superintendent in entire charge of the $20,000,000 Norris project. No general pool of cars was maintained in that locality, and the superintendent had his car always at hand, ready to travel a mile or two at a time—from the dam-site to the office, to the paymaster's office, to the warehouse. Certainly, an efficient private firm would have ridiculed the suggestion that such a man should call on a central pool for a car, or else walk around from place to place. On the other hand, the case of large mileage and low cost involved the daily commutation of the assistant superintendent from his home in Knoxville to the job at Norris, a distance of twenty-five miles. Actually, this was bad management, and as soon as a house was available for him in the town of Norris, he was moved there. The General Accounting Office position in both cases was exactly the reverse of that which would be taken by the managers of any efficient enterprise.

From the viewpoint of the Tennessee Valley project alone, there is little question that a large measure of freedom creates the opportunity for the optimum in efficiency, progressiveness, and economy. The most powerful administration is potentially the best administration. Apart from the theoretical possibilities of dishonesty and unconscionable extravagance under such a system—for it is worth repeating that these evils have so far been conspicuous by their absence in T.V.A. experience —the greatest danger is that of "bureaucratic self-expansion." Respecters of democratic government will not be left entirely untouched by moderate and dispassionate statements in Congress that the T.V.A. has engaged in programs, projects, and expenditures beyond those envisaged even by its supporters in the national legislature, although impassioned and vituperative attacks upon "rampant, wild-eyed, voracious bureaucracy" merit no reply. When firsthand observation convinces one that T.V.A. activities with few, if any, exceptions are both well purposed and beneficial, objections tend to dissolve.

Specifically, the advantages and benefits claimed for administrative freedom by Dr. Morgan are convincingly real. The avoidance of delays, the flexibility of progressive management, the economies resulting from the exercise of expert judgment, the fostering of morale through a feeling of accomplishment, the absence of overhead expense caused by restrictive procedures—all of these blessings have appeared in the Tennessee Valley. The efficiency of the Authority's construction projects is not mere braggadocio on the part of Dr. Morgan; it is a recognized fact, and administrative freedom has contributed largely to that end. If government operations are to measure up, in efficiency, to private enterprise, much of the red tape which has been built up to surround the old-line governmental departments must be circumvented.

Looking at the entire governmental process, one must recognize a measure of truth in the contention of Mr. McCarl and those congressmen who favor more strict control over T.V.A. finances. The exercise of freedom has inevitably revealed some shortcomings.[53] Furthermore, a strict accounting for public funds, and a feeling of responsibility for public stewardship, are of undeniable value. That government regulations have corrected and prevented many abuses and extravagances during the past decade is unquestioned; that Congress should determine major policies and guide the Tennessee Valley de-

[53] Dr. Morgan himself admitted the validity of some of the criticisms in the General Accounting Office audit report, as for example the maladjustment of house rents at Norris (see *Hearings before Military Affairs Committee, May, 1935*, p. 732). Dr. Morgan also recited an instance in which he had authorized expenditure of $8,000 on a house at Wheeler, while the actual cost was $17,000. "I feel as though they put it over on me a little bit so far as that house is concerned, and I am sorry" (*ibid.*, p. 733).

velopment is a simple axiom of representative government; that continued freedom will increase the dangers of abuse, as through degeneration in personnel or cumulative arrogation of unauthorized powers, is an argument worthy of consideration.

Meritorious as these arguments may be, it does not follow that most of the desirable results therein advocated are sacrificed under the system for which the T.V.A. has contended. No claim of irresponsibility is made; no lack of accountability need result. The following plea made by Dr. Morgan in committee hearings is pertinent:

I think that that discussion [proposed consultation of the committee with the Comptroller-General] should be in reference to the exceptions that are made to our actual conduct. If the actual working out of this situation in our hands has saved the disruption of the construction program, I think that that ought to come into the discussion, and not just a theoretical consideration.

If this criterion be accepted, the case of the T.V.A. for freedom from regular governmental procedures and strict General Accounting Office control is a strong one.

CHAPTER VII

THE RECONSTRUCTION FINANCE
CORPORATION GROUP

THE RECONSTRUCTION FINANCE CORPORATION

FROM a financial standpoint, by far the largest and most powerful of the federal corporate agencies is the Reconstruction Finance Corporation. As of March 31, 1937, the assets of the R.F.C. totaled $5,369,546,091.62,[1] which represents approximately half of the total assets of all government corporations as reported by the United States Treasury. Let us see what measure of freedom R.F.C. officials have enjoyed in the handling of such vast sums of public money.

In creating the R.F.C., Congress was greatly influenced by its predecessor in the industry financing field, the War Finance Corporation, and consequently there is a marked similarity between the two organic acts. Both agencies were created to meet a national emergency by the extension of credit, and both were left free to operate without serious restrictions other than those expressly included in the statutes. Thus an examination of the R.F.C. Act reveals the following provisions:[2]

1. The corporation is authorized to make loans "upon such terms and conditions not inconsistent with this Act as it may determine."[3]

2. The corporation may select and fix the compensation of its employees "without regard to the provisions of other laws" dealing with employment and compensation.[4]

3. The board of directors of the corporation shall determine and prescribe the manner in which its obligations shall be incurred and its expenses allowed and paid.

---

[1] *Report of RFC for the First Quarter of 1937*, p. 86.   [2] 47 Stat. 5 ff.

[3] It must be recognized that the major purposes of these loans are set out in the statutes, together with the classes of banks and other institutions to which loans may be made.

[4] However, a $10,000 limit on salaries was placed by the act of January 31, 1935 (49 Stat. 1).

4. Moneys of the corporation not otherwise employed may be deposited with the Treasurer of the United States subject to check by authority of the corporation or in any federal reserve bank.

5. Notwithstanding any other provision of law, the Reconstruction Finance Corporation is authorized and empowered to use as general funds all receipts arising from the sale or retirement of any of the stock, notes, bonds, or other securities acquired by it pursuant to any provision of law.[5]

From these provisions, it may be seen that the R.F.C. is not bound by the restrictive laws and regulations governing the use of public funds by the departments and establishments generally. An initial capitalization of $500,000,000 and the authorization to borrow some $5,500,000,000[6] have freed the corporation from annual appropriations. Actually, over $4,000,000,000 in notes of the R.F.C. was outstanding as of September 30, 1935, and over 90 per cent of this amount had been borrowed direct from the United States Treasury. All of such moneys constitute a revolving fund for carrying on the work of the corporation.

On the other hand, Congress, in addition to prescribing the major classes of loans which may be made, has set up certain general restrictions of which the following are merely illustrative. The aggregate amount of advances made to any one corporation is limited. Loans must be for a period not exceeding three years, or, with renewals, five years. Loans to railroads must not exceed at any one time $350,000,000. All loans must be "fully and adequately secured."[7]

The original R.F.C. act required the corporation to make

[5] This provision was not in the original act but is to be found in the act of January 31, 1935 (49 Stat. 5). It was designed, according to committee report, "to clear up any ambiguity which may exist at present as to the use and disposal of funds received by the corporation from the sale of obligations legally acquired by it" (see *House Report 10* [74th Cong.], p. 10).

[6] The limit set by 47 Stat. 714 is six and three-fifths the subscribed capital stock, but subsequent acts have added approximately $2,000,000,000 for various specific uses (see *R.F.C. Act as Amended* [revised March, 1937], p. 14, n. 35).

[7] Sec. 5, R.F.C. Act.

and publish a quarterly report of its operations to Congress, and the Emergency Relief and Construction Act of 1932 prescribed in addition a monthly report to the President and to Congress of activities and expenditures, together with a statement showing the names of the borrowers to whom loans and advances were made, and the amount and rate of interest involved in each case.[8]

Aside from the need for speed and flexibility in the conduct of a complex credit business such as that to be undertaken, the temporary nature of the R.F.C., as originally conceived by Congress, unquestionably had influence upon the measure of freedom actually granted. As Mr. Jesse Jones, chairman of the R.F.C. board, stated in 1932: "Congress undoubtedly had in mind that within a period of three years—five at the most—there should be such recovery and return to normal conditions as to make the lending by this governmental agency—the RFC—no longer necessary."[9]

In any event, no provision may be found in the statutes requiring an audit or the exercise of any control on the part of the General Accounting Office. When the original bill was being considered on the floor of the Senate, Senator Blaine offered an amendment as follows:

> *Provided*, That the Comptroller General of the United States, who may act personally or through such persons as he may designate or may employ without regard to the provisions of other laws of the United States and who shall be paid by the corporation at his request, compensation fixed by him, shall be the comptroller of the corporation with authority to prescribe the accounting procedure and *to determine the legal availability of the uses of the corporate assets.*[10]

In support of his amendment Senator Blaine argued that the work of the R.F.C. would be a very large undertaking

---

[8] For an interesting attack upon the secrecy surrounding R.F.C. loans prior to the passage of this act on July 21, 1932, see John T. Flynn, "Inside the RFC; An Adventure in Secrecy," *Harper's*, January, 1933. See also speech of Senator Norris, December 22, 1932, favoring complete publicity of R.F.C. loans (*Congressional Record*, LXXVI, 871–72).

[9] Quoted in *Congressional Record*, LXXVI, 875.

[10] *Ibid.*, LXXV, 1703. (Italics ours.)

and that some accounting procedure would be necessary; that the General Accounting Office was equipped and organized for that accounting procedure and was also equipped to determine the legal availability of the sums which might be appropriated under the act; and finally that "as a mere matter of business we ought to arrange for the accounting-system procedure, and also for some check of the activities of this board within the law as it may be passed." However, the question was immediately put, and the amendment was rejected without further discussion.

After the original act had been passed, Senator Blaine made another attempt when an amendatory bill was before Congress. He offered an amendment making the Comptroller-General the comptroller of the R.F.C. with power to prescribe and administer an accounting system, but omitting the section of his previous proposal which pertained to the legal availability of funds. Said Senator Blaine:

Mr. President, the amendment speaks for itself. The Senate will appreciate that the corporation, in case the pending bill is passed, will have under its control, as I understand, assets of about $3,500,000,000 or more. There is no provision made for the auditing of the accounts of the corporation. There is no business in the United States that can be conducted in a proper way without some system of auditing. The Comptroller General is the auditor for the United States respecting all other undertakings in which the Government has a financial interest, including the administration of the several departments of government.[11]

Upon his assurance that this was "simply a provision for auditing," Senator Blaine's amendment was agreed to by the Senate, but it was lost in the conference committee, and the entire bill was vetoed by President Hoover. Subsequent attempts to place the R.F.C. under the jurisdiction of the Comptroller-General have likewise failed.[12]

When the 1935 bill to extend the functions of the R.F.C. for two years was being considered, the following provision was inserted at the request of the Secretary of the Treasury:

[11] *Ibid.*, pp. 13580–81.

[12] See, e.g. S. 5572 (73d Cong.), "Requiring the RFC to be subject to the provisions of the Budget and Accounting Act of 1921."

No obligations, contingent or absolute, shall be incurred for the expenditure or other disposition of funds heretofore, hereby, or hereafter appropriated, or otherwise obtained for the carrying out of functions of Reconstruction Finance Corporation unless within estimates of such obligations and expenditures approved by the Director of the Budget; and, to the extent that the Secretary of the Treasury may consider practicable and under such rules and regulations as he may prescribe, there shall be maintained on the books of the Treasury Department such accounts as may be necessary to give full force and effect to this provision.[13]

Chairman Jones, when testifying before the House Committee on Banking and Currency, was careful to state that the foregoing section was inserted at the request of the Secretary of the Treasury; that to his knowledge there had been no controversy between the R.F.C. and the Secretary; and that it "is for you gentlemen to determine what you want."[14] He would not reply directly to a question about his own opinion as to the desirability of the section. However, upon further examination, he admitted that the effect would be to give the Budget Director and the Secretary of the Treasury a veto with reference to the amount and quality of R.F.C. loans, and that the work of the corporation *could be* hamstrung thereby.[15] Consequently, the House Committee rejected the provision, and it was also stricken out as undesirably restrictive by the Senate Banking and Currency Committee.

While such attempts to regulate the lending operation of the R.F.C. have failed, the use of funds for administrative expenses has not gone entirely unrestricted. In accord with presidential policy put into effect through executive orders in August and September of 1935, the R.F.C. has had to submit fiscal-year estimates of administrative expenses to the Budget Bureau in

---

[13] S. 1175 (74th Cong.), sec. 10.

[14] "To Extend the Functions of the RFC," *Hearings before House Committee on Banking and Currency, January, 1935*, pp. 18 ff.

[15] "QUESTION: 'They could ham-string you, if they took a notion to, with that section, could they not?' MR. JONES: 'I assume that is the effect of it; yes'" (*ibid.*, pp. 19–20).

advance of incurring obligations for such expenses.[16] Since the Director of the Budget was given the discretion to modify apportionments "upon the happening of some extraordinary emergency, or unusual circumstance," this requirement has not handicapped to any appreciable extent the operations of the corporation. On the other hand, it has encouraged careful budgetary planning.

In June, 1936, however, Congress, in passing a deficiency appropriation act, included a rather obscure section which appeared to be of serious portent. Section 7 prohibited the incurring, after June 30, 1937, of any obligations for administrative expenses except pursuant to an annual appropriation specifically therefor, on the part of over a dozen New Deal agencies, among which were included the following corporations: R.F.C., Commodity Credit Corporation, R.F.C. Mortgage Company, Electric Home and Farm Authority, Export-Import Bank, H.O.L.C., Federal Savings and Loan Insurance Corporation, Federal Surplus Commodities Corporation, and Federal Farm Mortgage Corporation.[17] Several questions immediately arose. What did the term "administrative expenses" embrace? Would "appropriation" be accompanied by the application of the statutes and rules governing expenditure of public funds generally? Would the General Accounting Office now have control over accounts and expenditures? Officials of the corporations named were quite understandably apprehensive of the outcome.

Actually, the worst fears of corporate officials have not been realized. Through consultation with the Budget Bureau, a comparatively satisfactory plan was evolved. To illustrate: the R.F.C. "appropriation" for administrative expenses during the fiscal year 1938 became rather an *authorization* for the use of $9,500,000 of the corporation's funds, and was so legislated by Congress.[18] The following were to be included in "adminis-

---

[16] See executive orders Nos. 7126 (August 5, 1935) and 7150 (August 19, 1935).

[17] See 49 Stat. 1648.

[18] See Pub. No. 171 (75th Cong.), approved June 28, 1937.

trative expenses": personal services; travel expenses; printing and binding; books and periodicals; procurement of supplies, equipment, and services; typewriters, adding machines, and other labor-saving devices, including their repair and exchange; rent; and use of the services and facilities of the federal reserve banks. From the corporation's point of view, however, the two provisos of the act are most important. The first declares that all necessary expenses in connection with the acquisition, operation, maintenance, improvement, or disposition of any real or personal property belonging to the R.F.C., or in which that corporation has an interest, including expenses of collections of pledged collateral, "shall be considered as non-administrative expenses for the purposes hereof." The second provides that except for the limitation in amount and the requirement that travel expenses be in accord with government travel regulations, "the administrative expenses and other obligations of the corporation shall be incurred, allowed, and paid" as before, i.e., in the manner prescribed by the board of directors.

In practice, therefore, the board of directors of the R.F.C. has exercised a wide latitude in financial operations, within statutory limits, and is responsible only to Congress and the President. In securing funds above the initial capitalization, the approval of the Secretary of the Treasury is necessary,[19] but, once borrowings are actually made, the board itself is the final authority in the utilization of such funds. Lending policy and determination of the amount and quality of loans are subject to the supervision of no other governmental agency. All funds may be used in general operations, but it has been the policy of the board to keep a minimum above repayments to the Treasury on R.F.C. notes; interest charges are kept down in this way.

[19] Chairman Jones stated before a House committee that, "of course, we can only lend the money that the Secretary of the Treasury permits us to lend, because if he does not buy our notes, lend us money, or permit us to sell our notes, we would have no funds" (*Hearings, House Committee on Banking and Currency, January, 1935,* p. 19).

Expenditures such as the purchase of supplies and travel allowances have not been governed by ordinary governmental regulations but are determined by the corporation itself.[20] In practice, governmental regulations have been followed wherever practicable—thus most materials are purchased from the General Supply list—but in an emergency, or wherever deemed desirable, expenditures approved by the board are quite legal. An illustration may be taken from the feverish days of the bank crisis in 1933, at which time resolutions passed by the board were telegraphed to field agents at considerable cost. These messages sent out at night were designed to permit threatened banks to open the next morning upon the assurance of a loan, and many banks were saved. Much was at stake; there was little place for red tape here! In the matter of ordinary purchases, such as furniture and office supplies, the R.F.C. does not have anything like the serious problem which confronts the T.V.A. in its huge construction projects.

Finally, in the matter of accounting, the R.F.C. has its own auditing division, which maintains a continuous internal audit of the Washington office, and makes periodical examinations of custodians and loan agencies. In addition, it has been the practice of the directors to have an outside audit made annually for their own information.

Before leaving the R.F.C., we should notice the attitude of Comptroller-General McCarl. In the first place, Mr. McCarl recognized that the statutes exempted the R.F.C. from any control or audit by his office.[21] Regarding the advisability of this freedom, however, the first Comptroller-General was hardly so resigned, as the following excerpt from his 1932 report reveals:

It is appreciated that when the Government undertakes the conduct of a corporate activity, commercial in nature, there may frequently be required expenditures, which, because of the nature of the activity, can not be allowed by the accounting officers under laws applying to government

[20] Travel expenses were finally brought under regular government regulations in 1937 (see Pub. No. 171 [75th Cong.]).

[21] *Annual Report of the Comptroller General, 1932*, p. 15.

transactions generally. It does not, however, necessarily follow that because this is true the expenditures of the activity as a whole should be devoid of or immune from an independent audit by this office. Rather does it mean that in framing the independent audit provision for incorporation in the legislation creating the corporate activity language should be embodied—in the form of a proviso or otherwise—to the effect that in auditing such of its expenditures as otherwise are correct credit shall be allowed for those necessitated solely by the nature of the activity without regard to their conformity with laws applicable to public expenditure generally.[22]

In accordance with this view, Mr. McCarl recommended in 1932 that administrative expenses of the R.F.C., as opposed to loaning transactions, be controlled and audited in his office.[23] Subsequently, in 1933, he suggested the bringing of all R.F.C. funds under his control with a proviso authorizing his discretionary allowance of expenditures "not otherwise allowable, if and when established to be reasonably necessary to a proper functioning of the legally authorized activities of the corporation."[24] In the latter instance, the Comptroller-General stated:

As to the wisdom and advisability of enacting the proposed legislation, I may say that since the capital of the corporation is derived from funds appropriated by the United States, no sound reason is apparent why the corporation should be exempted from the accounting prescribed by law for governmental agencies generally merely because by the act creating it the corporation is given the status of a private corporation.

Mr. McCarl was probably correct in his assertion that the mere fact of corporate status offers no sound reason for exemption of the R.F.C. from regular governmental auditing control. Yet this does not meet the issue. It is not contended that corporate status is the justification for exemption; rather

[22] *Ibid.*, pp. 14-15.

[23] Unpublished MS, April 21, 1932. Mr. McCarl stated that the existing procedure "might be necessary and proper with respect to the money to be used for loans and other authorized financial transactions of the Corporation, but with respect to funds to be used for the payment of salaries and other administrative expenses of the Corporation . . . . no reason is apparent why they should not be carried in the Treasury as are other appropriated moneys and disbursed and accounted for as such."

[24] Unpublished MS, February 21, 1933.

is the business activity to be undertaken of such a nature as to warrant a freedom from regular governmental procedures, and utilization of the corporate device is largely the result of this need for freedom. In view of Mr. McCarl's attitude toward other corporate enterprises such as the Fleet Corporation and the Tennessee Valley Authority, it is doubtful whether the Comptroller-General, with his legal and accounting approach to the problem, is the proper official in whom there should be exclusively vested the administrative and discretionary power of determining "necessary expenditures." To date, as we have indicated, Congress has not adopted Comptroller-General McCarl's proposal that the jurisdiction of the General Accounting Office be extended to include transactions of the Reconstruction Finance Corporation.

THE COMMODITY CREDIT CORPORATION

The Commodity Credit Corporation is in reality an arm of the Reconstruction Finance Corporation. While technically there is no connection other than the presence of several R.F.C. officers on the board of the commodity agency, the latter has actually been made an integral part of the R.F.C. in order to avoid expense and duplication. R.F.C. field agencies act as examiners and distributors of the money that is loaned on corn and cotton. Direct disbursements on loans to farmers are made by the R.F.C. agents, but the bookkeeping transaction records a loan by the R.F.C. to the Commodity Credit Corporation and a subsequent loan by the latter corporation to the farmer. In this manner the money "borrowed" by the Commodity Credit Corporation does not pass through its hands at all, except as the R.F.C. employees may be considered its agents.

Because of this close tie-up, and because of the fact that operations of the Commodity Credit Corporation have been carried on almost entirely with funds borrowed from the R.F.C.,[25] any significant control of financial transactions, for

[25] As of December 31, 1935, over $600,000,000, of which approximately $300,000,000 was then outstanding, had been borrowed from the R.F.C. This

example, on the part of the General Accounting Office, is contingent upon control of the R.F.C.

Several questions have arisen, however, and the one which has been the subject of most dispute is that as to the utilization of earnings, or interest, in administration and operation. This question arose in July, 1934, when a letter from the Comptroller-General called attention to Executive Order 6549,[26] prescribing an audit of corporation transactions, and to the appropriation act providing funds for such audit purposes. Mr. McCarl's letter stated that accounts of all receipts and expenditures must be regularly filed in the General Accounting Office for settlement and adjustment as in the case of regular departments and establishments, that all funds except from the sale of stock should be deposited in the Treasury for withdrawal on accountable warrants, and that interest and earnings on funds must be covered into the Treasury as miscellaneous receipts, to be withdrawn only after congressional appropriation.[27] With respect to funds disbursed (direct to farmers) by R.F.C. to the account of the Commodity Credit Corporation, Mr. McCarl said that this was purely a bookkeeping transaction, and the corporation need render no accounting therefor. However, when borrowed funds from the R.F.C. were actually received, all interest earned thereon[28] must be covered into the Treasury and thus be lost to the corporation.

The reply of the Commodity Credit Corporation[29] expressed a willingness to co-operate in the rendition of accounts but disagreed as to the covering of funds into the Treasury. Funds

---

may be compared to the Commodity Credit Corporation's capital stock, which amounted to only $3,000,000 at that time. The subsequent issue of $97,000,000 additional stock, subscribed by the R.F.C. in accordance with 49 Stat. 1191 has decreased the ratio of borrowings to capital.

[26] Quoted on p. 129, above.   [27] Unpublished MS, July 5, 1934.

[28] Because funds were borrowed from the R.F.C. at 3 per cent and reloaned to farmers at 4 per cent, it was possible for the Commodity Credit Corporation to net 1 per cent in the transaction.

[29] August 6, 1934.

of the corporation were not "appropriated" funds; therefore, interest on invested funds both from stock and borrowings should remain available for further use. Such earnings were needed for administrative expenses and also as additional collateral on R.F.C. loans, which must be "adequately secured."

The Comptroller-General reiterated his position,[30] said that the $3,000,000 allocated from National Industrial Recovery funds for purchase of capital stock was really an appropriation, and again maintained that all earnings actually received by the corporation must be covered into the Treasury. He opined, however, that the corporation's problem of administrative expenses could be taken care of by the interest earned on R.F.C. funds which were "borrowed" but not actually handled. This latter ruling quite rightly puzzled corporation officials since any such earnings to be used in administrative expenses must have been "received" by the corporation, and according to Mr. McCarl's position must immediately be covered into the Treasury.

Consequently, on December 1, 1934, the Comptroller-General modified his position by ruling that all interest earned on money borrowed from the R.F.C. might be used in operation, *provided* that at the end of business on June 16, 1935, all which remained should be covered into the Treasury.[31]

In the meantime, however, compliance with the Comptroller's rulings was not given, and legislation was sought to extend the life of the corporation and to settle the question of utilizing earnings. As a result, the Act of January 31, 1935, which extended the R.F.C., also gave the Commodity Credit Corporation legislative sanction, extended its life, and provided that "the corporation is hereby authorized to use all its assets, including capital and net earnings therefrom, and all moneys which have been or may hereafter be allocated to or borrowed by it, in the exercise of its functions as such agency, including the making of loans on agricultural commodities."

[30] Unpublished MS, September 5, 1934.

[31] Unpublished MS, December 1, 1934.

The Comptroller-General acquiesced in this congressional sanction of the corporation's use of earnings.

Like the R.F.C., the Commodity Credit Corporation has been required to submit annual estimates of administrative expenses to the Budget Bureau and, since June, 1937, to have the total approved in advance by Congress. While the General Accounting Office contended that from the latter date such funds should be considered as appropriated moneys subject to regular accountable procedure, corporation officials have refused to accept this interpretation. They consider the statutes[32] as limiting the amount of corporation funds which may be used for expenses, yet without changing the status of those funds.

In practice, the Commodity Credit Corporation has carried in a checking account with the Treasurer of the United States an amount deemed sufficient to meet current operating expenses. All other funds are paid to the R.F.C. for application upon the indebtedness of Commodity Credit Corporation, under an arrangement whereby the R.F.C. has agreed to refund, from time to time, funds, within the limitation of the original commitments granted to the commodity corporation, to replenish the operating expense account carried with the Treasurer of the United States.

In the matter of expenditures, the Commodity Credit Corporation has not considered itself bound by the regular governmental regulations. An illustration is the contract granted in 1935 to the American Cotton Cooperative Association, for reconcentration[33] of cotton which had been pledged to the corporation to secure loans. The contract was a large one, and when disappointed low bidders complained, the corporation

[32] See 49 Stat. 1648 and Pub. No. 171 (75th Cong.). The Commodity Credit Corporation received substantially the same treatment as the R.F.C. (see above, pp. 161–62).

[33] Storage charges in rural areas were proving to be so high that economy demanded the gathering and restorage of the cotton in larger quantities and in fewer localities.

explained the transactions as follows: (1) Government regulations were not binding. The problem was to get the best bargain on a business basis. (2) A large amount of cotton was to be shipped. All firms capable of handling the matter were informed, so no advertising was necessary. Only two proposals were submitted for moving the entire amount.[34] The corporation considered the matter carefully and was thoroughly satisfied as to the reliability, facilities, and personnel of the American Cotton Cooperative Association, whose offer was considered the best bargain.

Thus the Commodity Credit Corporation considered that the facts would have justified the contract even under government regulation and previous rulings of the Comptroller-General. Without conceding the exemption from government regulations, which he had maintained were applicable, Mr. McCarl upheld the contract "in view of the facts as reported."[35] This is an instance in which the government regulations were liberally construed in favor of administrative judgment.

Another instance of administrative flexibility is the policy of the Commodity Credit Corporation to waive underpayments of less than one dollar and to make no refunds on overpayments of less than one dollar (unless requested to do so by the producer) in the matter of collecting on producers' notes. The complex collection procedure frequently results in small errors, due, for example, to the exact calculation of interest. In the view of the corporation, the attempted correction of all minor errors would result in an overhead expense far exceeding the value of the transactions; hence they are disregarded. Such a

[34] It may be noted that many "lower bids" were by small firms which desired to move only a part of the cotton.

[35] Unpublished MS, September 6, 1935. Mr. McCarl stated that complaints of other bidders need not be heeded since "it has been administratively concluded to be necessary to have one organization in charge of the reconcentration movement which could operate throughout the cotton producing area." Furthermore "the record discloses that every organization deemed qualified to conduct satisfactorily a movement of the volume contemplated had knowledge of the plans for reconcentration of the cotton and had an opportunity of submitting a proposal with respect thereto."

policy is good business, but it would be heresy for a regular governmental establishment!

Ordinary purchases of the Commodity Credit Corporation are made through the R.F.C. and in the same manner, that is, in conformance with governmental regulations except in extreme cases.

Accounts covering administrative expenses are submitted regularly to the General Accounting Office for a continuous post-audit. Accounts of money borrowed from the R.F.C. are not included. So far, no serious controversy has arisen concerning the General Accounting Office audit. As a matter of fact, exceptions taken by the Comptroller-General could only be in the form of protests; no power of coercion exists because there is no control over the sources of the corporation's funds. To repeat, effective General Accounting Office control of the Commodity Credit Corporation could come only through control of the Reconstruction Finance Corporation.

THE R.F.C. MORTGAGE COMPANY

While industries, farmers, and homeowners were being extended credit by existing governmental agencies, a need was felt in 1935 for some organization to give financial aid to distressed hotels, apartments, and other urban income-producing property. Although such assistance could not be given directly by the R.F.C., officers of that agency incorporated the R.F.C. Mortgage Company as a private mortgage loan company under the laws of Maryland.[36] All the capital stock was purchased by the R.F.C. under a general statutory authorization to purchase capital stock of mortgage loan associations or companies. All of the directors of the R.F.C. Mortgage Company are officers of the R.F.C., and managers of the R.F.C. field agencies act as agents for the mortgage company.

To supplement capital from the sale of stock, funds are borrowed from the R.F.C. just as any private company might

---

[36] The certificate of incorporation is similar to that of any private mortgage company organized in the state of Maryland.

do.[37] All moneys are used as a revolving fund. There is no question of covering into the Treasury, or of congressional appropriations. Surplus funds for operation are deposited with the R.F.C., and repayments on loans are made to that agency from time to time.

Purchases are made through the R.F.C., and in the same manner as by that corporation. No annual report is required; none has as yet been made. Accountability is to the R.F.C. as stockholder, rather than to the general government.

The General Accounting Office in 1935 declined to recognize the R.F.C. Mortgage Company as a governmental agency. Mr. McCarl's attitude was revealed by a ruling in which he refused to assign a governmental symbol for use in front of serial numbers on corporation travel requests. The Comptroller-General pointed out that Congress had not expressly authorized the R.F.C.—an instrumentality of the United States—to organize independent corporations under state laws for the purpose of carrying out its functions. Consequently, he stated that the action of Alley, Schwulst, and Slacks, employees of the R.F.C.,

. . . . in organizing the RFC Mortgage Company under the laws of the state of Maryland must be regarded as action in their individual capacities and not as officials or representatives of the United States. And while this office does not question the authority of the RFC, with the approval of the President to purchase the entire capital stock of the mortgage corporation created by said individuals, the said corporation remains a private corporation rather than an agency of the Federal Government.[38]

The deficiency appropriation act of June, 1936, however, numbered the R.F.C. Mortgage Company among those governmental agencies whose administrative expenses must be approved by Congress. When this provision was put into effect in June, 1937, the legislators merely provided that the

[37] As of December 31, 1935, $25,000,000 in loans to the R.F.C. Mortgage Company had been authorized by the R.F.C. (see *RFC, Summary of Activities, January, 1936*, p. 5).

[38] Unpublished MS, August 6, 1935.

$9,500,000 for administrative expenses of the R.F.C. should cover the mortgage company as well.[39]

THE ELECTRIC HOME AND FARM AUTHORITY

Whereas the original Electric Home and Farm Authority had been incorporated in Delaware as a subsidiary of the Tennessee Valley Authority, its capitalization was taken over in 1935 by a second Electric Home and Farm Authority, incorporated in the District of Columbia, and designated as an agency of the United States by the executive order of August 12, 1935.[40] This latter corporation, which is not confined in its operations to the Tennessee Valley area, is technically distinct from the R.F.C., but in view of the fact that its directors are officers of the R.F.C., and since its success is contingent upon the guaranty of R.F.C. credit, we may consider it as one of the related group.

In carrying on its operations, the E.H.F.A. is dependent upon short-term borrowings from commercial banks. This supply of funds is necessary because the ordinary receipts of the corporation are in the form of collections, or instalments, on contracts relating to electrical appliances purchased by individual customers. Bank loans are negotiated in anticipation of collections. The E.H.F.A. has had no trouble negotiating these loans at favorable interest rates, largely because each loan is covered by an R.F.C. commitment of the same amount, under an arrangement which is virtually a guaranty of such loans by the R.F.C. Actually, the lower interest rates of the private banks are secured, and no money is borrowed from the government lending agency.

In the drawing-up of the present E.H.F.A. charter, the Comptroller-General was consulted as to a borrowing limitation, with the result that the corporation can borrow only up to the amount of commercial paper held by it. Actually, whatever may have been the intention of the General Accounting Office, the limitation is quite elastic because borrowings are

---

[39] Pub. No. 171 (75th Cong.).   [40] Executive Order No. 7139.

used to make more contracts; hence more commercial paper is received; hence more loans are possible. In short, the "limitation" is capable of indefinite expansion.

The E.H.F.A. prides itself on the fact that its operations are conducted on a business-like basis. For example, in the negotiation of contracts, prospective customers are checked as to character, ability to pay, job prospects, etc. Contracts with dealers call for repurchase by them of equipment upon which payments are defaulted by the individual customer. When the E.H.F.A. was an integral part of the Tennessee Valley Authority program, the distribution of an attractive photo-pamphlet was deemed necessary to get people interested and informed regarding the services of the corporation. The Comptroller-General objected to these pamphlets, which cost approximately twenty-five cents apiece, but they were considered a part of sound business policy by corporation officials.

E.H.F.A. officials do not consider themselves bound by regular governmental regulations in the matter of expenditures. This position is taken in spite of the following ruling made by the General Accounting Office with respect to the first Electric Home and Farm Authority:

Executive Order No. 6514, December 9, 1933, by which the formation of the Electric Home and Farm Authority, Inc., is authorized, expressly designates such corporation as a government agency within the purview of the National Industrial Recovery Act and it is considered that as such, the said corporation is required to conform as nearly as possible to well established principles in the transactions of its business. All moneys of the corporation are Government moneys and expenditures therefrom should not be otherwise than subject to the same safeguards and rules and the same accountability as attend expenditures of public moneys by other departments and agencies of the Government.[41]

However, ordinary purchases do not present any serious problem, and government rules are ordinarily followed as a matter of policy, both to protect the corporation from criticism and to forestall unnecessary altercations with the General Accounting Office.

[41] Unpublished MS, October 31, 1934.

The only serious dispute with the Comptroller-General has been with regard to the handling of collections, or receipts, and surplus funds; in this respect, the case is similar to that of the Commodity Credit Corporation. E.H.F.A. funds are kept in a checking account with the Treasury of the United States in the name of the corporation treasurer. Collections are used to maintain this operating fund, which can be drawn upon as needed, as well as in the repayment of private bank loans. The Comptroller-General has objected to this practice and has demanded that a special deposit account be set up on the books of the Treasury, from which withdrawals should be made only upon requisitions approved by him.

As the Electric Home and Farm Authority has been designated an agency of the United States in Executive Order No. 7139, dated August 12, 1935, its funds which have heretofore been carried in an official checking account with the Treasury of the United States in the name of its treasurer . . . . should be transferred from the checking account *supra*, deposited into the Treasury of the United States, withdrawn therefrom on accountable warrants, and accounted for pursuant to law.[42]

The corporation, on the other hand, has taken the position that there is no legal authority for such a demand, that rather does its corporate status include the right to use funds as needed, and that, since administrative freedom might be endangered, compliance will not be given.

Annual estimates of E.H.F.A. administrative expenses are approved by the Budget Bureau and Congress. The 1937 appropriation act expressly excepts from the $400,000 limitation (as "nonadministrative") "all necessary expenses (including special services performed on a contract or fee basis, but not including other personal services) in connection with the acquisition, care, repair, and disposition of any security or collateral now or hereafter held or acquired by the Authority."

Until 1936, no annual report was required of E.H.F.A. However, the act of March 31, 1936, which continued the Authority as an agency of the United States and sanctioned the use of its

---

[42] Unpublished MS, December 14, 1935.

funds in operation, required in the future an annual financial and business report. In the matter of auditing, accounts have been submitted to the General Accounting Office for continuous post-audit. This was done voluntarily by corporation officials even before January, 1934, at which time the executive order which we have already noted extended the jurisdiction of the Comptroller-General to New Deal corporations. This arrangement is quite satisfactory to the corporation as affording an exact check on collections and disbursements. No outside private audit is made, but in addition to its continuous checkup, the General Accounting Office made upon request a thorough examination of all books in the E.H.F.A. offices at the time of the creation of the second corporation.

Some minor exceptions have been taken to E.H.F.A. accounts by the Comptroller-General, but no serious trouble has arisen. Should such exceptions not be voluntarily acquiesced in, it is difficult to see how they could be enforced, unless the Comptroller-General should acquire some control over the corporation's sources of funds. Of course, that control would exist should the E.H.F.A. agree to the deposit of its funds for withdrawal upon accountable warrants for which the Comptroller's signature is required.

THE EXPORT-IMPORT BANK OF WASHINGTON

The Export-Import Bank of Washington is distinct from the Reconstruction Finance Corporation, but the influence of the latter agency is felt through the presence of R.F.C. officers on the bank's board of directors and through the R.F.C.'s subscription to the preferred stock of the bank. As of December 31, 1936, the R.F.C. had subscribed to $20,000,000 of stock and had committed itself to purchase an additional amount of $15,000,000 on demand of the bank. In view of this supply of funds from the R.F.C., the Export-Import Bank's power to borrow money, with the approval of the Secretary of the Treasury, has not been exercised.

The Export-Import Bank is engaged in extending credits to

exporters and importers, supplementing ordinary commercial bank credits, to meet the abnormal situation in the foreign credit field produced in the depression years. The intricate nature of such a banking business has been recognized by the Comptroller-General as incompatible with strict requirements of his office, although the exact nature of the relationship which should exist between the two agencies has been the subject of disagreement.

In practice, purchasing regulations of the government are followed as a matter of policy. The purchasing problem of the bank has been of slight importance, and consequently there has been no disposition to question the legal applicability of government rules. The same is true of travel regulations and other incidental rules governing the expenditure of public funds. However, in May, 1934, the Comptroller-General ruled that no legal objection would be made if the special adviser to the President on foreign trade undertook to make certain purchases and to handle some administrative work for the Export-Import Bank in the interest of economy—the bank to make reimbursement for the expenses involved.[43]

A serious altercation with the Comptroller-General was prevented by the passage of the act of January 31, 1935, extending the R.F.C. In addition to extending the life of the Export-Import banks and giving them a statutory basis as "agencies of the United States," section 9 of this act provided that "they are hereby authorized to use all of their assets, including capital and net earnings therefrom, except such earnings as may be required from time to time to pay dividends upon their preferred capital stock, and to use all moneys which have been or may hereafter be allocated to or borrowed by them, in the exercise of their functions as such agencies."[44] Prior to this act, Mr. McCarl had taken the position, just as in the case of the Commodity Credit Corporation and the E.H.F.A., that earnings should be covered into the Treasury and not used in operation. The Export-Import Bank had not complied, how-

---

[43] Unpublished MS, May 19, 1934.   [44] 49 Stat. 4.

ever, and the provision was designed by bank officials as a sanction of their position. Actually, earnings have been used in operations and for meeting administrative expenses, and a checking account has been maintained with the United States Treasury. Like the other corporations in the R.F.C. group, the Export-Import Bank has been limited in the amount of such expenses by advance approval of the Bureau of the Budget and Congress.

In the matter of accounting, the Export-Import Bank has complied with executive order and submits accounts to the General Accounting Office for a continuous post-audit.

SUMMARY

The largest and most powerful of all federal corporations, the Reconstruction Finance Corporation, was conceived as a temporary agency for ameliorating distressing economic conditions in the United States through the extension of credit to private financing institutions. The complexity of such a huge banking business and the urgency of the economic situation were undoubtedly responsible for the congressional grant of a large degree of freedom and discretion in the utilization of public funds. The restrictions upon R.F.C. transactions that do exist are to be found in the statutes directly relating to that corporation, and complete freedom from General Accounting Office control is enjoyed. The original R.F.C. act is of particular interest because it is the first instance in which Congress expressly authorized a government corporation to "determine and prescribe the manner" of incurring obligations and allowing and paying expenses. In practice, the R.F.C. has normally followed governmental regulations regarding expenditures, but the discretionary power to meet exceptional or emergency situations has been retained and occasionally exercised. An elaborate accounting and auditing system has been set up within the corporation itself, and an annual audit by private accountants has been ordered by the directors. Congress and the President are kept informed concerning R.F.C. transactions through monthly reports of activities and expenditures and through complete reports of operations four times each year.

Closely related to the R.F.C. in one way or another are the Commodity Credit Corporation, the R.F.C. Mortgage Company, the Electric Home and Farm Authority, and the Export-Import Bank.[45] These corporations are all engaged in banking or credit operations and are managed with a considerable degree of freedom from regular governmental procedures. Disputes with the Comptroller-General regarding the use of earnings have been settled in the case of the Commodity Credit Corporation and the Export-Import Bank by express congressional sanction of the position taken by corporation officials that such funds should be available for continued use in operations. While the R.F.C. Mortgage Company was declared a private agency by Mr. McCarl, the Commodity Credit Corporation, the E.H.F.A., and the Export-Import Bank all submit accounts to the General Accounting Office for continuous post-audit. However, the Comptroller-General, because of his lack of control over the sources of corporation funds, has not had coercive powers. The submission of accounts for audit has not been objected to, but the details of such an audit have been continuously under discussion. Complete General Accounting Office control, such as that exercised over government departments, is impossible so long as the Reconstruction Finance Corporation remains without the Comptroller-General's jurisdiction.

Estimates of administrative expenses of all the "R.F.C." corporations have been controlled by the Budget Bureau since 1935, and since the declaration of a congressional policy in June, 1936, such estimates must be approved annually in appropriation acts.

---

[45] The recently created Disaster Loan Corporation has hardly established separate identity, and as yet may be considered as a phase of Reconstruction Finance Corporation activity.

CHAPTER VIII
OTHER NEW DEAL CORPORATIONS

THE HOME OWNERS' LOAN CORPORATION

THE Home Owners' Loan Corporation was created distinctly as an emergency agency. Its purpose was to give immediate relief to financially distressed home-owners who otherwise would lose their homes through foreclosure or who, even if they had no mortgage on their property, were finding it impossible to obtain money from private sources with which to pay taxes and provide for necessary maintenance and repair. The urgency of the situation, the need for prompt action, undoubtedly influenced Congress in giving the corporation a large measure of freedom in financial matters.[1] Thus, we find in the organic act authorization for the board of directors to determine the amount of capital stock;[2] to issue bonds; to select and compensate employees "without regard to the provisions of other laws"; to declare dividends to the United States if desired; to liquidate the corporation when its purposes are accomplished and to pay at that time "any surplus or accumulated funds" into the Treasury of the United States; and to prescribe by-laws, rules and regulations for "the accomplishment of the purposes and intent" of the act.[3] Furthermore, the corporation "shall determine its necessary expenditures under this Act and the manner in which they shall be incurred, allowed, and paid, without regard to the provisions of any other law governing the expenditure of public funds." It will be noted that this authorization is even stronger than the some-

---

[1] Cf. Mr. Boylan's statement in the House, April 28, 1933: "The Gentleman knows this is emergency legislation. The Gentleman knows also that were we to wait for Civil Service examinations, and whatnot, perhaps the exigency necessitating this legislation will have passed" (*Congressional Record*, LXXVII, 2569).

[2] Up to a $200,000,000 maximum.   [3] 48 Stat. 129 ff.

what similar one given the R.F.C. because of the express exemption contained in the last clause, which is not included in the R.F.C. Act. The potential difference is illustrated in the following decision of the Comptroller-General regarding expenditures of the Federal Home Loan Bank Board, which by law are to be made in the same manner as are those of the R.F.C.:

Section 19 of the Federal Home Loan Bank Act which provides that the board "shall determine its necessary expenditures under this act and the manner in which they shall be incurred, allowed and paid," relates to administrative procedures not otherwise controllable by law and *does not dispense with the provisions of Sections 3709 and 3743, Revised Statutes*. Purchase of a rug in the open market will not be further questioned but future purchases must be made from the General Supply Committee or in compliance with Section 3709, Revised Statutes.[4]

The H.O.L.C.'s freedom did not go entirely uncontested in Congress, however. When the establishing act was under discussion, Mr. Goss proposed to strike out the clause "without regard to the provisions of any other law governing the expenditure of public funds" and to substitute therefor the words "subject to such restrictions as the Budget Director or the President of the United States may prescribe."[5] In explanation, Mr. Goss stated: "In other words, as long as we are doing away with the provisions of the law governing the expenditure of public funds, I thought it only proper to put it under the direction of the Bureau of the Budget as well as of the President of the United States."

This suggestion, however, was voted down by the House, and the original language was accepted. Consequently, the role of the Director of the Budget became an advisory rather than a controlling one. This fact is brought out in an interesting col-

[4] Unpublished MS, October 12, 1932. (Italics ours.) The Federal Home Loan Bank Board, as a noncorporate agency, does not have the presumption of financial freedom that has come to characterize most government corporations. Thus Mr. McCarl's ruling is not surprising, but the inclusion of the language "without regard to the provisions of any other law" would have made such a decision impossible.

[5] *Congressional Record*, LXXVII, 2568.

loquy which occurred in 1934, when Congress was considering the guaranty of H.O.L.C. bonds to insure a plentiful supply of funds:

Mr. Busby: Why is it that you have to so carefully take into consideration what the Director of the Budget may say about the funds that are available to you?

Mr. Fahey (Chairman HOLC Board of Directors): Only that the Director of the Budget watches all of these operations.

Mr. Busby: He knows that you are authorized to use $2,000,000,000, does he not?

Mr. Fahey: Yes.

Mr. Busby: Do you regard it his business to censure the amount you shall have from time to time?

Mr. Fahey: No, sir.

Mr Busby: Does he do that?

Mr Fahey: No; he does not.

Mr. Busby: Do you want a free hand to go ahead and apply that $2,000,000,000 as speedily as may be done to relieve these distressed people?

Mr. Fahey: Absolutely.[6]

Again in 1935, the Director of the Budget was thrown into the picture when amendatory legislation was under consideration. Just as we have noted in the case of the R.F.C., the Secretary of the Treasury proposed a provision which would make all obligations and expenditures of the H.O.L.C. and the Federal Savings and Loan Insurance Corporation contingent upon the Budget Director's approval.[7] When this section was considered in committee, Chairman Fahey, just as R.F.C. Chairman Jones before him, was very reluctant about criticizing it because of its origin.[8] Finally, however, he declared that the

[6] "To Guarantee Bonds of HOLC," *Hearings before House Committee on Banking and Currency* (73d Cong., 2d sess. [March, 1934]), p. 83.

[7] S. 1771 (74th Cong.), sec. 22. The language of this provision was identical with that in the R.F.C. case (see above, p. 160).

[8] "Senator Bulkley: What position does your Board take about it?

"Mr. Fahey: We have not taken any specific attitude with reference to it at all, Mr. Chairman. It was proposed by the Budget and the Treasury, and we included it in the bill.

[Footnote continued on following page]

submission in advance of anticipated expenditures would be a "pretty difficult thing for this corporation to do."

Here we have hundreds of thousands of applicants for loans now in process, some of which are rejected at various stages of the procedure, so that, as a matter of fact, we only know from week to week and month to month how many bonds we will actually issue, and the same thing is true with reference to cash. So far as cash is concerned, we cannot, and we do not sell any bonds in order to provide cash, except with the approval of the Secretary of the Treasury and at appropriate times, so that the cash end of it is taken care of.[9]

General Counsel Russell was more outspoken than Mr. Fahey, and, after pointing out that the proposed section would give the Budget Director even more control than he exercises over the regular departments, he asserted that "it seems to me it is a question of who should exercise the discretion in a large business operation of this kind."

It seems to me that the Congress has already recognized the difference which this amendment attempts to wipe out, in setting this up as a corporation and comparing it, therefore, with a business establishment, instead of with a governmental agency in this respect. This amendment would attempt to wipe out that distinction, and to say that this is a governmental agency in all respects, that can anticipate in detail its expenditures and operations a year in advance. . . . . I think, as the language is written, Senator, the corporation could not either incur an obligation or expend any money unless the Director of the Budget approved it.

"SENATOR BULKLEY: Do you think it would be a practical thing?

"MR. FAHEY: We really could not say that.

"SENATOR BULKLEY: We have to rely on you to tell us what you think. We are trying to come to a wise conclusion.

"MR. FAHEY: I suppose we could take that up in the Board and discuss it and give you our opinion on it.

"SENATOR BULKLEY: If you do not think it is practicable, I think you ought to say so. We are interested to hear what you do think.

"MR. FAHEY: Frankly, we do feel that it would certainly complicate the operation to a certain extent" (*Hearings, Subcommittee of Senate Committee on Banking and Currency, March, 1935*, p. 214).

[9] *Ibid.*, pp. 214–15.

In conclusion, and in reply to the question as to what extent the H.O.L.C. should be permitted to incur obligations for the expenditure of money, Mr. Russell said:

In my opinion, it should be permitted to incur obligations, as the statute says, in the discretion of the board of directors, and that is in accord with the Reconstruction Finance Corporation, for which you have just recently passed a law and left this section out. It is in accord with the administration of all these business agencies that the Government is dealing with.[10]

This view was accepted by committees of both houses of Congress, and the section recommended by the Secretary of the Treasury was eliminated.

Since the intent of Congress seems quite clear, it will be interesting to review a number of the Comptroller-General's decisions respecting expenditures of the H.O.L.C. Soon after the passage of the original act, and in view of the provisions thereof, Mr. McCarl ruled that employees of the H.O.L.C. were not subject to 15 per cent reduction in compensation, or to general statutory restrictions on annual and sick leave; that purchases of equipment for the corporation need not be made from General Supply Committee contractors; that printing for the corporation was not required to be done at the Government Printing Office; and that travel and subsistence expenses of employees were not necessarily governed by the standardized travel regulations.[11] However, the corporation could not pay the compensation of clerks, or for equipment installed, in the Treasury Department by reason of additional work resulting from the activities of the corporation. Quoting section 4(j) of the H.O.L.C. act,[12] Mr. McCarl stated:

The above quoted provision is the only one authorizing payment by the HOLC of the expenses of another Government agency, and, having

---

[10] *Ibid.*, p. 217.   [11] Unpublished MS, June 28, 1933.

[12] This section reads in part: "The corporation shall pay such proportion of the salary and expenses of the members of the Board [Federal Home Loan Bank Board] and of its officers and employees as the Board may determine to be equitable, and may use the facilities of Federal Home Loan Banks, upon making reasonable compensation therefor as determined by the Board."

thus specified the expenditures permissible, it excludes reimbursement or advances to any other Government agency for expenses to which it may be put solely by reason of the additional work which may result from the activities of the corporation.[13]

A month later, however, the Comptroller-General agreed to the handling of H.O.L.C. bonds by the Public Debt Service of the Treasury, which was fully organized and equipped to handle such bonds at considerably less expense than would be incurred if the corporation were to set up its own organization. Either a special working fund or reimbursement to the appropriation originally charged with the cost of the work was agreed to by Mr. McCarl, who cited section 601 of the act of June 30, 1932,[14] and declared that, "under the circumstances as presented, the matter may be considered as work performed by one agency of the Government for another as contemplated."[15]

A ruling of March 1, 1935, stated that there was no legal objection to the H.O.L.C.'s use of funds and personnel in furnishing to members of Congress information as to identity of applicants for loans or the status of employees, and that the propriety of furnishing such information was for administrative determination.[16] On the other hand, the action of the corporation's board in agreeing to allow regularly employed attorneys to act as fee attorneys of a homeowner at his expense was vigorously objected to by the Comptroller-General; such a private practice would make the attorneys ineligible for com-

[13] Unpublished MS, October 16, 1933.

[14] "Any executive department or independent establishment of the Government, or any bureau or office thereof, if funds are available therefor. . . . may place orders with any other such department, establishment, bureau, or office for materials, supplies, equipment, work, or services, of any kind that such requisitioned Federal agency may be in a position to supply or equipped to render, and shall pay promptly by check to such Federal agency as may be requisitioned, upon its written request, either in advance or upon the furnishing or performance thereof, all or part of the estimated or actual cost thereof as determined by such department, establishment, bureau, or office as may be requisitioned" (47 Stat. 417).

[15] 13 C.G. 138, November 15, 1933; affirmed in unpublished MS, January 3, 1934.

[16] 14 C.G. 675.

pensation from the corporation. In rendering this decision, Mr. McCarl took the following position:

Authority given by law "to determine its necessary expenditures" does not place the corporation beyond all law or accountability with respect to its expenditures but imposes a responsibility to determine as a fact as necessary to the carrying out of its public duty any expenditure not in conformity with law or sound public policy, and in advance of the incurring of the obligation.[17]

Officials of the corporation asked Mr. McCarl for a reconsideration and reversal of this ruling, but without success.

In another instance, upon the H.O.L.C.'s explanation that its board could not always regulate detailed actions of agents in the field, the Comptroller-General agreed to the making of general regulations providing for travel expenses, and, as a part of such regulations, the authorization of travel by air transportation in emergencies when such travel is approved by a named executive of the corporation.[18]

It will be seen that these Comptroller-General decisions have not been very restrictive on the H.O.L.C.'s freedom of action in expenditures; the statutory provisions were hardly susceptible to restrictive interpretations. Subsequent events, however, have altered the picture somewhat. The H.O.L.C. and F.S.L.I.C. were both among the agencies which were required by the President in 1935 thereafter to submit administrative expense estimates to the Director of the Budget. They were also affected by the congressional policy announced in the deficiency act of June, 1936.[19] Among those who had fought section 7 of the latter act in committee hearings,[20] H.O.L.C. officials were most outspoken, with arguments similar to those with which Chairman Fahey and Mr. Russell had opposed control by the Budget Bureau.

The subsequent implementation of the new congressional

[17] 14 C.G. 755, April 30, 1935.

[18] Unpublished MS, May 8, 1935.   [19] See above, p. 161.

[20] See "First Deficiency Appropriation Bill for 1936," *Hearings before Subcommittee of the Committee on Appropriations, United States Senate, on H.R. 12624,* (74th Cong. 2d sess.), pp. 293 ff.

policy, however, as in the R.F.C. case, was minus its potential teeth. Corporation, rather than appropriated, funds were to be used for administrative expenses. True, a limitation of $30,000,000 for the fiscal year 1938 was set, travel expenses were expressly brought under government regulations, and only $500 could be spent for periodicals. However, expenses connected with property were declared "nonadministrative," and, aside from the limitations mentioned, the power of the board to "determine the manner" of expenditures was reaffirmed.[21]

In the matter of receipts and earnings, the Home Owners' Loan Corporation has been free to utilize such funds without any question as to covering into the Treasury. Thus a statement of assets as of December 31, 1934, included above loans, property, and investments an item of $126,863,505.49 representing cash on hand and in banks.[22] All moneys constitute a revolving fund, and, as we have noted, any surplus upon liquidation will then be covered into the Treasury.

The accounting procedure of the H.O.L.C., as might be expected in such a complex financing business, presented a highly complicated problem. Detailed methods and forms were worked out in conjunction with the Comptroller-General, who detailed a unit to the H.O.L.C. Washington office for this purpose. Originally, loan accounts were sent from the states to the Washington office for recording, auditing, and examination. However, as the business grew, decentralization became necessary, and eleven regional offices were created primarily as supervising agencies. These regional offices now carry the ac-

---

[21] See Pub. No. 171 (75th Cong., June 22, 1937). That the liberal language of this appropriation bill is hardly in accord with the original intention behind sec. 7 of the deficiency act of 1936 is evidenced by Representative Buchanan's protest in the 1937 hearings. In so protesting, Mr. Buchanan revealed that he had been the father of "Section 7" (see "Independent Offices Appropriation Bill for 1938," *Hearings before Subcommittee of Committee on Appropriations, House of Representatives* [75th Cong., 1st sess.], pp. 644–46).

[22] *Second Annual Report of Federal Home Loan Bank Board, 1934*, p. 85. Of this amount, $126,819,455.49 was held in a checking account with the United States Treasury.

counting and auditing, the appraisal supervision, and legal supervision of the transactions of the various state offices. In justifying this regional plan before a congressional committee, Chairman Fahey declared: "As we have tried to explain, all the problems of accounting, handling of bonds, and the handling of cash, are so complicated that . . . . it is utterly impossible to concentrate them here in Washington."

This statement in a large measure explains the accounting relationship to the General Accounting Office of the United States. The H.O.L.C. comes within the purview of Executive Order 6549, and has offered to submit accounts to the General Accounting Office, but the hugeness of the task together with the overworked condition of the latter agency has prevented the acceptance of this proposal.[23] The corporation feels that its own thorough audit makes a continuous examination by the General Accounting Office unnecessary, but its books and accounts are open for inspection at any time. Unquestionably, this willingness to submit to the Comptroller-General's audit is occasioned largely by the express statutory exemptions which would prevent any such control as is usually connoted by a governmental "audit." One is tempted to hazard a guess that the same factor was influential in the first Comptroller-General's lack of enthusiasm in the matter.

To summarize: Financial operations of the H.O.L.C. are directed by the board of directors, whose freedom within statutory limits is practically complete; expenditures are not subject to general governmental regulations, although the purchasing procedures, for example, are followed where an exception is not clearly advantageous; all funds may be used in operations; finally, an elaborate accounting and auditing system is maintained by the corporation itself, and accounts are not submitted to the General Accounting Office.

[23] In a list of government agencies not under audit of the General Accounting Office submitted to Congress in 1935, the H.O.L.C. was included, but after its name appeared in parentheses the words "offers to account" ("Independent Offices Appropriation Bill, 1937," *Hearings before Subcommittee of House Committee on Appropriations, December, 1935*, p. 265).

THE FEDERAL SAVINGS AND LOAN INSURANCE CORPORATION

It will be recalled that the Federal Savings and Loan Insurance Corporation, like the H.O.L.C., is managed by the Federal Home Loan Bank Board acting as a board of directors, or trustees. However, it should be pointed out that all transactions and accounts are kept separate in each case.

In creating the insurance corporation, Congress granted it freedom in appointing and compensating employees, the power to borrow money, and the power to invest its funds not required for current operations in United States obligations or to deposit such funds in the Treasury or in any federal reserve bank.[24] This is a measure of freedom not enjoyed by ordinary government departments, but nothing was said in the act about the manner of expenditures. As a consequence, Comptroller-General McCarl ruled that the corporation could not incur any expense except in accordance with the statutes of the United States. Thus it must have its printing done at the Government Printing Office, rather than by private printing companies. Also, purchases of supplies must be made subject to the regular statutes and regulations, such as those relating to purchase from the general supply list, the advertising for bids, and the acceptance of the lowest bid.[25]

Compliance with government regulations regarding expenditures was of most serious concern to corporation officials when they began to anticipate the liquidation of defaulting institutions. In this connection, the original act had provided:

In connection with the liquidation of insured institutions in default, the Corporation shall have power to carry on the business of and to collect all obligations to the insured institutions, to settle, compromise or release claims in favor of or against the insured institutions and to do all things that may be necessary in connection therewith, subject only to the regulation of the court or other public authority having jurisdiction over the matter.

[24] 48 Stat. 1256 (1934).

[25] See *Hearings before Subcommittee of Senate Committee on Banking and Currency, March, 1935*, p. 180 (testimony of Mr. Russell).

It was this duty of liquidation, which had not yet been exercised, that formed the basis for the corporation's recommendation in 1935 of amendatory legislation giving it freedom in expenditures under exactly the same language as found in the H.O.L.C. act. Thus, Mr. Catlett, a member of the board of trustees, made the following statement when supporting the amendment before a congressional committee:

> Mr. Russell and the Board are concerned about the situation, so that when we are compelled to administer these institutions and liquidate them at a distance, we can actually do so without being so hampered by the regulations here in Washington as we are now. As those of you who are lawyers recognize the fact that when we have to handle these liquidations in times of emergency in the different states, we are going to be decidedly hampered if we have to comply with all the regulations thrown around the operation here in Washington. And that is the reason behind this suggestion which appears in the Senate bill.[26]

Upon Senator McAdoo's query as to specific illustrations of the restrictions and red tape which corporation officials hoped to eliminate by the amendment, the following points were brought out:

1. If the assets of a defaulting institution were purchased and the corporation had to sell the real estate under the regulations affecting government departments, or do repair work on the buildings under the regular rules, prompt and efficient liquidation would be seriously handicapped.

2. If the corporation were engaged in a liquidation in California, for example, it would be disadvantageous to have all the printing done at the Government Printing Office.

3. Under existing authority, the corporation could not hire local attorneys for a particular piece of work, with a lump-sum payment, but in order to employ them must put them on the Washington payroll. Yet in cases involving the local associations, it was desirable and almost necessary to have local attorneys handle the matters because they were more familiar with the procedure of the local courts than was anyone from Washington.

[26] *Ibid.*, p. 179.

The Senate committee was convinced that what was desired was not freedom from accounting but rather "freedom in administration," so the provision that the corporation might determine, incur, and pay its expenditures without regard to the provisions of any other law was reported favorably and later passed the Senate vote.

On the floor of the House, however, the corporation's "freedom" found a different reception. In the debates on the activities of the Federal Home Loan Bank Board and its corporate arms, Mr. Buchanan declared:

If we do not stop forming corporations and giving them carte blanche to spend money, we will soon have a Government run, and its powers controlled, by soulless corporations throughout this country. This Congress should maintain supervisory authority to investigate the need for every dollar of public money that goes through the hands of any government corporation.[27]

When Mr. Williams proposed an amendment to strike out the section giving the Federal Savings and Loan Insurance Corporation more freedom in expenditures, the House assented, and the pending bill went to conference with this difference, among others, between the House and Senate versions. The conference report upheld the Senate position in this particular, and the act as approved on May 28, 1935, contained the independence for which corporation officials had contended.

As we have already noted, estimates of F.S.L.I.C. administrative expenses were later subjected to approval of the Budget Bureau and the national legislature. Like the other corporations so treated, the F.S.L.I.C. has continued to use its own funds and, aside from the specific statutory limitations, has continued to prescribe the manner of expenditures without regard to other laws.

For almost two years, funds of the loan insurance corporation were kept in the Treasury subject to accountable warrants. Accounts were submitted for the regular audit procedure of the General Accounting Office, although an unusual freedom

[27] *Congressional Record*, LXXIX, 3261.

in expenditures had been guaranteed by law. Since the early part of 1937, however, corporation funds have been transferred to a checking account. This was done in the belief that there was no legal requirement for the accountable procedure and that the easier access to funds would be advantageous. Post-audit by the General Accounting Office has been continued.

THE FEDERAL DEPOSIT INSURANCE CORPORATION

The Federal Deposit Insurance Corporation is unique in that, while its capital stock is divided almost equally between the United States and private banks, complete control is exercised by the government. Yet it has been vigorously contended that the corporation is a private rather than a government agency because of its function of insuring accounts in private banks and because it is expected to be a self-sustaining venture from the assessments levied against the insured institutions.[28]

The Comptroller-General has ruled that the corporation is a department of the government within the meaning of the Post Roads Act of July 24, 1866, and is entitled to government rates on official telegrams. After citing the Supreme Court decision holding the Fleet Corporation to be similarly privileged,[29] Mr. McCarl declared that "there is, also, the further and compelling fact that the intended and actual function of the Federal Deposit Insurance Corporation is wholly in the field of public service. It does not in this respect compete with private enterprise."[30] In view of the government's investment, the detailed statutory provisions controlling the operations of

---

[28] "Now this corporation, according to this bill, is not a Government corporation, it is a private corporation to be operated under the direction of the Government and therefore it is no more entitled to the free use of the mails than is the Federal Reserve or any other private corporation. I hope we will not make the mistake of leading the people to believe that this is a Government corporation" (Mr. Ayers, *Congressional Record*, LXXVII, 3964). "This corporation is a private corporation . . . . I think it will be self-sustaining by reason of the assessments on the depositors of the banks under this system" (Mr. Patman, *ibid.*, p. 4039).

[29] *Emergency Fleet Corporation* v. *Western Union*, 275 U.S. 415.

[30] Unpublished MS, December 5, 1934.

the corporation, and the management by two presidential appointees plus the Comptroller of the Currency, sitting as a board of directors, it would appear that the F.D.I.C. cannot be realistically called anything other than a governmental agency.

While the statutory provisions are long and detailed,[31] the board of directors of the corporation is given a large measure of freedom in considering applications for insurance; in making examinations; in acting as receiver for, and administering the assets of, closed banks; in organizing new national banks to assume insured deposits; and, generally, in managing the insurance business of the corporation. Under the act, the board determines and prescribes the manner in which its obligations shall be incurred and its expenses allowed and paid. In practice, it has not been bound by the regular governmental statutes and rules. The purchasing problem is not a serious one, and such routine matters as travel expenses are strictly regulated by the board of directors. Following President Roosevelt's executive order of August 5, 1935,[32] the Deposit Insurance Corporation has been put under the Director of the Budget in so far as estimates of administrative expenses are concerned. So far, this relationship has developed no serious controversy.

Another of the statutory provisions reads as follows: "Money of the Corporation not otherwise employed shall be invested in obligations of the United States or in obligations guaranteed as to principal and interest by the United States, except that for temporary periods, in the discretion of the board of directors, funds of the Corporation may be deposited in any Federal reserve bank or with the Treasurer of the United States."[33] Thus, it may be seen that there is no danger of funds being lost to the corporation through reversion to the general funds of the Treasury. As of December 31, 1936, $332,642,349.08 had been invested in United States securities, while an additional

[31] See 49 Stat. 684 ff.

[32] Executive Order No. 7126, as amended by Executive Order No. 7150.

[33] 49 Stat. 698.

$9,089,127.20 in cash was on hand and the surplus balance totaled $54,105,323.78.[34] As might be inferred from these figures, the corporation has had no occasion to exercise its borrowing power as outlined in the law.[35]

Accounts of the corporation are maintained by a fiscal agent and chief accountant, together with his staff. At the same time, a continuous internal audit is carried on by the corporation auditor, who also supervises the preparation of budgets and their control, and acts as co-ordinator of the operations of the corporation. No accounting or auditing relationship exists between the General Accounting Office and the Federal Deposit Insurance Corporation. Rather has a private firm been employed for each annual audit.

The Comptroller-General has apparently not attempted to examine the corporation accounts in pursuance of Executive Order 6549. This is perhaps due in part to the large percentage of privately owned stock, as well as to the added load which would necessarily be placed upon a General Accounting Office staff already overworked.

THE FEDERAL SURPLUS COMMODITIES CORPORATION

Another unique creation of the Roosevelt administration has been the nonstock, nonprofit corporate agency originally christened "Federal Surplus Relief Corporation." Financed through grants from the state relief administrations operating under F.E.R.A., this corporation used federal funds only indirectly. Indeed, an attempt by the Federal Emergency Administrator of Public Works to allocate $25,000,000 from the National Industrial Recovery Appropriation to the F.S.R.C. for expenditure was frustrated by Comptroller-General McCarl early in 1934. The proposed allocation was in pursuance of a resolution of the Special Board for Public Works to the effect that a "certain program of projects of public works of the Surplus Relief Corporation be included in the comprehensive pro-

---

[34] *Annual Report of the Federal Deposit Insurance Corporation, 1936*, p. 37.

[35] See above, p. 62.

gram," but Mr. McCarl refused his countersignature on the warrant for the following reasons:

It is not disclosed in this resolution or otherwise by the record what program of projects of public works is proposed to be carried out or performed by the Surplus Relief Corporation, whether such projects are covered by the NIR Act, and whether the corporation possesses authority to carry out or perform such projects of public works. It is understood this corporation was organized primarily to distribute for relief purposes surplus agricultural commodities . . . . and under such circumstances it is not clear how it has or may become involved in public works projects.[36]

When the purpose intended (purchase of land for various uses) was explained to the Comptroller-General, he agreed to the legitimacy of the expenditures under the N.I.R. Act, but still refused to countersign the transfer warrant.

The serious matter is the proposal to take the moneys from the appropriation and hand them over to a Delaware corporation for expenditure. . . . . If the proposal were to transfer the moneys for expenditure by an agency clearly within the Government, such as a department or establishment, or, for instance, the Federal Emergency Administration of Public Works, or other statutory agency, no objection by this office would be necessary.[37]

In spite of its inability to receive federal funds, the F.S.R.C. had an active life. The first major activity was that of purchasing commodities for the state relief organizations. All purchases were made through the corporation's division of procurement, which had been put under an officer detailed from the Supply Corps of the United States Navy. Purchasing and collateral operations were carried out in accordance with United States Navy procedure, bids being required on commodities or services desired by the corporation.[38] The peculiar nature of all F.S.R.C. purchases may be seen in the fact that a policy of handling only surplus[39] commodities was adopted.

[36] Unpublished MS, January 24, 1934.

[37] Unpublished MS, February 12, 1934.

[38] See *Monthly Report of the FERA, July, 1935*, p. 23.

[39] A report of the F.E.R.A. defines surplus as follows: "A surplus may be defined as that part of a supply which, at a given supply price, cannot be sold. In practice, the surpluses purchased under the surplus commodity program origi-

Thus the problem was quite different from the ordinary one of securing supplies or materials necessary for operation.

The second major activity of the F.S.R.C. was the processing of purchased commodities in anticipation of delivery to the various states for relief consumption. A 1935 ruling of the Comptroller-General was to the following effect:

> If it be administratively determined that it is in the interest of the United States to obtain the necessary beef products for distribution for relief purposes by paying the expense of processing cattle rather than by purchasing the finished product, the General Accounting Office will interpose no objection to the use of the appropriation involved in making advances to the Federal Surplus Relief Corporation for the payment of processing expenses.[40]

Contracts for the processing of commodities have been made, subject to the approval of the Comptroller-General and general governmental rules. The same is true of contracts for storage of commodities, which is a third main function of the corporation. Problems of a peculiar nature sometimes arise in this connection, as in September, 1935, when a warehouse in which some $450,000 worth of canned meats of the F.S.R.C. were stored, collapsed. The Comptroller-General ruled that he would "make no objection to the use of moneys available for the conduct of the corporation's business in contracting at reasonable cost for salvage operations."[41]

Finally, the transportation of commodities was a function of the F.S.R.C. Mr. McCarl suggested that all corporation funds be placed in the Treasury subject to withdrawal on accountable warrants, in order that an "effective" audit of freight accounts could be rendered.[42] This, however, corporation officials refused to do, and funds were retained in a checking account.

---

nated in part under the marketing control agreements of the Agricultural Adjustment Administration. In other instances the presence of surpluses was determined by reference to the usual carry-over or the usual crop outturn and the price of the commodity" (*ibid.*, p. 25, n. 2).

[40] Unpublished MS, January 9, 1935.

[41] Unpublished MS, January 9, 1935.

[42] Unpublished MS, March 17, 1934.

While F.S.R.C. accounts were submitted to the General Accounting Office pursuant to Executive Order 6549, corporation officials insisted that a post-audit rather than an administrative or pre-audit was the proper procedure. The status of the corporation has been greatly altered, however, since the Federal Surplus Commodities[43] Corporation has been placed under the Secretary of Agriculture and directed to use funds previously appropriated to the Department of Agriculture.[44] While the corporation may use such funds "for purchasing, exchanging, processing, distributing, disposing, transporting, storing, and handling of agricultural commodities and products thereof . . . . without regard to the provisions of existing law governing the expenditure of public funds," nevertheless, the new account set up in the Treasury is under accountable procedure, and thus expenditures will be under General Accounting Office control.

THE PUBLIC WORKS EMERGENCY HOUSING CORPORATION

The Public Works Emergency Housing Corporation was incorporated by Public Works Administrator Ickes under the laws of Delaware, and was almost immediately designated an agency under Title II of the National Industrial Recovery Act by an executive order of President Roosevelt.[45] Its powers were broadly defined both in the certificate of incorporation and in the executive order, and it was expected to be of great service in expediting the low-cost housing program of the Public Works Administration.

After this auspicious beginning, however, the corporation's history is for all practical purposes told in a single decision of Comptroller-General McCarl, who refused to countersign two warrants transferring $100,000,000 and $1,000, respectively, to the P.W.E.H.C. from National Industrial Recovery funds. The request for the transfer had been made by Administrator

[43] As noted above (p. 39), the change in name was made on November 18, 1935.

[44] See Pub. No. 165 (75th Cong.), approved June 28, 1937.

[45] Executive Order No. 6470, November 29, 1933.

Ickes in accordance with a resolution of the Special Board of Public Works. Mr. McCarl pointed out that the moneys available to carry out the provisions of the N.I.R. Act were appropriated moneys, and declared:

The creation of a corporation involves organization and other expense, not necessarily great but which amount, in this instance, might be otherwise beneficially employed as it must come from the appropriation for carrying out the provisions of the NIR Act, and should be avoided as unnecessary unless clearly in the public interest.[46]

Calling attention to the almost limitless powers contained in the Housing Corporation's charter, the Comptroller-General continued:

In view of the things stipulated as authorized in the basic law and the much wider authority outlined in the Articles of Incorporation it seems probable there exists a misunderstanding and that an agency in corporate form was determined upon in the belief that through creating a corporation and transferring appropriated moneys thereto such moneys would lose their appropriation status and become available for uses otherwise prohibited by law. Such is not the case as appropriated moneys remain appropriated moneys no matter where lodged and their uses are prescribed accordingly.

While admitting that Congress could grant statutory corporations an extraordinary measure of freedom, the Comptroller-General declared that corporations created as administrative agencies by executive authority could exercise no wider powers than if operating as unincorporated units in the executive branch. He also stated that there was room for doubt that the authority given by the N.I.R. Act to create additional agencies was intended to authorize the creation of corporations, but that his office, wishing to avoid placing any unnecessary restraint upon those administering the law, had felt justified in withholding objection where there seemed no serious danger involved.

In the instant matter, however, inasmuch as the powers and authority outlined in the Articles of Incorporation appear to contemplate operations beyond statutory authority, and which condition unless rectified in ad-

[46] Unpublished MS, January 11, 1934.

vance of operations may lead to the incurring of obligations which may not lawfully be paid from the appropriation, it seems highly desirable that these things be now brought to attention in order that they may be worked out before there is opportunity for serious complication.

After receiving the Comptroller-General's ruling, Mr. Ickes submitted several questions pertaining to the housing corporation to the Attorney-General of the United States, and the decision of the latter on pertinent points may be summarized as follows:[47]

1. Title II of the N.I.R. Act was sufficient authorization for the President to create corporations as "agencies" for carrying on the purposes of the act.

2. Such corporations might be created under state laws.[48]

3. The power to create and utilize such corporate agencies necessarily included the authority to defray the expenses of their organization.

4. On the other hand, the corporate powers of such an agency must not be in excess of those necessary to carry out any program of public works authorized by the N.I.R. Act, since Congress intended that the funds appropriated to effectuate the purposes of the N.I.R. Act should be used only for such purposes.

These opinions of the Attorney-General, while upholding the legality of nonstatutory corporate agencies of the federal government, had no influence on Mr. McCarl's refusal to sign the warrants for the transfer of funds to the Public Works Emergency Housing Corporation. As a consequence, the corporation was never utilized, and has been dissolved. This instance is illustrative of the power wielded by the Comptroller-General where withdrawals of appropriated funds from the Treasury are involved.

[47] Opinion of the Attorney-General of the United States, February 7, 1934.

[48] However: "In conclusion, may I suggest for your consideration that there are some reasons, in my opinion, why it may be preferable to organize corporate agencies of this character in the District of Columbia rather than in Delaware or any other state" (*ibid.*).

FEDERAL SUBSISTENCE HOMESTEADS CORPORATION

The National Industrial Recovery Act initiated another phase of the federal government's housing activity under the designation "subsistence homesteads." In section 208 of that act, $25,000,000 was made available to the President, "to be used by him through such agencies as he may establish," for the financing of the program. It was after President Roosevelt had delegated his powers under this section to Secretary of the Interior Ickes that the Division of Subsistence Homesteads was established in the Department of Interior and the Federal Subsistence Homesteads Corporation organized as the administrative arm of the division.

The creation of the F.S.H.C. was decided upon by Secretary Ickes after consultation with the Attorney-General[49] and in the belief that the purchases, constructions, sales, and loans to be made under the subsistence homesteads program could be most expeditiously and efficiently handled through a business corporation. He also concluded that it would be advisable to organize a subsidiary corporation for the establishment of each project, thus localizing management and providing a procedure whereby future independence could be achieved by the homesteaders themselves. Consequently, thirty such subsidiaries were organized by March, 1934—all with common stock of $1,000 subscribed for by the F.S.H.C. Through the power to select and remove the local directors, the parent-corporation retained the control of major policies. Funds were advanced by means of a loan contract which stipulated the procedures and plans to be followed in establishing each project. Yet the subsidiary corporations were to be the actual operating units—making purchases, holding title to land, and selecting and making contracts with homesteaders.

Thus organized, the subsistence homesteads program got under way. Capital consisted of the $25,000,000 provided in the N.I.R. Act. These funds were never formally transferred

[49] See P. M. Glick, "The Federal Subsistence Homesteads Program," *Yale Law Journal*, XLIV (June, 1935), 1324.

to the F.S.H.C., but were expended by the disbursing officer of the Division of Subsistence Homesteads in the name of the corporation. The act itself had provided that the "moneys collected as repayment of said loans shall constitute a revolving fund to be administered as directed by the President for the purposes of this section,"[50] and hence the question of covering receipts into the Treasury did not arise.

Other knotty problems did appear, however. The corporate agencies had been established with the idea that expenditures could be made in the manner of private business companies and without compliance with regular governmental procedures. The question of expenditures was, of course, closely tied up with the question of General Accounting Office control over accounts, and the solicitor of the Department of Interior had given an opinion to the effect that the accounts of the F.S.H.C. and its subsidiaries were not required, under the law, to be settled in the General Accounting Office.[51] While the corporations began to operate on this basis, it is doubtful whether the Comptroller-General would have agreed upon the legal point. However, a decision by Mr. McCarl was forestalled, and the moot question of accountability apparently settled, by President Roosevelt's executive order of January 3, 1934.[52] With accounts now subject to settlement and adjustment in the General Accounting Office, the directors of the subsistence homesteads program felt that in losing the "hoped-for freedom from required observance of the established procedural rules," they had lost perhaps the main advantage of the corporate device.[53] Consequently, the difficulties inherent in operating the subsidiary corporations under strict governmental regulations, together with increasing doubt as to the superior efficiency of the decentralized plan, led to a decision by Secretary Ickes, in April of 1934, to discontinue operations of the local units, and to substitute therefor direct operation by the federal personnel. The name of the Federal Subsistence Home-

[50] 48 Stat. 205–6.

[51] Glick, *op. cit.*, p. 1342.

[52] See above, p. 129.

[53] Glick, *op. cit.*, p. 1344.

steads Corporation continued to be used in acquiring land titles and making contracts, but actually the corporation had no existence independent of the Division of Subsistence Homesteads. The director of the division served as general manager of the corporation; the latter agency employed no personnel of its own; and operations were carried on under all governmental regulations and procedures.

Thus, the Federal Subsistence Homesteads Corporation became only a name soon after its creation. When all subsistence homesteads functions were transferred to the Resettlement Administration in May of 1935, the F.S.H.C. was retained only in order to simplify the holding of property and the completing of unexecuted contracts, prior to transfer of the entire assets to the United States by a single deed.

FEDERAL PRISON INDUSTRIES, INC.

When Congress was considering the creation of a corporation to take over the duties of the Attorney-General[54] with respect to federal prison industries, there was considerable discussion relative to the financial powers of such an agency. The bill as introduced provided for a permanent appropriation of all funds and earnings of the corporation for use as operating capital, while at the same time stating that "the corporation shall from time to time deposit with the Treasurer of the United States to the credit of miscellaneous receipts, so much of its earnings as shall, in the judgment of its board of directors, exceed the amount needed for a reasonable operating capital and surplus."[55] After a debate in which objection was made to this permanent appropriation as one of a series of "back door Treasury hand-outs,"[56] the bill passed the House and was sent to the Senate. Here it was amended so as to provide that:

1. All funds of the corporation must be deposited in the

[54] See act of May 7, 1930. 46 Stat. 391.

[55] See *Congressional Record*, LXXVIII, 10160.

[56] See views of Mr. Blanton and Mr. Taber (*ibid.*, pp. 10157 ff.).

Treasury and withdrawn only on accountable warrants or certificates of settlement issued by the General Accounting Office.

2. Such funds, including future earnings, might be used as operating capital "in accordance with the laws generally applicable to the expenditures of the several departments and establishments of the Government."

3. Accounts of all receipts and disbursements must be rendered to the General Accounting Office in such manner, to such extent, and at such times as the Comptroller-General may direct, for settlement and adjustment.

4. The Comptroller-General might, in his discretion, sanction the uses of moneys and allow credit for items not otherwise allowable in accordance with law if and when established to be reasonably necessary to a proper functioning of the legally authorized activities of the corporation.[57]

In a letter to the Attorney-General, Mr. McCarl construed this proposed section as dispensing with the necessity of annual reappropriations, as subjecting the corporation to the same procedure in expenditures as is followed by regular government departments, and as requiring rendition of accounts to the General Accounting Office in the manner customary to disbursing officers except that the frequency of submission might be varied as conditions warranted. With specific reference to the fourth point enumerated above, the Comptroller-General declared that it had no bearing on legally authorized expenditures, that its purpose was only to allow him to sanction exceptional expenditures otherwise illegally made, and that the meaning was "not to extend the authority of the Comptroller General beyond that otherwise authorized by law over the expenditures or disbursements of the corporation herein created nor make him an administrative officer in the affairs of the corporation."[58]

Nevertheless, when the Senate amendments were before the House, this latter provision was particularly attacked. As Mr. Taber stated:

---

[57] See *ibid.*, p. 11305.   [58] Letter quoted in *ibid.*, p. 12466.

I have been over this, and there is one part of it that seems to me to delegate administrative authority to the Comptroller General. The gentleman from Georgia (Mr. Tarver) has suggested that that proviso be striken out, and that he would move to concur with an amendment striking out that last proviso.[59]

The House accordingly struck out the language giving the Comptroller-General discretionary power to allow otherwise illegal expenditures, and accepted the other three points, which were incorporated in the organic act approved by the President, June 23, 1934. The incident is of particular interest because it represents the nearest approach to enactment of this discretionary power which has been repeatedly recommended by the Comptroller-General as a possible solution to the expenditure problem of government corporations.

Federal Prison Industries, Inc., then, as finally organized represents a peculiar combination of freedom and regulation. As we have noted in an earlier chapter, the availability of funds without annual congressional review and appropriation has been considered a great blessing by corporation officials because of its augury of a continuity of policy previously impossible.

In addition, the original desire of the officials concerned had been to secure freedom from regular governmental expending and auditing procedure, so as to operate most effectively in selling goods at competitive market prices. The law, however, was unequivocal on this point, and the by-laws of the corporation recognize the application of the regular statutes and rules.[60] Purchases, for example, are made after advertisement

[59] *Ibid.*, p. 11778.

[60] E.g., By-law 20, adopted at first meeting of the board of directors, December 27, 1934, provides:

"Since the funds of this corporation must be expended in accordance with the laws generally applicable to the expenditures of the several departments and establishments of the Government no moneys standing to the credit of the corporation shall be withdrawn from the Treasury of the United States except on accountable warrants issued pursuant to requisitions, properly signed by the Commissioner of Industries or his duly authorized representative, and he or his

and the receipt of bids. All such transactions must be approved by the Comptroller-General.

What is of significance in this connection, however, is the fact that, while freedom was originally desired, corporation officials later felt that the application of rigid governmental procedure in matters of expenditure and auditing had caused no difficulty in practice. On the contrary, it had come to be looked upon as a protection to the officers of the corporation and the board of directors.

TENNESSEE VALLEY ASSOCIATED COOPERATIVES, INC.

As one of the smaller of the New Deal corporations, the Tennessee Valley Associated Cooperatives, Inc., exhibits several distinctive features. Without any direct statutory authorization, it was incorporated in the state of Tennessee by the three directors of the T.V.A., acting in their private capacity, and in the view of T.V.A.C. officials it "is not regarded as a 'government corporation' as that term is generally used." However, while it has not received any direct congressional appropriations, the corporation is nevertheless supported by federal funds, and its financial features merit a brief consideration.

Upon its creation in 1933, the T.V.A.C. was granted $300,000 from the Federal Emergency Relief Administration. This grant was made in the same manner as F.E.R.A. grants to local self-help co-operative associations, that is, upon application therefor by the governor of the state, and for the same purposes, namely, to encourage and assist co-operative ventures which might remove people from public relief rolls and keep others from becoming relief clients. The distinguishing feature, however, was the fact that the T.V.A.C. was to be an intervening agency which could study co-operative problems, and could advise, encourage, supervise, and make loans

---

representative shall also sign all vouchers and payment thereof shall be made by Government check issued by the proper disbursing agent of the United States, as required by laws."

and grants to the individual co-operative associations, which in other jurisdictions were the direct beneficiaries of F.E.R.A. funds. In other words, the task of the T.V.A.C. has been to administer its funds for the benefit of other associations, rather than in its own interest.

The 1933 allocation of F.E.R.A. funds and the earnings on this original $300,000 have been the only sources of T.V.A.C. capital; no further appropriation or allocation of any kind has been received. The purpose and nature of the corporation are such that the only income derived from its activities results from interest on bank deposits or certificates of deposit, incidental to the safekeeping of the funds administered by it, and from interest charged on loans made to co-operative associations. Interest rates on such loans are low and are imposed, according to corporation officials, "not as a means of obtaining income but rather because of the psychological benefits to be derived by the beneficiary associations from an adherence to customary business practices and principles."[61] All income of the corporation becomes a part of the working capital and is available for use for the same purposes and in the same manner as the original grant.

Expenditures of the T.V.A.C. are determined by its board of directors,[62] in the manner of a private corporation. Government regulations are not applicable, and matters such as the determination of projects to be undertaken or sponsored and the making of necessary purchases rest in the judgment and discretion of the board. Actually, during the first three years of its existence the corporation did not have to incur any administrative expenses because of the co-operation of the Tennessee Valley Authority. Under its planning and development programs for the valley area, the Authority detailed for part-

[61] Letter from administrator of T.V.A.C., dated April 24, 1936.

[62] The original board was composed of the three directors of the T.V.A., but as of April, 1936, membership consisted of the chairman of the T.V.A., an official of the Alabama Relief Administration, and an adviser to the Resettlement Administration.

time work in the administration of T.V.A.C. affairs enough of
its own personnel to meet the needs of the smaller corporation.
The object was to acquire and interpret the information derived from the activities of the T.V.A.C. as well as to assist in
the economic betterment of members of the local co-operatives.

Books of the T.V.A.C. are kept, and periodic audits made,
by T.V.A. accountants who devote a small portion of their
time to that work. Financial statements and reports prepared
by such accountants are prepared primarily for the information
of T.V.A.C. directors, rather than for the inspection of the
Authority, although such information is, of course, available
to the latter agency. The T.V.A.C. submits no accounts to the
General Accounting Office and is not subject to any control
or audit by the Comptroller-General.

Compared to our larger government corporations, the Tennessee Valley Associated Cooperatives represents a very mod-
est financial investment. It is primarily an agency for administering relief funds in a particular manner and does not possess
the characteristics of a large and competitive enterprise. Hence
it may hardly be said that the nature of its operations is the
basis for the T.V.A.C.'s freedom from governmental procedures
in matters of expenditure, income, and accounting. Rather has
that freedom grown out of the peculiar origin of the corporation and the fact that no directly appropriated funds have been
received.

SUMMARY

The eight New Deal corporations dealt with in the foregoing
chapter present a varied picture as regards financial powers and
characteristics. The Home Owners' Loan Corporation and the
Federal Savings and Loan Insurance Corporation have both
been authorized by Congress to determine their expenditures
"without regard to the provisions of any other law governing
the expenditure of public funds," and an identical board of
directors manages the affairs of both corporations with a large
degree of administrative freedom. In each case, however, Con-

gress has provided statutory guides and restrictions in some detail. While the Comptroller-General audits the accounts of the F.S.L.I.C., he has no comptrolling power over either the H.O.L.C. or the F.S.L.I.C. comparable to that exercised over government departments.

The Federal Deposit Insurance Corporation is closely guided by detailed statutory provisions, but, within those limits, power of the board of directors to make expenditures and manage operations is unrestricted. No relationship exists between the F.D.I.C. and the General Accounting Office.

The Federal Surplus Commodities Corporation has had its status changed since the days when it operated primarily as a relief agency financed by state funds. More recently, it has been placed under the Secretary of Agriculture and now operates with appropriated moneys subject to the regular General Accounting Office controls. In the statutes, however, Congress has recognized the peculiar nature of the F.S.C.C.'s transactions and exempted them from the application of general laws.

In contrast to the large majority of government corporations, Federal Prison Industries, Inc., has found General Accounting Office control, imposed by Congress yet not originally intended by officials of the corporation-to-be, quite satisfactory in practice as a measure of protection to the nonsalaried board of directors. It should be noted, however, that the permanent appropriation of all funds and earnings is enjoyed by the corporation.

The Public Works Emergency Housing Corporation, established by executive action under a vague statutory authority to create "agencies" in carrying on the public works program, was paralyzed by Comptroller-General McCarl's refusal to transfer appropriated funds for its use and hence never functioned. The Federal Subsistence Homesteads Corporation, in turn, ceased active operations after it had been put under complete General Accounting Office control through executive order. Finally, the Tennessee Valley Associated Cooperatives has operated under a limited allotment of relief funds, under

the wing of the T.V.A., yet free from the regular governmental
controls and procedures.[63]

[63] Since this chapter was written, the Farmers' Home Corporation, the United
States Housing Authority, and the Federal Crop Insurance Corporation have
been established. The F.H.C. and the U.S.H.A. must make expenditures subject
to audit and regulation by the General Accounting Office, although both are
exempted from regular purchase procedure when amounts of less than $300 are
involved. The Crop Insurance Corporation, however, may make its expenditures without regard to regular laws, under what is clearly intended to be merely
a post-audit by the General Accounting Office (see sec. 513 of Pub. No. 430
[75th Cong.]). The Housing Authority is given extensive borrowing power,
while all three of the corporations may deposit their funds subject to check and
use their earnings in operations.

CHAPTER IX
CONCLUSIONS

THE government corporation is a hybrid development on the hazy borderline between government and business. Recent recognition of its advantages for administering certain governmental activities marks a significant step in the art of public administration. Indeed, the corporate device represents one answer to the charge that government is so poorly organized and so beset by red tape that public operation of economic enterprise is inevitably sluggish and inefficient.

One is immediately faced, however, with the problem of determining which activities of government are suitable for utilization of the corporate device. While no infallible criteria appear, it is submitted that the government corporation is most frequently advantageous in the case of activities which possess one or more of the following characteristics:

1. Intimate business contacts with individuals and companies in rendering them goods or services for which unit payment is made upon receipt rather than through a lump-sum payment of taxation

2. Self-liquidation, or an approximate balance of nonappropriated income with expenditures

3. Competition with private businesses, especially when a "yardstick" for determining costs is intended[1]

No better example can be found than transport, and in citing the reasons for organizing a public corporation to deal with the London passenger transport problem, Mr. Herbert Morrison has stated:

Transport is or ought to be a very live and adaptable industry. It has intimate contact with the public. It is important that it should be quick

[1] The corporate device per se answers no pressing questions of social and political philosophy. The problem of the extent to which government should undertake economic activities though of great importance, is beyond the scope of this study.

to respond wherever possible to public wishes and desires; nay more, that it should anticipate them before they become vocal. Transport is a vital instrument of trade and commerce. It is desirable that it should be able with speed and decision to adapt itself to the changing needs of the modern world.[2]

In the United States today, over a score of federal enterprises of a business or commercial nature are being conducted through government corporations. The increasing number of these corporations and the tremendous breadth and importance of the activities involved warrant more careful study and a determined effort to bring about improved methods of administration and control. One of the most significant problems of all is that of determining the manner in which financial transactions shall be conducted and controlled. Important aspects involve the securing of funds, the manner of expenditures, the disposition of receipts and earnings, and accounting and auditing procedures.

From an examination of the corporations dealt with in the preceding chapters, it becomes evident that without exception they have enjoyed a measure of freedom in financial matters which differentiates them from the regular departments and establishments in the federal administrative branch. Even the Federal Prison Industries, Inc., which must observe all governmental laws and regulations in matters of expenditure, and which is subject to complete audit control of the General Accounting Office, nevertheless enjoys a permanent appropriation and consequently is freed from the necessity of annual appearances before Congress in order to secure funds. At the other extreme, such agencies as the Inland Waterways Corporation have the perennial use of their capital, freedom in expenditures from regular governmental procedures, unrestricted power to retain and utilize earnings, and complete freedom from the jurisdiction of governmental accounting and auditing officers. In between these extremes, the majority of corporations enjoy

[2] Herbert Morrison, *Socialisation and Transport* (London: Constable & Co., Ltd., 1933), p. 137.

varying degrees of freedom—a freedom in some cases rather clearly outlined in the statutes, in others the subject of differing interpretations and even dispute.

The primary reason for extending to government corporations a large measure of financial freedom has to do with the nature of the activity which is undertaken. The corporate device has been with but few exceptions utilized in the conduct of business undertakings of a character ordinarily associated with private enterprise rather than in the administration of functions more clearly "governmental" in nature. Thus, the majority of federal corporations have been directly engaged in banking and credit activities; others have operated transportation services in particular localities; still others have engaged in such business undertakings as the purchase and distribution of foodstuffs, the production and sale of hydroelectric power, and the construction and maintenance of housing facilities. These functions are of a dynamic nature which demands different treatment from that afforded routine governmental activities. Hence, it has been realized that regardless of the value of general restrictions and regulations for controlling the financial transactions of the relatively stable old-line departments, the successful entry of the government into commercial and competitive fields demands flexibility and an absence of red tape in administration. This flexibility might have been achieved in several ways. There is undoubtedly much truth in the following statement of Mr. Louis B. Wehle:

To a great extent, the phenomenal growth of the government controlled business corporation in America could have been avoided, if an early distinction could have been made between the static regulatory function and the dynamic business function, and if there could have been lent to the performance of the business function by departmental officers a reasonable freedom from abstractly sound, yet antiquated, restrictions upon their procedure.[3]

However, the answer of Congress to the need for flexibility in commercial enterprises has been the government corpora-

[3] "Government-controlled Business Corporations in America and Europe," *Tulane Law Review*, X (1935), 94.

tion. District Judge Mayer, referring to the Sugar Equalization Board in 1920, made the following comment:

> The very incorporation of defendant, the Sugar Board, demonstrates that the ordinary methods of transacting business by executive departments was inadequate, and doubtless subject to embarrassment by a maze of unworkable statutes and regulations, and that the elastic powers of a business corporation would enable the purchase and sale of sugar to be engaged in with the same facility as such transactions ordinarily go forward at the hands of individuals or business corporations.[4]

The case of the Federal Barge Lines is another excellent illustration. From 1920 until 1924 this wartime heritage was operated under the Inland and Coastwise Waterways Service, an agency dependent upon annual congressional appropriations and subject to the regular governmental purchasing and auditing procedures. The results were discouraging, and particularly did the helplessness of the Service in the face of emergencies requiring immediate but unforeseen expenditures prompt officials to make an urgent request that Congress remedy the situation. As a consequence, the Inland Waterways Corporation was created in 1924 as an agency which could effectively test the economics of water transportation by operating the Federal Barge Lines in competition with the railroads and other carriers. Conducted along the lines of a private business, with ample funds and freedom from governmental restrictions, the I.W.C. has been very successful in contrast to its predecessor.

Another significant factor has been the need for speed in carrying on a temporary or emergency progam. The urgency of the situation was frequently pointed to as justifying the large powers granted the wartime corporations, at a time when action and accomplishment took precedence over cautious restrictions and controls. Unquestionably, the temporary nature of the corporations created was a factor in securing the acquiescence of many who would have viewed any such grants of

[4] *Federal Sugar Refining Co.* v. *U.S. Sugar Equalization Board*, 268 Fed. 575, 587.

freedom on a permanent basis as fraught with danger.[5] Perhaps to a slightly lesser degree the economic emergency of the 1930's influenced Congress and the President in defining the powers of the New Deal corporations. Illustrative is the H.O.L.C., which was organized to give prompt relief to distressed home-owners on as large a scale as possible. As Congressman Boylan said in the House when opposing restrictive provisions: "The Gentleman knows this is emergency legislation. The Gentleman knows also that were we to wait for Civil Service examinations, and what not, perhaps the exigency necessitating this legislation will have passed."[6] Another example is the Reconstruction Finance Corporation, which was designed as a temporary agency and empowered to give immediate relief to financing institutions caught in the depth of the depression. Speed was an important factor; and, in establishing an agency which could extend relief with as little delay as possible, Congress drew upon the emergency War Finance Corporation as a model. Wartime and depression experience thus indicates that government corporations created for emergency purposes have been granted extraordinary powers largely, if not primarily, because of the urgent need for quick and untrammeled action.

There have always been those who oppose the grant of any extraordinary financial powers to government agencies operating in corporate form. Various reasons are brought forth, but in general the argument progresses along somewhat the following lines: public money is expended and received, and Congress has the duty of exercising control thereover; general re-

[5] E.g., consider the following statement of Paul M. Warburg, vice-governor, Federal Reserve Board, with respect to the proposed War Finance Corporation: "I would like to make it as emphatic as I can that I think this is only an emergency institution for this war, and that it would be a very unfortunate thing if an institution of this kind were to be permitted to exist after the conclusion of peace; and that is one of the reasons why I think these powers are better lodged in the corporation than in the Government, because the corporation automatically ceases to have power to operate, yet upon the conclusion of peace the government could go on" (*Hearings before House Committee on Ways and Means, February, 1918*, pp. 41–42).

[6] *Congressional Record*, LXXVII, 2569.

strictions and procedures have been developed to insure honest administration, and they should be applicable to government corporations as well as to noncorporate agencies; there is no sound reason why corporations should not be subject to the jurisdiction of Congress' central "watch-dog," the General Accounting Office; and, finally, there is great danger that "freedom in financial transactions" will grow into "waste, extravagance, and irresponsibility."

There can be no disputing the fact that government corporations must be held adequately responsible for their stewardship of public funds. Under our form of government this means that they must be held responsible to Congress, either directly or indirectly, since that body is the guardian of the public treasury. In the broadest sense, congressional control is maintained through the statutory definition of the major purposes to be served by a particular corporation. Such provisions vary widely in nature and in the length of detail, but every corporation is provided with these major statutory guides, and all financial operations must be governed accordingly. This is true not only of the corporations expressly created by federal statute but also of those organized under executive order. The case of the Public Works Emergency Housing Corporation is illustrative, since both the Comptroller-General and the Attorney-General ruled that the corporate powers of that agency could not legitimately exceed those necessary to carry out the public-works program as outlined by Congress in the National Industrial Recovery Act.

Congressional determination of the major purposes and policies of government corporations is indisputably desirable. Within this larger framework, however, there are several alternative degrees of control. On the one hand, such detailed regulations and restrictions may be imposed in the statutes that administration is hampered and the advantages of the corporate device nullified. At the other extreme, a corporation may within its vague statutory guides enjoy complete freedom in financial transactions, and may be free from any periodic checkup by Congress or its agents, thus dangerously approaching irresponsibility. Finally, there is a large middle ground where administrative freedom may be so guided through adequate controls as best to serve the public interest. It is this latter field which needs to be outlined. Because of the great variation in organization, purposes, and activities which characterizes our federal corporations, generalization is hazardous, but, in any event, the attempt to pick out some guiding considerations seems worth the effort.

With regard to the supplying of capital, Congress has freed most of its corporate agencies from the necessity of annual appropriations by subscribing to an amount of capital stock varying according to the nature of the enterprise concerned. Where Congress has determined as a matter of policy the desirability of undertaking a particular business activity, and desires maximum efficiency and continuity of administrative policy in the conduct of that business, the practice of subscribing to capital stock is quite satisfactory. It leaves with Congress the determination of the amount which the government should invest in the activity, and yet has the following advantages over a system of annual appropriations: the danger of a half-completed program, curtailed by lack of funds, is minimized; the removal of uncertainty surrounding the annual supply of funds is conducive to continuity of policy and administrative efficiency; the danger of congressional interference in the details of administration, as through restrictive riders on appropriation bills, is done away with; and, finally, the corporation's operations are not paralyzed for several weeks each year while laborious and detailed preparation is made for the annual appearance before congressional appropriations committees. A system of stock subscription, however, should by no means be made the cloak for uncontrolled expansion and entry into new fields of activity. The utilization of capital within the broad limitations and purposes of the incorporating statute should prevent such abuses, and capital outlays in new though related fields should require express congressional authorization. Illustrative are the periodic expansion of R.F.C. lending powers through congressional action,[7] and the extension of I.W.C. activities to additional river systems.[8] Where a field of business activity can be fairly well delineated and congressional policy with respect thereto well defined, the corporate device, with its permanent capitalization, reaches its greatest serviceability as an administrative vehicle.

In addition to initial capitalization, many of the federal corporations have secured supplementary funds through their borrowing power. This is particularly true of the banking and credit corporations. It has been the practice of Congress to place a maximum limitation upon the borrowings of the several corporations, and this seems to be a desirable yet not too restrictive measure of control. For the most part, borrowings must be made on the corporation's own credit and security, and thus there is a tangible advantage in sound condition and good management. Occasionally, however, the guaranty of corporation bonds has been resorted to by the government in order to secure needed funds on the most favorable terms. The sacrifice of self-reliance has been justified on the grounds of the urgency of the program concerned and the immediate need of funds. In the case of activities primarily of an emergency and relief nature, such as the work of the R.F.C. and the H.O.L.C., the justification seems sufficient, whereas in other more permanent corporate undertakings the government guaranty of borrowings is not desirable. Where large bond issues are concerned, and particularly where government guaranty is provided, Congress has often required the approval of the Secretary of the Treasury in corporation borrowings. This is done in order to secure harmony with the borrowing activities of the government itself, and such an arrangement provides a reasonable and desirable measure of control.

Experience indicates that the majority of business enter-

---

[7] See *Reconstruction Finance Corporation Act as Amended* (currently revised in R.F.C. offices), *passim.*

[8] See 49 Stat. 958.

prises carried on by government corporations cannot be subjected to the general restrictions and regulations which usually surround the expenditure of public funds without seriously endangering efficiency and economy. However, it is only in recent years that express statutory authorization has been given government corporations to "determine the manner" in which their expenses shall be incurred, allowed, and paid. In the conduct of a complex banking business, it is inevitable that immediate action without compliance with governmental red tape will continually be required. Let us take an illustration from the experience of the Export-Import Bank. An American manufacturer selling goods abroad wishes to know, before submitting his bid, the terms on which the bank will finance him. A protracted delay means loss of the business. Unless the bank can make an immediate commitment, without submitting it to the Comptroller-General for approval, such applicants cannot be given financial assistance. A huge construction program like that of the T.V.A. can be most efficiently carried on if purchases and contracts are made intelligently, without blind adherence to rigid rules regarding acceptance of the lowest bid, the drawing of lots in cases of identical bids, etc.; the engineering judgment so valuable to private construction undertakings is just as valuable when government takes upon itself similar activities. Purchasing operations like those of the Panama Railroad Company's commissary division can be successful only if discretion and ingenuity may be exercised. Advertising for bids is quite satisfactory as the normal procedure in purchasing matters, but when as a strict requirement it prevents taking advantage of favorable market prices in particular instances, the net result is an added expense that should not be inflicted upon a business enterprise.

The importance of the purchasing problem is much greater for some of our federal corporations than it is for others. In the case of the banking and credit agencies, the purchase of office supplies and equipment is such a small part of total financial operations as to be relatively insignificant. Such purchases can be standardized and conducted under regular governmental rules without serious handicap to administrative efficiency. Purchases of standard supplies from the regular government contractors may indeed be economical while at the same time preventing possible abuses under a more flexible arrangement. On the other hand, where government corporations are concerned with the construction, maintenance, and operation of huge physical plants or the securing of products and materials for resale in a competitive market, the purchasing problem is of vital importance to the success of the enterprise, and purchases must be made with a freedom conducive to the greatest efficiency and economy.[9]

The rigidity of other governmental rules such as that which prohibits the alteration of any contract unless in the government's favor also frequently works a hardship upon public enterprises and destroys friendly relations with private companies. Van Dorn cites an interesting case in which the Inland and Coastwise Waterways Service had contracted with a private firm for the remodeling of several of its barges.[10] The terms provided for delivery of the barges to the company on a certain date and their return, fully remodeled, before a specified time. The failure of the private firm to complete the work on schedule was due to a delay on the part of the service in delivering the barges, and the administrator, recognizing this fact, refunded the $2,500 which the company had forfeited under the contract. Both parties were satisfied, but the Comptroller-General demanded the re-collection of the forfeit on the ground that the contract had been altered not in favor of the government. As a consequence, the company sued the service

---

[9] After years of experience in the management of one of England's public enterprises, Mr. Frank Pick made the following statement: "Private enterprise may buy whatever it pleases and on whatever terms it pleases. A public utility undertaking, being open to challenge on preferences, on favouritism, on even baser grounds, protects itself by going to tender and accepting the lowest tender, other things being equal. *Yet this is maybe the least efficient way of buying*" (*Public Administration*, XIII, 135 [italics ours]).

[10] *Government Owned Corporations* (New York: Alfred A. Knopf, 1926), p. 267.

because of its failure to deliver the barges on time, and the final cost to the United States was $35,000.

The overhead cost of settling small claims against a business undertaking in the regular governmental manner, that is, through adjustment and settlement in the General Accounting Office, often would exceed many times over the amount of the claim involved. Much more economical is the practice of the T.V.A. with respect to claims arising in connection with its reservoir clearance activities. Minor damages to cultivated ground are paid for on the spot, and the delays and expense involved in adjudication by the General Accounting Office are avoided. Also, banking corporations upon occasion wisely write off small errors. A centralized and overly formalized procedure in such matters is an unnecessary handicap to business success.

Occasionally, as in the case of Federal Prison Industries, Inc., with its relatively small expenditures, the application of regular statutes and rules does not work a hardship. This is exceptional, however, and it is interesting to note that even former Comptroller-General McCarl, the chief advocate of strict regulation in expenditures, has conceded now and again that the business operations of certain government corporations cannot be successfully carried on under regular procedures.[11] Mr. McCarl's plea that exemption, if intended by Congress, be expressly given, is a reasonable one, and explicit provisions in the R.F.C., H.O.L.C., and Federal Savings and Loan Insurance Corporation Acts are a marked improvement over earlier exemptions which though apparently intended, were only implied.

One outstanding characteristic of most government corporations has been the sale of goods or services from which the receipts and earnings have comprised an essential part of the expendable funds. In contrast to receipts of the regular departments and establishments, corporation earnings have with few exceptions been available for operating expenses, capital

[11] See, e.g., the *Annual Report of the Comptroller General, 1932*, p. 15.

improvements, and the building up of reserves and surpluses. The immediate deposit of earnings into the federal Treasury as miscellaneous receipts has seldom been required. Sometimes the retention of earnings is expressly authorized in the statutes; sometimes the excess over operating expenses is committed to a particular use such as the building up of reserves; frequently, the right to retain and utilize earnings has been asserted as an implied corporate power.

There are several advantages, as Congress has recognized, in the availability of earnings for further use in the particular enterprise from which they arise. In the first place, such a system goes a long way toward making a successful corporation self-sufficient and beyond the need for further appropriations; the large majority of federal corporations meet their operating expenses from their own proceeds. Second, the incentive to keep operating expenses well within earnings and still show a surplus is a valuable aid to efficient operation. Corporation officials, whether in private or public fields, take pride in a commendable financial record and strive to maintain and better previous standards. The Panama Railroad Company, with its enviable record, is a case in point. In the third place, serious capital impairments may be prevented, and needed replacements and improvements may be made. For the banking and credit agencies, it is essential to maintain unimpaired capital and to build up reserves and surpluses with which to meet unexpected losses from loan transactions. If earnings may be retained for these purposes, the business position of the corporations is greatly strengthened. On the other hand, the Panama Railroad Company, the Inland Waterways Corporation, the Tennessee Valley Authority, and other such corporate enterprises which involve the maintenance and operation of large physical plants have a problem not shared by the banking agencies, namely, that of making needed replacements and improvements in physical plant and equipment. Reserves for depreciation must be accumulated, and such factors as increased business, technological advances, and competition will from time to time demand outlays for new property and equipment if the enterprise is to be progressively conducted. The Panama Railroad Company, for example, has been able to increase its capital assets from approximately $11,000,000 in 1904 to over $34,000,000 in 1936 through the employment of part of the company's earnings for the purchase of rolling stock and equipment and the improvement of property. Congressional sanction of the use of earnings for such purposes is very desirable. Finally, the use of earnings normally insures the availability of operating capital for the meeting of emergencies and unforeseen contingencies without expensive delays. One of the greatest blows to the Inland and Coastwise Waterways Service resulted from its inability to meet a serious emergency caused by an unprecedented drop in the river level in 1922. Much business was lost as a result of the fear of shippers that the service would be discontinued.[12] Such an eventuality would have been impossible if the Inland Waterways Corporation, with its power to retain earnings and build up reserves, had been in existence.

Empowering government corporations to retain and utilize earnings does not mean that the government is deprived of any ultimate profits which may accrue. Thus, temporary agencies such as the wartime corporations or the R.F.C. have been required to turn over all assets upon liquidation, and rightly so. In the case of the more permanent corporations, provision may well be made for the return of any excess profits to the federal Treasury—witness the annual dividends of the Panama Railroad Company. However, profits such as those made by the P.R.C. are exceptional, and in operations such as the extension of credit, in which the policy of the government is to keep interest rates as low as possible while covering expenses, the question will not arise.

The problem which has been least satisfactorily settled in so far as our government corporations are concerned is that of providing suitable methods of accounting and auditing con-

[12] See Van Dorn, op. cit., p. 220.

trol. Some corporations are entirely free from any form of governmental audit, and the only periodic checkup of their financial transactions is that made in the annual audit conducted by private accountants. Others are subjected to all the regular governmental procedures and must submit complete accounts and supporting papers for a continuous audit by the General Accounting Office. The majority, however, have been on a middle ground which is often poorly defined, with the result that auditing matters become the subject of debates and frequently bitter disputes with the governmental accounting officers. Neither of the two extremes seems to secure the proper responsibility in the use of public funds together with the flexibility needed for efficient administration. However, while the ideal solution lies somewhere in between, it should be possible to define the procedure in such a way as to eliminate much of the uncertainty and bickering which have so frequently appeared in the past.

The subjection of all government corporations to the "auditing" control of the General Accounting Office as that agency is now constituted would be a serious mistake. The President's Committee on Administrative Management has quite rightly pointed out that the Comptroller-General's present function of allowing or disallowing current expenditures by governmental agencies results in inefficient administration and is properly a function which should be lodged in the Treasury—i.e., within the administration itself.[13] If the exercise of a comptrolling function on the part of the General Accounting Office is a handicap to the most efficient management of the regular administrative agencies of the federal government, it is an even greater obstacle in the conduct of business enterprises by government corporations. Where flexible management is most to be desired, General Accounting Office control would substitute legalistic interpretations, excessive centralization, and the sac-

[13] See President's Committee on Administrative Management, *Report with Special Studies* (Washington: Government Printing Office, 1937), pp. 21–25, 159–67, 173–207.

rifice of efficiency, if need be, to the observance of regularized and formal procedures. The conviction of governmental accounting officers that legal details must be strictly observed "regardless of what may be considered administratively efficient" can hardly be attacked from the standpoint of law, but is far from inviolable as a business principle. Purchases, for example, would be watched with an eye to legal authorization, proper form in negotiating, incurring, and paying the obligation, but with little or no attention to the most important thing of all—that is, whether the article was needed and whether it was of a quality and at a price best calculated to meet the need. Even if the Comptroller-General and his men were qualified in every other way to exercise the comptrolling function—that is, to examine continuously, allow and disallow corporation transactions—the delays which would inevitably result in such a huge undertaking would seriously handicap the operating unit. Tentative commitments, with a long wait for approval from above, would have to be resorted to, with an accompanying loss of business vigor and efficiency.

Legal authorization for the financial transactions of government business corporations is indeed important, but minute regulation of the details of management must be avoided. Individual transactions should be considered in relation to major purposes and policies and with a sympathetic eye to their bearing upon total efficiency, broadly conceived. Standard procedures are undoubted aids to efficiency, but they are simply means to an end, and to exalt and rigidify technical details is unsound business. The entire comptrolling function is a fundamental part of management, and in the case of complex business activities of government corporations should be exercised within the corporations themselves. The Tennessee Valley Authority case is an outstanding illustration of the inadvisability of having the comptrolling function exercised by the Comptroller-General and his legal and accounting staff.

The question of auditing is quite different. The exercise of external control through some system of periodic examination and post-audit of the accounts of government corporations should properly be in the hands of a government agency. The practice of having an audit made only by a private firm has sometimes been followed, but theoretically this does not adequately discharge the corporations' responsibility to Congress and the taxpayers. The selection of auditors who will give "favorable reports" is one possible abuse. A type of safeguard which might be provided in such cases is that illustrated in the case of the British Broadcasting Corporation, whose accounts are annually audited and certified by private auditors. The B.B.C. is placed by statute under the control of the postmaster-general and provision is made for the latter official to have his comptroller and accountant-general audit corporation accounts if at any time that seems desirable.[14] This power is not frequently exercised, but its existence insures a governmental audit when any cause for suspicion appears.

However theoretically sound a governmental audit of corporation accounts may be, in practice the auditing activities of the General Accounting Office have been unsatisfactory as applied to our federal corporations. This is true for several reasons. Auditing, as practiced by the General Accounting Office, is a continuous process and is inextricably bound up with the comptrolling function. Ordinarily, the "audit" is conducted in Washington and necessitates a detailed submission of accounts, contracts, checks, and all supporting schedules which is too laborious and expensive for corporations engaged in complex field activities of a business nature. Some of the corporations have found it necessary to maintain two sets of accounts —one to conform to General Accounting Office requirements, the other to meet their own needs in business operations. Again, the emphasis of the General Accounting Office, as we have indicated, is on legalistic and procedural detail designed to govern more or less regularized and routine activities. This emphasis may be clearly seen upon examination of the Comp-

[14] See M. E. Dimock, *British Public Utilities and National Development* (London: Allen & Unwin, 1933), p. 275.

troller-General's reports respecting audits of Fleet Corporation and T.V.A. transactions. In the case of the Fleet Corporation, the fact that the statutory mandate was for the Comptroller-General to make an audit "in accordance with the usual methods of steamship or corporation accounting," apparently had little effect, and corporation officials rightly complained that Mr. McCarl's audit was conducted along regular governmental lines, and with his usual approach. For example, exceptions were taken to such transactions as the following: compromise settlement of claims against the corporation when it had not been proved that "the action could be sustained at law"; expenditures for insurance on property contrary to the "long established policy of the Government not to carry insurance"; purchase of automobiles for use of corporation officials; and payment of premiums on fidelity bonds required of corporation employees. These practices, all quite common and legitimate for a private corporation, were nevertheless condemned by Mr. McCarl as being illegal for a governmental agency.

Furthermore, the attitude taken by the Comptroller with with respect to his auditing duties has been such that his reports are filled with many exceptions that are easily explainable, and hence give an entirely erroneous impression concerning the degree of efficiency with which a corporate activity is being conducted. The first T.V.A. audit report, with its misleading and often ludicrous exceptions, is a good illustration. Reports in which the exceptions are of this character are of little value to a Congress interested in safeguarding the efficient administration of corporate enterprises. Reasonable criticisms and suggestions for improvement are lost in a maze of exceptions which merit, and hence receive, scant consideration. The opportunity to make the reports valuable as efficiency audits and guides for future congressional action is lost.

A final reason for the unsatisfactory nature of the General Accounting Office audit has been a shortage of funds and personnel. The job of examining in detail every financial transaction of an increasing number of government agencies is indeed a tremendous one, and the Comptroller-General has not been given the facilities necessary for its prosecution. The General Accounting Office is sometimes referred to as the most over-worked staff in the federal service, and yet its job as conceived by Mr. McCarl is such that it is behind months and even years in the treatment of many accounts.

In contrast to the auditing methods of the General Account-ing Office might be suggested some that are more appropriate to the external control of government corporate enterprises. In the first place, the continual submission of detailed accounts and all supporting papers should not be required, but rather should all books and accounts be kept in such a condition as to be ready at any time for a thorough and searching audit in the corporation offices. Periodic audits should be made by an in-dependent agency, but neither the legalistic and regularistic emphasis of the General Accounting Office nor the employee-accuracy-and-honesty emphasis of the private auditing firm entirely meets the need. Much good might be accomplished if the audit could be more than a financial or fidelity audit, if it could be a service or efficiency audit, by an agency having the power thoroughly to investigate operations and to make recom-mendations to Congress as to efficiency as well as honesty in administration. The tendency in the national government of Great Britain has been for the comptroller and auditor-general increasingly to call attention to extravagant and inefficient practices when making his audit reports to parliament, and the conclusion of an American commission especially studying British financial administration was to the effect that "this is a duty which should be discharged to a far greater extent than it apparently is."[15] In the case of our federal corporations, an efficiency audit and report should be of great value in guiding congressional action. It is true that the value of such reports would depend largely upon the manner in which they are re-

[15] W. F. Willoughby, W. W. Willoughby, and S. M. Lindsay, *The System of Financial Administration of Great Britain* (Washington: Brookings Institution, 1929), p. 226.

ceived by Congress. Under the British system, a special public accounts committee carefully considers the reports of the comptroller and auditor-general, and its excellent work has been cited as one of the most valuable phases of parliamentary control of governmental finance.[16] A similar development in this country would be an improvement over present congressional methods. Mr. A. E. Buck is authority for the following statement regarding the Budget and Accounting Act of 1921:

It should have created at the same time a single Committee on Public Accounts for the two houses, abolishing the present committees on public expenditures which are largely ineffective. The reports of the Comptroller General cannot be very useful unless carefully reviewed by Congress to the end that the executive and the administration may be required to carry out the desirable recommendations contained in these reports. A congressional Committee on Public Accounts, functioning along the general lines of the English Public Accounts Committee described above, seems indispensable to the proper handling of this work.[17]

The type of audit which we have been considering is not entirely foreign to American experience. The work of the Farm Credit examiners, as they tend more and more toward efficiency audits, is a case in point; and T.V.A. Chairman Morgan's suggestion that the Comptroller-General furnish competent engineers at the Authority's expense to go over T.V.A. work, "to keep track of it, in any field that he wants to explore, to see whether it has a good honest tone to it, to see whether anything ought to be looked into further"[18] is somewhat along the same lines.

It is quite possible that an auditing agency with the duties which we have suggested could accomplish much yet save considerable in work and expense by making judicious use of some form of test audit. It is not too much to expect that a corps of trained men, used particularly for the audit of government corporation activities and hence familiar therewith, could with respect to certain corporations follow a complete audit one

[16] *Ibid.*, pp. 228 ff.

[17] *Public Budgeting* (New York: Harper & Bros., 1929), p. 560.

[18] See above, p. 137.

year with a quick survey and several spot tests the next without losing the ability to detect and ferret out any major defects upon the slightest suspicion. Occasional and unannounced examinations, such as those made in the case of national banks, for example, would be useful in this connection.

The best solution to the problem of providing our federal corporations with an external audit is contingent upon a thoroughgoing redefinition of the powers and functions of the General Accounting Office along the lines recommended by the President's Committee.[19] The comptrolling function would be exercised within the administration. For the regular departments this would mean the establishment of an effective comptrolling agency within the Treasury Department. In the case of the governmental business corporation, this internal financial control would properly be exercised within the corporation itself. The General Auditing Office, a legislative agency independent of the administration, would become a real post-auditing body, designed to keep an external check upon financial transactions. A particular division of this office would have the specialized duty of auditing, thoroughly investigating, and making efficiency reports upon the financial operations of governmental business corporations, and its personnel and methods could be adapted to this problem. Comparisons and constructive suggestions could be made, and Congress would have reason to give close consideration to the reports which were prepared.

Short of this desirable change in the status of the General Accounting Office, other solutions must be found. Congress should, in the first place, clarify the relationship between corporations and the Comptroller-General. There should be no occasion for disputes such as that which has arisen in the case of the Tennessee Valley Authority out of the statutory provision that the Comptroller-General "shall audit" the transactions of the corporation. In such instances, it should be made clear whether Congress intends a complete submission of ac-

[19] See above, p. 222.

counts and schedules, as Mr. McCarl maintained, or a post-audit in the corporation offices, as contended by T.V.A. officials. If the Comptroller-General is to be given the power of auditing the accounts of government corporations, the nature of that audit should be defined in the statutes. A provision such as that in the amended T.V.A. act to the effect that the corporation shall have opportunity to examine and answer the exceptions contained in the audit before the report is made to Congress may well be included.

It must be admitted that the auditing arrangement just sketched is not entirely satisfactory. The General Accounting Office has exhibited no enthusiasm for such curtailed auditing powers—witness the Fleet Corporation case—and it is doubtful whether the audit would be conducted in the desired manner without the reappearance of the old emphasis on legalism and the interference in administration which have characterized past efforts. It might be feasible, particularly in the event the number of government corporations continues to increase, to create an additional governmental auditing agency, specifically with the function of examining corporate business enterprises. Such an agency would have the same functions as those outlined above for the "corporation division" of a reconstituted General Auditing Office. That is to say, a trained staff would specialize in making post-audits, both fidelity and efficiency in nature, of government corporation transactions and would report thereon to Congress. An entirely different approach from that of the General Accounting Office could be developed. The expense of such an agency need be hardly any greater than that necessary to supply the General Accounting Office with additional funds and personnel, and the benefits to be derived should more than compensate for the cost.

Where a number of related corporations are grouped together under an overhead organization such as the Farm Credit Administration, a satisfactory independent audit can perhaps be made by the central agency. Such an arrangement makes unnecessary the regular controls usually applied to transactions of governmental agencies, and hence the subsidiary corporations should be entirely free from any direct control or audit by the General Accounting Office. The experience of the F.C.A. seems to offer encouragement to the further extension of the scheme. The central agency is sufficiently distinct from the subsidiary corporations to insure an independent examination of individual corporation transactions; and yet through familiarity and sympathy with the major objectives of the group as a whole it may lend to its examinations a reasonableness and sense of perspective which is greatly to be desired. Opportunity for improvement through comparison of the individual corporations is afforded, and an audit becomes a preliminary step to better and more efficient methods as well as a check on honesty in administration. Control of financial transactions may be made effective without imposing an administrative straitjacket upon the operating units.

A final alternative is to free individual corporations from any control or audit by a governmental agency, as has been done in the case of the Panama Railroad Company, the Inland Waterways Corporation, and the Reconstruction Finance Corporation. Where the decision lies between this type of freedom, on the one hand, and complete General Accounting Office control as ordinarily exercised on the other, there are strong arguments in favor of the former. Where this choice is made, however, statutory provision should be made for periodic audits by reputable private firms as well as for financial reports by the corporations themselves. The Inland Waterways Corporation Act, which makes no mention of any audit or report whatsoever, goes to an unsatisfactory extreme. In providing for the periodic audit, Congress may well place the selection of the private firm in the hands of the President or some other official or agency which is not directly responsible for the management of corporation activities.

In surveying the total picture, the great differences in size, organization, powers, and purposes which characterize our many federal corporations cannot be overlooked. Many of these variations are the necessary result of the activities under-taken; compare, for example, the administration of federal prison industries with the gigantic task of giving financial relief to distressed homeowners in every locality of the United States, or the encouragement of local co-operative ventures in the Tennessee Valley with the operation of a railroad and numer-ous other economic enterprises in the Panama Canal Zone. Some corporations are closely related, and can be rather uni-formly dealt with—perhaps co-ordinated as are those under the Farm Credit Administration. Others, such as the Inland Waterways Corporation, are more unique, and independent.

In spite of the fact that government corporations created for different purposes must of necessity exhibit many variations, the suggestion of Mr. O. P. Field[20] that Congress should enact a carefully drawn statute under which all corporations federally owned and operated should be incorporated is worthy of con-sideration. The value of such a general statute would, of course, depend upon the success with which fundamental prin-ciples and policies were determined and enunciated without imposing a rigid mold of detail. As far as our particular prob-lem of financial powers is concerned, there should be no reason why Congress could not retain its major controls over cor-porate business enterprises, while, as a general pattern, freeing them from the need for annual appropriations, the application of general rules regarding governmental expenditures, the ne-cessity of immediately surrendering earnings, and the burden of a governmental audit, as now practiced.

The government corporation is primarily an administrative device and is so designed. It reaches maximum administrative efficiency when granted a large measure of freedom in manage-ment and in financial matters. If it is used for partisan pur-poses or is otherwise mismanaged, its very virtues become vices. Desirable financial freedom becomes the shield of favor-itism and corruption. Fortunately, the experience of the fed-

[20] See "Government Corporations: A Proposal," *Harvard Law Review*, XLVIII (1935), 775.

eral government with its corporate agencies is reassuring on this point. Corporation officials must and can be chosen for their ability and integrity without any reference to partisan or political considerations. The entire divorce of the Tennessee Valley Authority from spoils practices is only one of the encouraging signs in recent corporate developments. In the last analysis, the selection of public-spirited and able men to direct the operations of our government corporations is the real safeguard to the public interest, and, when this is accomplished, the freedom conducive to progressive administration can profitably be granted.

BIBLIOGRAPHY

BOOKS

BAIRD, FRIEDA, and BENNER, CLAUDE L. *Ten Years of Federal Intermediate Credits*. Washington: Brookings Institution, 1933.

BECK, JAMES M. *Our Wonderland of Bureaucracy*. New York: Macmillan Co., 1932.

BENSON, GEORGE C. S. *Financial Control and Integration*. New York and London: Harper & Bros., 1934.

BERNHARDT, JOSHUA. *Government Control of the Sugar Industry in the United States*. New York: Macmillan Co., 1920.

BUCK, A. E. *Public Budgeting*. New York and London: Harper & Bros., 1929.

CHASE, STUART. *Government in Business*. New York: Macmillan Co., 1935.

DIMOCK, MARSHALL E. *British Public Utilities and National Development*. London: George Allen & Unwin, Ltd., 1933.

———. *Government-operated Enterprises in the Panama Canal Zone*. Chicago: University of Chicago Press, 1934.

———. *Developing America's Waterways*. Chicago: University of Chicago Press, 1935.

FORBES, RUSSELL. *Governmental Purchasing*. New York: Harper & Bros., 1929.

LANGELUTTIG, ALBERT. *The Department of Justice of the United States*. Baltimore: Johns Hopkins Press, 1927.

MORRISON, HERBERT. *Socialisation and Transport*. London: Constable & Co., Ltd., 1933.

SCHMECKEBIER, LAWRENCE F. *New Federal Organizations*. "Institute for Government Research, Studies in Administration." Washington: Brookings Institution, 1934.

SEIDEMANN, HENRY P. *Manual of Accounting and Reporting for the Operating Services of the National Government*. "Institute for Government Research, Studies in Administration." Baltimore: Johns Hopkins Press, 1926.

SHEALEY, R. P. *The Law of Government Contracts*. 2d ed. Washington: Federal Publishing Co., 1935.

SMITH, DARRELL H. *The General Accounting Office: Its History, Activities, and Organization*. "Institute for Government Research, Service Monograph," No. 46. Baltimore: Johns Hopkins Press, 1927.

SMITH, DARRELL H., and BETTERS, PAUL V. *The United States Shipping Board.* "Institute for Government Research, Service Monograph," No. 63. Washington: Brookings Institution, 1931.

SURFACE, FRANK M. *The Grain Trade during the World War.* New York: Macmillan Co., 1928.

THURSTON, JOHN. *Government Proprietary Corporations in the English-speaking Countries.* Cambridge: Harvard University Press, 1937.

VAN DORN, HAROLD A. *Government Owned Corporations.* New York: Alfred A. Knopf, 1926.

WILLOUGHBY, W. F. *Government Organization in War Time and After.* New York and London: D. Appleton & Co., 1919.

———. *The Legal Status and Functions of the General Accounting Office of the National Government.* "Institute for Government Research, Studies in Administration." Baltimore: Johns Hopkins Press, 1927.

WILLOUGHBY, W. F., WILLOUGHBY, W. W., and LINDSAY, S. M. *The System of Financial Administration of Great Britain.* Washington: Brookings Institution, 1929.

WILLOUGHBY, WOODBURY. *The Capital Issues Committee and War Finance Corporation.* "Johns Hopkins University Studies in Historical and Political Science," Ser. LII, No. 2. Baltimore: Johns Hopkins Press, 1934.

ARTICLES

ABBOTT, CHARLES C. "The Government Corporation as an Economic Institution," *Harvard Business Review*, spring, 1937.

ASHBURN, T. Q. "The Inland Waterways Corporation," *Military Engineer*, XXV (May-June, 1933), 249.

BROWN, W. R. "Incorporation of Federal Agencies," *Illinois Law Review*, XLVIII (April, 1934), 1082.

CHASE, STUART. "How Can the State Do Business?" *Current History*, XLII (May, 1935), 126.

COOKSEY, GEORGE R. "Work of the War Finance Corporation Reviewed," *Congressional Digest*, December, 1931, p. 302.

COREY, HERBERT. "Uncle Sam Finds a Formula for Competing with the Carriers," *Public Utilities Fortnightly*, VIII, No. 7 (October 1, 1931), 388.

"The Corporation as a Federal Administrative Device," *University of Pennsylvania Law Review*, LXXXIII (January, 1935), 346.

CULP, M. S. "Creation of Government Corporations by the National Government," *Michigan Law Review*, XXXIII (February, 1935), 473.

FIELD, OLIVER P. "Government Corporations: A Proposal," *Harvard Law Review*, XLVIII (March, 1935), 775.

FLYNN, JOHN T. "Inside the RFC: An Adventure in Secrecy," *Harper's Magazine*, January, 1933, p. 161.

GLICK, PHILIP M. "The Federal Subsistence Homesteads Program," *Yale Law Journal*, XLIV (June, 1935), 1324.

"Government Corporations in Business," *Columbia Law Review*, XXXII (May, 1932), 881.

LILIENTHAL, DAVID E. "Business and Government in the Tennessee Valley," *Annals of the American Academy of Political and Social Science*, March, 1934, p. 45.

McDIARMID, JOHN. "The Financial Powers of Government Corporations as Defined in Acts of Congress," *Texas Law Review*, XV (June, 1937), 437.

———. "Reorganization of the General Accounting Office," *American Political Science Review*, XXXI, No. 3 (June, 1937), 508.

McGUIRE, O. R. "Government by Corporations," *Virginia Law Review*, XIV (January, 1928), 182.

———. "Some Problems Arising from Government Corporations," *University of Pennsylvania Law Review*, LXXXV (June, 1937), 778.

McINTIRE, JOHN A. "Government Corporations as Administrative Agencies: An Approach," *George Washington Law Review*, IV (January, 1936), 161.

MANSFIELD, HARVEY C. "Judicial Review of the Comptroller General," *Cornell Law Quarterly*, XX (June, 1935), 459.

MORGAN, ARTHUR E. "Purposes and Methods of the Tennessee Valley Authority," *Annals of the American Academy of Political and Social Science*, March, 1934, p. 50.

NEHEMKIS, PETER R., JR. "The Public Authority: Some Legal and Practical Aspects," *Yale Law Journal*, XLVII (November, 1937), 14.

PRITCHETT, C. H. "The TVA as a Government Corporation," *Social Forces*, XVI (1937), 120.

REED, STANLEY. "Government-owned Business Corporations in the United States," *Tulane Law Review*, X (December, 1935), 79.

ROBINSON, HAROLD. "Some Problems Confronting the Public Works Emergency Housing Corporation," *Cornell Law Quarterly*, XIX (June, 1934), 548.

SCHNELL, R. H., and WETTACH, R. H. "Corporations as Agencies of the Recovery Program," *North Carolina Law Review*, XII (February, 1934), 77.

SEIDMAN, JOEL I. "Business Operations of the Federal Government," *Editorial Research Reports*, Vol. II, No. 11 (1934).

THURSTON, JOHN. "Government Proprietary Corporations," *Virginia Law Review*, XXI (February and March, 1935), 351, 465.

WATKINS, LOWE. "Federal Ownership of Corporations," *Georgetown Law Journal*, XXVI (January, 1938), 261.

WEBBINK, PAUL. "Government Owned Corporations," *Encyclopaedia of the Social Sciences*, VII, 106.

WEHLE, LOUIS B. "Government-controlled Business Corporations in America and Europe," *Tulane Law Review*, X (December, 1935), 94.

OTHER SOURCES

Official sources provide a great deal of valuable material. The reports of the various government corporations—annual and special—are indispensable. The same is true of the annual reports and published decisions of the Comptroller-General. The latter official has also made several special audit reports on the transactions of government corporations. A wealth of material may be found in his reports on the Fleet Corporation (*House Document No. 111* [71st Cong.] and *House Document No. 217* [72d Cong.]) together with the replies of corporation officials (*House Document No. 695* [71st Cong.] and *House Document No. 321* [72d Cong.]), and in his April, 1935, audit report on T.V.A. transactions with its detailed rebuttal by the T.V.A. directors. Many volumes of congressional committee hearings are invaluable, particularly when there has been for consideration the creation of a corporation, the amendment of existing laws, or the appropriation of funds for corporation use. Finally, the *Report of the President's Committee on Administrative Management* (January, 1937), with its special studies of the General Accounting Office and of government corporations, will be found useful.

INDEX

INDEX

Ashburn, General T. Q., 54, 55, 100, 101, 104
Attorney-General of the United States, rulings of, 79, 198
Audit, governmental
comparison of, with private audit, 17–18
nature of, 16
Austin, Senator Warren R., 132, 133, 134
Ayers, Representative Roy E., 191 n.

Baird, F., 30 n.
Bank of North America, 21
Barbour, Senator W. Warren, 140, 141
Beck, James M., 6 n., 26 n., 28 n.
Benner, C. L., 30 n.
Berle, A. A., 48 n.
Blaine, Senator John J., 158, 159
Blanton, Representative Thomas L., 56 n., 83
Boylan, Representative John J., 179 n., 213
British Broadcasting Corporation, xii, 224
Britten, Representative Fred A., 105
Buchanan, Representative James P., 20, 142, 190
Buck, A. E., 227
Budget and Accounting Act of 1921, 9, 15
Budget Bureau; *see* Director of the Budget
Bulkley, Senator Robert J., 68, 181 n.
Busby, Representative Jeff, 181

Catlett, F. W., 189
Celler, Representative E., 3
Central Bank for Cooperatives
general characteristics of, 37
supervision of, 110
use of earnings of, 119–20
see also Farm Credit Administration
Collins, Representative Ross A., 78
Commodity Credit Corporation
audit and accounts of, 170

general characteristics of, 39–40
legislative sanction of, 167
manner of expenditures of, 168 ff.
relation of, to Reconstruction Finance Corporation, 165
relations of, with Comptroller-General, 166 ff.
use of earnings of, 166 ff.
Comptroller-General of the United States
control of government corporations by, criticized, 222 ff.
discretionary power of, 15
functions of, 8 ff.
proposal for redefining, 228
recommendations of, regarding
Inland Waterways Corporation, 103–5
Panama Railroad Company, 81
Reconstruction Finance Corporation, 164–65
Tennessee Valley Authority, 139, 142
regulations of, governing public expenditures, 12 ff.
relations of, with
Commodity Credit Corporation, 166 ff.
Electric Home and Farm Authority, 172 ff.
Export-Import Bank, 176–77
Farm Credit Administration, 121–22
Federal Deposit Insurance Corporation, 191–93
Federal Prison Industries, 202 ff.
Federal Savings and Loan Insurance Corporation, 188 ff.
Federal Subsistence Homesteads Corporation, 200
Federal Surplus Relief Corporation, 193–95
Home Owners' Loan Corporation, 183 ff.
Inland Waterways Corporation, 101
Panama Railroad Company, 81
Public Works Emergency Housing Corporation, 196–97
Reconstruction Finance Corporation, 163 ff.
R.F.C. Mortgage Company, 171

239

Date Due